MW01292734

In a highly personal and engaging style, Mary Steege beautifully illuminates the parallels between the teachings of Jesus and the Internal Family Systems model. I'm extremely grateful for this contribution to our understanding of IFS and spirituality.

Richard C. Schwartz, Developer of the IFS Model

With a voice that is fresh, funny, uncompromisingly honest, and at times irreverent, Mary Steege's The *Spirit-led Life* fluidly interweaves Christian scripture and theological reflection with Internal Family Systems theory and her personal experience. Talking with her parts, arguing with Jesus, and sharing vignettes of her life with wit and humor, Mary reveals how Christianity and this psycho-spiritual model of psychotherapy can help us come home to the Divine within and without. You won't be able to decide if you would want this author to be your pastor, your therapist, or your best friend.

Susan McConnell, senior trainer, Internal Family Systems

With wit and wisdom, Mary Steege puts words to things that many "know" (or want to know) but have not been able to name. Like her own self, Mary's writing is theologically articulate, humorous and moving, deeply engaging, and utterly true. The authenticity and accessibility of her own faith, doubt, and experiences of God graciously invite us into deeper knowledge of our own. Be ready to see the Spirit at work in every part of you.

Melanie Hammond Clark, co-pastor, Covenant Presbyterian Church

Mary Steege's first book is faithful, fresh, honest and amazingly wise. Her assertion that the Holy Spirit is operating in us to the extent we embody eight key virtues (the 8 C's) is the most practical and life-giving concept I have encountered in a decade. Add to that her dry wit and colorful storytelling and who wouldn't want to have her cloned? I can't thank her enough for making Internal Family Systems (IFS) a land bridge between the two continents of Christian spirituality and psychotherapy so I can travel between the two without perishing.

Victoria Millar, co-pastor, Covenant Presbyterian Church

The Spirit-Led Life:

A Christian Encounter with Internal Family Systems

By
Mary K. Steege

Includes:

Spirituality and the IFS Model:
Conversation with Richard C. Schwartz, Ph.D.

Printed in the United States.
ISBN: 1453619119
EAN: 9781453619117.

This book is lovingly dedicated to

David, Miranda, and Matthew Steege,

and to the people of Covenant Presbyterian Church,

Racine, Wisconsin.

Table of Contents

Introduction

By Richard C. Schwartz

      Until fairly recently collaborating in the writing of a book on IFS and Christianity had little appeal. The devout Christians I had known in my life had either repulsed me or hurt me. I grew up in Evanston, Illinois -- at the time, a very Christian town, and I was a Jew, at least that's what I called myself. My father had always identified himself as a Jew but because of being embarrassed by his immigrant parents in New York, and then his experiences in World War II, he renounced organized religion and considered himself an atheist. My mother attended the local Protestant church near the farm in Montana where she grew up, but never had strong convictions in that direction and converted to Judaism when she married my father to please his parents.

      While my parents didn't encourage my five brothers and me to attend temple or church when we were young, they wanted us to think. So my father would sit us down every Sunday morning for many years and lead us in his own version of Sunday school. He would read to us and then have us discuss many different sources like the Iliad and Odyssey, texts from the world's religions, his favorite poets, and also, we would read the Old and New Testament. While I remember dreading many of these family meetings because I was missing lots of neighborhood ball games, I have to say that my father was right when he used the old parental standby, "someday you'll thank me for this."

      I'm grateful for those sessions because my father didn't impose his atheistic biases. Instead, he pushed us to think for ourselves about many of the big questions we would face in our lives. The stance I learned there of opening to a philosophy or religion, trying out its basic positions on human nature and spirituality, and then listening inside to my intuition regarding what fit and what didn't, has served me well.

What I learned about Jesus from those early sessions, I liked. He was revolutionary, courageous, and loving and accepting of all -- implying that everyone was loved by God. On the other hand, most of my peers in Evanston were Christians and they didn't seem very Christ-like. What they told me they learned in church didn't feel right to me at all. It was all about how much God would punish them for misbehaving and how much he needed them to constantly praise him. The nuns who taught them seemed to be the extension of that God and were smacking them with rulers and scaring them about sex. I remember at around age nine spending the night at my best friend's house. I was in a cold sweat because I had tried to discuss religion with him and he told me with great authority that I was going to hell because I wasn't going to be baptized.

I had friends who told me that I was going to hell because I hadn't been baptized and yet I saw how the boys who went to Catholic school seemed like the biggest sinners. As a young man, the religious Christians I knew seemed stiff and superficial, judgmental and intolerant, as if the religion had squeezed the juice out of them. If Jesus turned people into that, I didn't want anything to do with him.

By the early 1980s, my disdain for religion had only grown and I had no interest in Christianity. The Internal Family Systems Model (IFS) was in the early stages of its development and I was teaching it to anyone who would listen. Several religious Christians got excited about it in those early days and tried to tell me why they were excited, but I wasn't interested. One, Russell Harris, even published a book that was a Christian version of IFS and, while I overtly supported his project, secretly I was embarrassed to have IFS so closely associated with Christian therapists.

As I used the model with clients through the eighties and

nineties, increasingly they began having what could only be described as spiritual experiences. These vicarious encounters with the mystical profoundly affected my own spirituality and I became interested in Buddhism, Hinduism, Taoism, shamanism, Kabala -- everything but Christianity. I gradually shifted my view of what I called the Self from being an innate human capacity for self-healing to being a spiritual essence comparable to Buddha Nature, Atman, the Tao, or the Ground of Being. Correspondingly, my view of IFS evolved from being a form of psychotherapy to being an integration of spirituality and psychology, or even to being a form of spiritual practice.

In 2001 I was asked to run an IFS training for evangelical Christian therapists in Jackson, Mississippi. I had many concerns. I worried that we would have to distort the model in order for it to fit into the fundamentalist framework, or that conservative Christians would co-opt it somehow and use it to proselytize or to further their political agenda. I was afraid that we would be emotionally assaulted as condemned sinners, just as my Christian peers had assaulted me in childhood. It didn't help when they asked that I exclude one of my most skilled trainers on the grounds that she was a lesbian. In addition, this was the beginning of the Bush administration and I was furious at evangelicals for hijacking our country.

You might say I had an attitude.

I viewed evangelicals as ignorant, fearful, rigid people who wanted to inflict their black-and-white worldview on the rest of us. I was also intrigued by the challenge. I saw this as an opportunity to convert the fundamentalists. Maybe by helping them with their fearful parts we could pry them loose from their dogma, and help them see that God isn't the vengeful, punitive narcissist they worshipped. Maybe IFS could be the cure for fundamentalism.

About 30 students enrolled for the first training. Many of them had graduated from Reformed Theological Seminary (RTS), where they had to complete double masters -- one in marital and family therapy and one in theology. Nearly all considered themselves fundamentalist and many had never interacted with "nonbelievers." Their religion was the center of their lives. RTS follows a strict Calvinist stance; they believe that people are inherently sinful until they accept Jesus into their hearts. I thought this might be a problem since we believed people are inherently good regardless of what they did with Jesus. It would be interesting to see if there was any common ground on which we could stand, but I was determined not to water down the basic premises of IFS. There would be no Trojan Horse strategy for us. They could take it or leave it, but we would keep our faith in the model.

Being neither hero nor fool, I decided to send down emissaries to explore the territory first. I recruited a team of IFS trainers, all of whom had been raised Christian. They taught the first three weekends of the training and came back with reports of being extremely provoked at times yet hugely moved at other times. The group had decided to hold off the theological debates until I came for the fourth weekend, but there had been a number of spontaneous outbursts which had set the trainers spinning. In addition, they were a bit intimidated because the group included two professors who taught in the RTS program.

The three subsequent training weekends I led were among the most intense, exhilarating, challenging, and rewarding of my career. They challenged my view of southerners, evangelicals and, most importantly, the teachings of Jesus. As we began the theological debates, all the obvious points of difference were in there in bold relief but the ability of many of the students to engage in open, curious, and respectful exchanges about these issues amazed me. One of the professors, Bill Richardson, set that tone with a statement that totally floored me. He said that what we are getting clients to do internally was what Jesus advocated in the outside world -- to love and see the good in all. IFS clients learn to seek out their internal outcasts and bring them home, befriend inner oppressors and offer them a new kind of life, go to "sinful" parts with compassion and heal, rather than judge, them. Bill said that discovering that this is possible internally had led him to reevaluate some of the ways that the church encouraged people to relate to their parts. I had never considered that parallel and, as I played with it, my interest in the teaching of Jesus began to pique. Was he the external embodiment of what I call Self?

The ability of Bill and many other students there to take a fresh look at elements of what they believed belied the stereotypes I brought with me and made me ashamed of how closed my mind had been to them and to the teachings of Jesus. Like me, they were seekers, had devoted their lives to discovering what felt true and would consider data that didn't fit the paradigm. They were committed to lives of service and wanted to know the best ways to serve even if it challenged their beliefs.

We talked about many of the theological issues including judgment, the role of Jesus, human nature, sin and salvation. There were, of course, many charged debates and moments of intense conflict. There were also points of irreconcilable difference. In general, it was exhilarating to speak honestly about issues of such import to both sides. We were all surprised to find how often debates would become quite tense and yet we could all come back to Self, remaining connected and respecting our differences. It felt good to know that the other took your perspective seriously even if he or she wasn't persuaded.

As students sensed the increasing safety in the group and came to trust that we meant it when we said that all their parts were welcome, they became increasingly eager to discuss how many of their parts were unwelcome in their church and why that might be. As one example of that, one student said he had some parts that not only didn't love God, but were very angry at God, and that he could never admit that in church. That opened the door for many others to disclose similar secrets and feel relieved to know they were not alone.

I was involved in training two different groups in Mississippi and I left those experiences with two important new perspectives. The first is that IFS has the ability to create an atmosphere in which it is possible to have a Self-to-Self connection between groups that profoundly disagree. The second one, beginning with Bill Richardson's profound observation about the parallels between Jesus' teaching about the external world and what IFS does internally, is that the wisdom of what Jesus actually said is well worth studying to both enrich and ground IFS. The more I learn about his actual teaching -- not how he has been interpreted by various influential but perhaps burdened followers -- the more excited I become.

While I left the Mississippi experience with a new interest in Christianity, I had little opportunity to explore this passion further. Through my workshops and trainings, I met many other Christians and came to appreciate the diversity within the tradition, but I still had parts that resisted churches or Bible study. I wanted to find someone with whom to dialogue who was well schooled in Christianity, was open-minded and intelligent, and knew IFS. I waited several years and then Mary Steege came to my retreat at Esalen. At the time she was serving as pastor of a Presbyterian church and studying IFS. She was also an extremely soulful, bright, and articulate person. We had many thrilling discussions there and later. When she began sharing with me the IFS-based sermons she had written and delivered to her congregation, I became ecstatic. It turned out that she was also a wonderful writer and had a way of excerpting the exact passages from the Bible that I wanted to explore.

Despite this new interest in the parallels between Jesus' teaching and IFS, I do not consider myself to be a Christian any more than I consider myself to be a Hindu, Taoist, Jew, Buddhist, or follower of any other indigenous or modern religion. There are amazing connections between IFS and the original texts of all the traditions I have examined and there are also passages that contradict IFS. What has changed is that my interest in spirituality has expanded to include Christianity along with those traditions.   I have been thrilled to find pieces of wisdom in some of Jesus' words that further confirm the perennial nature of the spiritual side of IFS. In the future I hope to participate in creating books that explore the connections between IFS and other spiritual traditions. For now, however, I've learned and grown from this collaboration with Mary and look forward to the dialogues this book inspires.

Richard C. Schwartz,
Oak Park, 2010

Back-story

There's something about light. We're drawn to it. The light of day. The light of flame. The light of stars that twinkle in the night. Light illuminates. It warms and it comforts. It makes me feel all snug inside, and this sense of well-being goes beyond physical sensation. Light seems to touch my very soul; it's how I've come to speak of God. Divine Light – it draws, it warms, it comforts, illuminates. It shines, and no darkness can overcome it. Jesus said: *you* are the light of the world.

Remain in light; this is what it takes to love and serve the Lord. It's not as easy as it sounds.

Holy Light shines into the dimmest corners of my being. It reaches into the outer edges of my life. There is no hide. It shines on things I would not see, reveals that which I would hide. It walks into my heart of fear. I once was blind, but now I see. Spiritual awareness has been the gateway of my redemption, an inner illumination that leads to healing and transformation. It fosters a continuing process of repentance and renewal. Yielding to the steadfast presence of God, softening into the warm embrace of unconditional love, I am made whole, and through this process I become light enough, unburdened enough, refined enough, transparent enough… enough so as to let the love of God shine in me and through me.

Awakening is slow and sure, except when it's not.

One day I woke up to my life. It was not a gentle awakening, not a soft fluttering up from sleep, or the gradual shift from darkness into dawn. It was more like the slam of floor when you fall out of bed, more like the smack of wall as you walk in your sleep. Awareness knocked the breath right out of me, and what I woke up to was this: the sudden realization that I am not enough – not strong enough, not smart enough, not good enough, not powerful enough to change the world and make it over in the image of how I think it ought to be. In short, I am not God. Waking up was such a disappointment.

Although I have to say it never felt to me like playing God. It felt more like trying to save the world, and save the people that I love. It felt like being responsible and doing all the right things. It felt like being faithful. I was good at it, and I got a lot of good results. So let's be clear about that. I'm not looking to diminish any of what I've done or to undermine any of the ministries to which I have been called, but I labored under what my friend Melanie calls "the curse of the competent." I was capable, spiritually capable even, and so it took an extra long time for me to run into my limitations. It took a long time before I finally smacked to a halt and came face to face with myself.

In the summer of 2005, some deep need rose up in me and could not be denied. I had been living into my roles as pastor, wife, and mother. I worked hard. I served a wonderful thriving congregation. I worked alongside a gifted and gracious co-pastor. Professionally, it doesn't get any better than what I'd got and I knew it. On the home front, I had a husband, gainfully employed; two bright and engaging children, a golden retriever, and a mini-van named Wesley. Still, there was a growing sense of dissatisfaction, an inner itch that couldn't be relieved by any amount of external success. On the outside, I was calm, but inside, I was growing resentful and ready, apparently, to rebel.

One night, I am in the next town over, out with friends and with one too many drinks on board. I shouldn't be driving. I know better, but still, I consider it. I even stop and think about the consequences of getting caught, the impact on my personal and professional life. Then, clear as if someone was standing right next to me, a voice whispers in my ear, "Well, it's one way out." I am taken by surprise. I think to myself: this is not a good sign. In the first place, I'm hearing things, and since when does driving drunk sound like a good idea?

Mind you, I am a good person and I'm not looking for any trouble. I wanted to keep on being a good person and I certainly didn't want to hurt anyone, but clearly I needed something. I needed relief, and I needed it yesterday.

This is a classic polarization of parts, though at the time I didn't know anything about that, about parts or polarizations. I only knew that something deep within me wanted out. I needed some form of healing for myself. And there was something more. Underneath it all, woven into the very fabric of my distress, I had a strong sense of call, the nagging, persistent restlessness that I have come to associate with the working out of God's divine will within me. A kind of leading, you might say, but with all the punch of a cattle prod.

After that, and after a particularly bad fight with my husband, I got myself a good therapist who introduced me to the Internal Family Systems model of psychotherapy. IFS took me to places I had never been and got me farther than I had ever gotten before. A taste of healing and I was pretty much hooked. I had a week of continuing education coming to me, so I tracked down Dick Schwartz, developer of the model. He was scheduled to lead a weeklong IFS retreat experience. As a bonus for me, it was at the Esalen Institute in Big Sur, California, right along the ocean. I flew out from the Midwest, drove down along the coast and checked into the conference center. Relief swept over me. For a whole week, someone else would worry about all those lost and wandering souls. For a whole week, someone else would arrange the schedules and cook the meals. For a whole week, I could come and go at will. It was all about me… for a whole week! The freedom was thrilling, and it was terrifying.

That first day, Dick began to talk about the model, and as he did, a wave of exhaustion swept over me. I woke up to find that I was worn out, drained physically, emotionally, spiritually. I woke up to the depth of my disconnect from God and from myself. I was often waiting on others, or waiting for others;

busy serving God, but not really taking the time to be with God, or to let God be with me. I was rarely still, and because of that, I rarely heard the still, small voice of God. Now I had a whole week, and it was time to tend my soul.

Internal Family Systems is a clinically valid model of psychotherapy and not identified with any particular faith system. At the same time, there is an inherent spirituality. IFS relies on the healing power of spiritual presence and it articulates a process of spiritual transformation. It makes no Christological confession of Jesus as Lord and Savior, and yet it resonates with the revelations of Christian scripture, reverberates with the very spirit of Christ.

"Self," as Dick calls it, is the nexus of our spiritual connection with God. Christians talk about this point of connection variously as being made in the image of God, as the in-dwelling of the Holy Spirit, having the mind of Christ, that of God within, Christ-consciousness, and so on. When Dick began to speak about the Self, I understood immediately that he was talking about the Holy Spirit, and that through Dick, God was speaking to me.

Dick talked about "managers" and as he did, I recognized familiar figures from the Christian faith, competent, committed people who meant well but got carried away with their abilities and their responsibilities. Determined to serve God, they actually got out ahead of God and in God's way -- people like Saul and David, the scribes and the Pharisees, and even the disciples who, in their zeal, would have kept the children from Jesus and sent people away hungry. I recognized many who fill our pews and head up our committees. There are many chefs in Christian kitchens. Then, too, I saw myself: my own efforts to manage the world around me and to manage my own inner world, the valiant attempt to maintain order in the face of a chaos that threatens to overwhelm.

As he spoke about the "exiles," Dick echoed the very words of Jesus. Dick is not a Christian and yet there he was, preaching the same good news of our gospel. Jesus was all about the exile. He reached out to widows and orphans, the despised and downtrodden, the ill and the alien and the outcast. "The Spirit of the Lord is upon me," Jesus said, "because he has anointed me to bring good news to the poor. He has sent me to proclaim release to the captives and recovery of sight to the blind, to let the oppressed go free, to proclaim the year of the Lord's favor."

IFS is radically compassionate in its approach to people and all their parts. It is consistent with the radical compassion of Christ. IFS confronts us with the conditional love that we often practice in the church and in our lives. When Dick talked "firefighters," I recognized the people that we often discount or dismiss, the angry, destructive, trouble-making ones who aren't really all that welcome at church, except for the 12 Step programs that meet in our basements. In truth, the Bible is filled with people like this, and even though they cause a lot of problems, God's love for them remains steadfast. Time and time again, God takes these ones and works in them for good. I was really glad that Dick got this key piece of the gospel, that Dick understood about the wild, extravagant, unmerited love of Christ which we call grace.

Best of all, even though he didn't know me, Dick knew what was wrong with me. It was all those burdens. At the time I was carrying a pretty heavy load – the sins of the fathers, the weight of the world, the carrying of too many crosses not my own. Now, here was a man and a model that spoke boldly of healing and hope. It was a different context and a different community, but it was the same good news: "Come to me all you who are weary and carrying heavy burdens and I will give you rest."

The irony of it all. I have traveled all this way, thousands of miles just trying to get away from it all, ready to leave my life behind. Instead I find IFS, and in IFS, I find a way back home. It is so God.

Back-story

After the workshop, I continued my personal search for healing. I returned home, energized and eager for renewed ministry. I began to explore the congruence between the Christian faith and the Internal Family Systems model. IFS illuminated familiar scriptures in fresh new ways. My sermons were enriched and my capacity for spiritual leadership increased. IFS became a form of spiritual practice, a process for discernment that has become an important part of my daily life. IFS has not in any way replaced my Christian faith, but it has certainly enhanced and enlivened it. It doesn't diminish my Christian walk, but it does give me resources that I never had before. IFS is not the only way to connect with God, but it is another way and one which has expanded my experience of God's presence.

One night over dinner, Dick says: you should write a book. I'm flattered, of course, but dismiss the whole idea. What do I know about writing a book? Who am I to write a book?

Later that night, Jesus weighs in. It's a good idea, he says. You should do it… write a book about me, about me and Dick.

I roll my eyes. I'm not sure that we should encourage either of them. But I can tell, Jesus is enthusiastic about the model and its potential for spiritual revitalization. Me, too.

So here within these pages you will find many points of connection between the Internal Family Systems model and Christian spirituality. The work relies on the Christian scriptures and touches on aspects of Christian theology. It is, for the most part, personal narrative. I write from what I know. Who I am is the gift I offer. I also believe that we can glimpse the universal as it is expressed in the particular; we find Holy Spirit hidden as it is in every single life.

I draw on my experiences as pastor, therapist and practitioner of IFS. This work is neither exhaustive nor definitive, and I am, by no means, the only one doing this kind of work. Many others have been exploring the relationship between spirituality and IFS and bringing it to their own communities of faith. This book is for all who are interested in this conversation and for all who know the power of spiritual presence as it works in us for healing and shalom.

Mary Steege,
Racine, 2010

A Brief Introduction to the Internal Family Systems^{SM} Model

The IFS Model views a person as containing an ecology of relatively discrete minds, each of which has valuable qualities and each of which is designed for, and wants to play a valuable role. (For the evolution of this theory and its relation to other theories of multiplicity, see below.) These minds, or parts, are forced out of their valuable roles, however, by life experiences that reorganize the system in unhealthy ways. A good analogy is an alcoholic family, in which the children are forced into protective and stereotypic roles (the scapegoat, mascot, lost child, and so on) by the extreme dynamics of their family. But these roles do not represent the essence of the children; on the contrary, once released from his or her role by intervention, each child can find interests and talents separate from the demands of the chaotic family. The same process seems to hold true for internal families -- parts are forced into extreme roles by external circumstances, but they gladly transform into moderate, more functional roles once they see that the system can safely operate that way.

What circumstances force these parts into extreme and sometimes destructive roles? Trauma is one factor, but more often it is a person's family of origin values and interactional patterns that create internal polarizations, which escalate over time and are played out in other relationships. Object relations and self psychology have observed these processes. What is novel about IFS is its understanding of all levels of human organization -- intrapsychic, family, and culture -- through the same systemic principles, and its intervention at each level with the same ecological techniques.

Parts: Managers, Firefighters, and Exiles

Most clients have parts that try to keep them functional and safe -- to maintain control of their inner and outer environments. They do this, for example, by keeping them from getting too close or dependent on others, by criticizing their appearance or their performance to make them look or act better, and by taking care of others' needs rather than their own. These parts that are in protective, managerial roles are called managers. When a person has been severely or chronically hurt, humiliated, frightened, or shamed, certain parts carry emotions, memories, and sensations from those experiences. To keep these feelings out of consciousness, managers try to keep vulnerable, needy parts locked in inner closets. These incarcerated parts are known as exiles. Whenever one of the exiles is upset to the point that it floods the person or exposes him or her to being hurt again, the third group of parts rushes to douse the inner flames of feeling, earning them the name firefighters. Highly impulsive, they push for stimulation that will override or dissociate from the exile's feelings. Bingeing on drugs, alcohol, food, sex, or work are common firefighter activities.

The Self

The aspect of the IFS Model that differentiates it most significantly from other models is the belief that, in addition to these parts, everyone is at their core a Self. The Self has leadership and healing qualities -- perspective, confidence, compassion, and acceptance -- crucial to our highest, most harmonious functioning. Even the most severely abused, symptomatic clients have this healthy and healing Self, although many have very little access to it initially. The goal of IFS therapy is to differentiate this Self from the parts, thereby freeing its resources for healing by helping parts out of their extreme roles and guiding them into harmonious collaboration.

Unlike other approaches to psychotherapy, IFS has as its goal leadership by the Self of the client's internal system of parts, and, in families, groups, and organizations, Self-leadership within each member. In contrast to other forms of psychotherapy, the IFS therapist does not have to teach clients how to correct the thoughts and emotions picked up by parts through their experiences. When clients are led by their Selves, they know, through internal communication, how to help each inner personality, what those parts need in order to feel safe, and how they can release their burdens. Led by the qualities of the Self, clients know how to provide what the parts need. The therapist's job is to guide clients to a Self-led state in which they become therapists to their own inner families.

In interpersonal relationships, when the therapist can help family members get their parts to step back and let their Selves communicate, long-standing issues are resolved with a minimum of guidance. Rather than reacting to each other's extreme views and positions, each Self-led person, sensing the hurt behind the protective walls of other's parts, automatically feels empathy, just as individual clients feel for their own parts. It is the Self's compassionate understanding of the parts' pain and shame, as well as the Self's availability to assist the parts again and again, that is healing.

This introduction is taken from the Center for Self-leadership website: www.selfleadership.org. You can learn more about the Internal Family Systems Model and how to work with it on this website. Books, articles, and DVDs/CDs about IFS are also available through the CSL Store.

But seek first the kingdom of God…
(Matthew 6:33)

Coyote Christ

Let me tell you, when I first met the model, being a spokesperson for Christian IFS was the last thing on my mind. When I met Dick, I wasn't running away from my life exactly, but I was willing to leave it – leave my marriage, leave my ministry and do whatever it would take to find myself and save my soul. I was looking for something, but I had no clue what. I felt the pain of my own suffering. That, and the unrelenting sense of being called to something else -- some new learning, some deeper healing, some greater understanding.

I fought it. Believe me, I fought it. I fought because I knew -- whatever it was, this leading would take me into uncharted territory. It would call for some form of reorganization, inside and out. And even if this was to be in the service of some greater good, I'm just not all that good at letting go. So I fought it and fought God and generally made myself miserable. Eventually I gave up and surrendered to God. Because, really, in the end, what else can you do? It just takes some of us longer to get there than others. But I felt good, good and open now, for the first time in a long time, ready for whatever God had in mind. I was ready for something new.

That's how I end up on the coast of California at the Internal Family Systems workshop being offered at the Esalen Institute. Seated on a pillow, I soak up the sun as it pours through the plate glass windows in a round building known as The Big Yurt. I gaze at the collection of humanity gathered in

1

this room. We are a diverse group with different dress, different skin color, different accents. We are from all over the world, and I say to myself: we're not in Wisconsin anymore. I say it with a sense of satisfaction. I might have been a little smug.

From his place on the pillow, Jesus starts to grin. I imagine he is pleased with himself, with himself and the little surprise that he has in store. Dick begins to speak and I am stunned… jaw-dropping, dumbfounded, dead-in-my-tracks stunned to hear Dick talk about the Holy Spirit and its power for permanent healing: thank you, Jesus!

OK, that may not be an exact quote. Dick doesn't call it Holy Spirit; he calls it *Self*, but I could see: it was one and the same. In the eight C's of Self, I recognized key characteristics of Christ, and the healing power of Self-energy sounds a lot like what I have come to know as the transforming power of God's Love. Self leadership is none other than a Spirit-led Life.

Go figure. I have come all this way looking for Retreat, and instead I find Revival. I give up, only to find what I have been looking for all along – an approach to human suffering that puts healing back in the place where it belongs: within the context of a trusting relationship between the holy and the human. I have come all this way, only to find myself right at home.

This is so God —ironic and perverse, never willing to leave me alone, never willing to leave my spiritual "well-enough" alone. Just when I think I have my life all figured out, my faith all figured out, Holy Mystery comes and opens me up to still more.

My friend Melanie has a nicer Jesus. Her Jesus is kind and caring. He always seems to have some words of gentle encouragement, and when it comes to giving guidance, he's firm but fair. I don't know where you get a Jesus like that. Mine is a meaner, mischievous twin to hers: Jesus of the Parable, who is more than willing to pull the rug out from under my feet, turn

2

my assumptions upside down, knock me on my end, if that's what it takes. Mine is the God of the Shell Game: now you see him, now you don't. Mine is the Coyote Christ, cousin to the Native American trickster -- a Jesus who turns up in so many disguises that I have learned now to look for him everywhere. Just when I catch a glimpse, just when divine nature is revealed, he laughs outright, and then he's off again.

Jesus has a lot of fun at my expense. He shows up with all his sleight of hand then waits for me to catch up and catch on. Oh, he's not every one's cup of tea, I know, but it's working pretty well for me. I see in him the Love he is. In him, I experience a Divine Presence that knows me and cares about me. Without fail, I am led to experiences of both grace and growth. My life unfolds, and in it all, God is at work for the good. So now I try to do my part; I try to play along.

The workshop comes to an end.

Some time later, I am back in my life. I'm in the kitchen, peeling potatoes and minding my own business when that something new finally shows up. My new call comes and it turns out to be an explication of Christian IFS. This new call comes and I don't think Jesus could be any more cheesy about it; it comes by phone. I mean, literally…the phone rings.

It's Susan.

I don't know Susan. I've never heard of Susan, but she has heard of me. I am a Christian pastor, of the Presbyterian Church, USA, persuasion and for several years I have been learning the Internal Family Systems model of psychotherapy. I have been downright immoderate, drinking in big IFS gulps, inhaling deep IFS breaths. I have been rolling around in the model, trying it on and trying to get the feel of it, how it fits with my faith.

Turns out, Susan is a Christian and she is just getting started with the model. Her experiences with IFS have been spiritually profound, and while this sounds like it is a good

3

thing, it's also a problem. She doesn't know how, or if, these experiences fit with her faith.

I feel like I'm losing my religion, she says. *I feel funny calling you up out of the blue like this, but I'm a little desperate.*

I listen, and at first a nice warm flush spreads through my body. I am pleased and secretly proud. At last the universe has acknowledged me as a person of extraordinary Gift. At long last, the cosmic consciousness has woken up to the wonder of me and recognized me for who I am: someone with an important part to play in the well-being of the entire world.

It's grandiosity, I know, but I find it only mildly appalling. On the whole, it's a nice change from the trashy things I usually say about myself. Self-aggrandizement is lovely, but doesn't last. Paranoia works its way back in.

Who has been talking about me? I want to know. *And what have they said?*

I have caught the eye of the unnamed Other and this kind of attention raises all the hackles of my hyper-vigilant self. A new level of participation calls for a new level of alert, but just who might be coming for me, and from what corner?

All this happens in a flash, and still, on the other end of the phone, Susan waits for some words of wisdom. She's waiting for me.

I don't know why. I am not a well person and I wish God would quit doing things like this to me, quit handing me myself, quit working on me, quit working through me – quit revealing strength in the very place of my weakness. And yet, this is so God.

It's Coyote Christ on the loose, in my life and in Dick's life as well. Dick is a marriage and family therapist, a Ph.D. who entered the field from a strictly scientific perspective. Empiricism and the scientific method have served as important standards in his work. Starting out, Dick also had a few things to prove about himself and his field, things that he wanted to prove to the scientific community in general, and to his

4

physician father in particular. That's what Dick had in mind, anyway, and that's what he did, but as his research and clinical work moved forward, the spiritual began to bubble up from within the scientific. The subjective claimed its place alongside the objective and Dick found himself developing a unique model of psychotherapy which is both clinically valid and spiritually sound. It bridges many ways of being.

There was still more. Dick began to have his own spiritual awakening and found himself drawn into a deeper awareness of divine presence as it manifests in our daily lives. He began having his own spiritual experiences and found himself in the company of other spiritual seekers.

And as if that wasn't enough, there was still more. As a child growing up quasi-Jewish in the suburbs of mostly Christian Chicago, Dick suffered at the hands of his classmates who met him with prejudice and persecution. He learned his lessons well. As an adult, he kept a careful distance from Christians, but then one day they came knocking on his door. The Christians were coming to *him* in search of healing and in the spirit of collaboration. What could he do?! He had to welcome them. He *had* to, because the whole idea of "welcome" is a cornerstone of his own model. These Christians began to learn the IFS model and Dick began to learn from them. In the unlikely place of oppression, Dick now found an opportunity to release some of his own burdens and, I must say, make some pretty good friends.

This is exactly how the Spirit works. God turns us back into the lives that we would leave behind; redeems all that we would consider waste. This is the way the Spirit moves, to tend our wounds and renew our life. This seeking of the lost, this healing of the hurt, this learning how to live with grace – it's where the Christian faith and the IFS model walk hand in hand.

The Spirit was at work in Susan's life as well. Coyote Christ up to his old tricks. Growing up with chaotic relationships at home, Susan learned about healthy relationships in the Christian community. Struggling with addiction, she found a 12 Step group that met in the church. Within the congregation itself she found the structure, sanctuary, and support she needed. Within the extended family of her church, she finally found a home. Life settled down and she settled in. But now, the Holy Spirit is stirring things up again; messing with her mind. She's having powerful experiences of spiritual presence, but they aren't coming from within a Christian context; they are happening within the context of the IFS community. She is encountering the grace of God, and these experiences of grace are both profound and profoundly disturbing.

These people aren't even Christians, she says. *This isn't a Christian group or anything, so how can Christ be there? It seems like God is there, but what if I'm wrong? What if I'm just deceiving myself? Can I really be a Christian and still do this?*

Good questions. Just the kind of questions that many Christians ask as they are introduced to the IFS model. Depending on your starting point, the model is more challenging for some Christians than it is for others. It may seem like a natural fit, or it may raise a few questions. It may lead us to look more closely at our own beliefs and reconsider the faith to which we belong, and though this process is not always comfortable, times of testing and reassessment are not all bad. Challenge helps us grow and spiritual challenge helps us grow in faith. That which is false, we lay aside. That which we have outgrown, we shed. And that which is true, we hold deeper in the heart.

It may come to us in different ways, but every grownup I know has gone through some kind of spiritual crisis. It just seems to hit harder for people like Susan whose faith is hard-won and central to her way of life. It's just not fair. People who invest the most have the most to lose. I get that, but some of us have been through enough already. Shouldn't we get some kind of break based on all the time and effort that we've already put into this little venture, some kind of *Get Out of Jail Free* card, or a little blood to dab on the doorpost? Couldn't we be spared the angels of spiritual angst?

But no, something in the outer world evokes a crisis in the inner world. We used to know how the world worked, but now we're not so sure. Once we had a firm foundation, but now we're shaken to the core. This does not feel good. In fact, it feels bad... very bad, like the rug is being pulled out from under my feet, like the whole world has suddenly tilted on its axis. When I lose my spiritual balance it feels a lot like falling. Things begin to spiral out of my control. Down I go, head over heels. Spinning and turning, it seems like the downward plunge will never end. Or if it does, that I will end up battered and broken, beyond all hope of even God's repair.

Lucky for me, not every life event sends me into this kind of spiritual tailspin. Usually it's the Big things in life that do that – the Big, Bad things like Death, Divorce, Disease, Disaster... anything that flies in the face of what I believe to be the truth about myself, about the world, or about God; when the life I have in mind collides with the reality of my life as it unfolds. The impact sends me reeling.

Here's the strange thing: Susan is not experiencing any of the Big, Bad things of life, none of those dreaded D's: no one is dying, no one divorcing, no one newly diagnosed. In fact, it's the exact opposite. Instead of a big D, she has come up against the big G. It's God. It's Coyote Christ. The Holy Spirit is showing up in a new way and now everything looks different. Susan is looking at life through a whole new lens, and while this may sound good, let me just say, clarity is not all that it's cracked up to be.

I was at the mall awhile back, picking up a new pair of prescription glasses. I put them on and right away my head begins to tilt at a funny angle. I begin to walk sideways, like a crab, or a drunk -- right into the wall. I bump into one thing

7

after another, and I think to myself: this cannot be right! This can *not* be right!!

In a remarkable, for me, display of assertive behavior, I go back to the optician and demand, "This can *not* be right. There must be something wrong with these glasses." He checks the prescription. Lo, and behold, it is just as it is meant to be. "It's your eyes," he says. "Your eyes have changed, your prescription has changed. It's going to take awhile, but you'll adjust. Trust me, in the long run, you'll see better."

What adjust?! What long run?! Clearly the man has no idea who he's talking to. I am not a patient person, and I am nothing if not nausea avoidant, disorientation averse. I think to myself: *You know what? I'll just go back to my old glasses.* Seriously. This is what I say to myself. *I can live with limited vision. I've been doing it this long; I don't see why I can't do it a little longer.* In the end, I give these new lenses a try. With a little time and a lot of bruising, I readjust. Eventually I learn how to walk in a straight line again, and I see more clearly than I have in quite some time.

New glasses are bad enough. Spiritual readjustment is worse. We run into God, or maybe it's God who runs into us. Either way, the encounter can leave us bruised and disoriented. We run up against the wall. Finding ourselves at a standstill, we are forced to stop and make sense out of our situation. We enter into a time of contemplation. We enter a time of discernment. We begin to ask questions. Good questions. Important questions. Hard questions.

Encounters with God bring greater spiritual awareness and they invite us into greater spiritual clarity, but the process of transformation doesn't end there. It continues. It ripples out into the world. Soul-searching questions lead us into life-realigning answers. Hearts change, and then we have to change our lives. Spirit heals, and then we have to live more whole.

It's hard work, but hard to get out of. In fact, you can pretty much count on it. God will do whatever it takes to wake you up and bring you to your senses, if not to your knees. As a preacher and a pastor, I am always talking up God and Jesus, but sometimes I think if people had any idea what I'm talking about, they would run me out of town.

Make no mistake. Jesus is a real pest, gnat of the highest order. Holy Spirit is tenacious, always stirring us up, always working to undo the shackles of spiritual oppression, and if we find such encounters with God unsettling, it's only because we ourselves have settled. We have settled for something less than what God has in mind. We have accommodated a lesser way of being. It doesn't matter how deeply we may have buried our sense of Self, Holy Spirit is the seed for Life and it will work its way up through the rocky ground of the most hardened heart.

Season after season, year after year, this spiritual energy is at work in us, coaxing, pushing, prodding, inviting us and in general doing whatever it takes to wake us up and bring us into a more abundant way of life. As with the ancestors of old, God will lead us out of our experience with slavery and servitude. The Spirit will gather us in from places of exodus and periods of exile. And if there are times of wandering and weeping, we understand it all as part of the journey. We see it all in the context of Something More. We are learning to trust in God, and becoming all the more people of God.

Susan's most recent adventure in spiritual awakening came to her through trainings in Internal Family Systems, but it doesn't really matter where it is that you encounter the Holy Spirit. Wherever you do, whenever you do, it's all the same. Come close to God, and your life will change. Look at the scriptures. The Bible is full of people with changed hearts and changed lives, people like Moses and Miriam, Abraham and Sarah, David, Samuel, Jacob and Noah, Elizabeth and Zechariah, Mary and Joseph, the disciples and countless others.

Jesus brings us the good news, but it doesn't always translate into good times. Mary had one of those encounters with the Holy Spirit. The angel of the Lord shows up, and her whole life changes. The whole world changes. In the long run, it works out for our good, but it was pretty darn costly for her. She ended up on the outside of her community, and her son ended up on a cross outside the city of Jerusalem. We may call her *blessed*, but most of us would far rather bless her than actually be her.

The Holy Spirit moves. It has a way of working with us and within us, whether we like it or not. The blind see, the lame walk, lepers are healed, and disciples leave their livelihoods; nothing stays the same. Some people call this healing. Some people call it conversion. I like to call it transformation. Transformation is a user-friendly word for whatever the Spirit is up to. Call it whatever you want. Jesus doesn't care. All he ever says is the same old thing: come and follow me.

You can say yes if you want to, but you should be forewarned. The Holy Spirit will draw you out to where you cannot return. Open your heart to God, and there will be no going back. You can't play it safe. This is what I say to Susan. You might end up renewing your congregation, but you also might end up leaving your church. You might give up some old beliefs, but you will find a deeper faith. You may wander in the wilderness for a long before you enter the Promised Land. It's a little risky.

As for me, I was already on the trail of Christ, the Coyote, with all his wily ways. I already knew to expect the unexpected.

There are no guarantees, I say. No guarantees, except for one: that God will work for good.

In the beginning, certain aspects of the IFS model were challenging for me. The whole idea of spending time with myself and learning how to love myself ran counter to much of what I had learned in the Christian church. It seemed to run contrary to the Christian culture of self-sacrifice. I had been taught to sacrifice myself for the good of others. I had been raised to deny my needs, and I don't mean just set them aside; I mean, forget that I had any, much less any right to honor them or tend to them.

Then I had one of those "light-bulb" moments, a flash of insight, or perhaps a moment of inspiration. I saw that we could treat our parts on the inside just as Jesus treated people on the outside. We could be compassionate with our parts, as Jesus was compassionate toward people. I realized that a more full and authentic faith would, in fact, have this kind of consistency; it would be congruent. There would be the same kind of spiritual leadership within as without. I got the goose-bumps. It was thrilling to think that I could embody Christ in this way, in all dimensions of my being and in all aspects of inter-relationship.

IFS turned out to be a path for spiritual awakening and transformation. It became a means through which I could enter into the presence of God. IFS opened up a whole new mission field; only this time, on the inside, on the inside of me. IFS opened me up to me. It put me in touch with a lot of different parts of me, including some that I didn't like and had tried hard to disown. It brought forth experiences that I had tried to put behind me, deny and forget. Tell the truth, I thought I had done a pretty good job of moving on. I thought I was leaving the past in the past. Turns out, I was wrong. I was simply saving up for later, and now I had quite the backlog. All that awareness -- it was a little overwhelming. I was awake for sure, but raw.

And then, too, I wondered what I was supposed to make of all those other people practicing the model. They were a diverse group. They came from all walks of life and practiced many different spiritual paths. They tuned in to another spiritual dimension. They heard things and saw things and got messages from the Divine. I wondered what kind of flaky, far-out thing I had gotten myself into. Mind you, these were the exact same things that I had been experiencing all along, but at least I knew better than to talk about it. I knew that such experiences were entirely consistent with scripture, it's just that, personally, I prefer a little more control… well, actually a lot more control. I'm big on spiritual experience; I just like to think it through first. Spiritual presence is fine so long as it gets filtered through my brain before I let it loose in the world.

But mostly, I could sense that something in me was about to shift. I didn't know what to think, and that scared me as much as anything.

Still, it all felt right, and much of what I learned made sense. I was familiar with the concept of a spiritual self and with Thomas Merton's concept of "True Self." The idea of multiple inner perspectives certainly fit with my experience. I was well aware of the arguments that raged in me, and inside most people I knew, even the Christians. *Especially* the Christians. I for sure knew the pain of wounding inside of me and I was staggering under the weight of all that I carried. And then too, I had experienced the healing power of Holy Presence long before I met Dick and his model.

So there I sat on the beautiful cliffs of Big Sur, soaking up the sun and the sounds of the surf. I tried to picture myself explaining all of this to the folks back home. I couldn't. How could I? I couldn't even explain it to myself.

Was I losing my mind?
Losing my way?
Or both?

I felt disoriented, and yet I knew… I *knew* that I was in the right place and on the right track. God was at work in me and I felt certain that the Holy Spirit was at work within this model. I saw many similarities between Christian spirituality and IFS. I saw them, not even so much as complementary spiritual paths, but as the same path only viewed through different lenses and discussed through a different vocabulary.

Still, I needed to know more. My inner theologian and my inner defense attorney were in strong agreement. They would not be satisfied until I did a more systematic exploration of IFS and its congruence with the Christian faith. I went back home and went to work.

I have studied the model and searched the scriptures. I have done this work and offer it gladly, but you should know up front that it won't be enough. Even if you, like me, are Christian, this book alone won't do it for you. Jesus may be The Way, but he has this funny way of walking us down different paths. My answers may not be your answers. My questions might not even be your questions. This book may serve as a guide, but some of the work you have to do for yourself. It's in your lesson plan.

There's more to it than that. I have satisfied my need to know, but knowledge alone is not enough. It's not enough to know *about* God; we have to *know* God, know God and experience God for ourselves -- develop our own personal trusting relationship with the Divine. In truth, the only thing that has ever satisfied my hungry heart and busy mind is presence of Holy Spirit -- God With Us.

As a pastor and a therapist, I take a fairly pragmatic approach. I use the IFS model because it works; people get the help and healing that they need. As an individual, I use the model for the exact same reason: it works. I get the help and the healing that I need. Through IFS, I enter into the presence of God. In the Spirit of Christ, I gather me in -- all my lost and exiled parts. Not only is it possible for me to be redeemed from my past, even the past itself is redeemed. God sanctifies to me my deepest distress. Yes, IFS helps me heal and it makes me whole. It does what Jesus does; it works as the Spirit works. At heart, IFS is the experience of God's amazing grace, and it makes more room for Christ in me. I was seeking and this is what I found. IFS: it's where the Spirit led, so in the end, what else could I do?

I don't know who you are or how you come to be reading this book, but I do know this: Coyote Christ is up to something.

Always is.

How is the Holy at work in you? What in you is waking up, stirring and stretching into life? More important, will you allow it? Make room for it? Welcome it, even, in the name of Jesus? Will you follow where the Spirit leads?

IFS is a resource right at hand and this Self-led way of life, this way of letting the Holy Spirit lead within you… it's quite the ride, wild and wonderful, and it will, if you let it, lead you into the very heart of Christ and into the very kingdom of God. And let me tell you, it doesn't get any better than that.

I do not understand my own actions.
For I do not do what I want, but I do the very thing I hate...
                                        (Romans 7:15)

Those conflicts and disputes among you, where do they come
from? Do they not come from your cravings that are at war
within you? ... Do you suppose that it is for nothing that the
scripture says, "God yearns jealously for the spirit that he has
made to dwell in us"?

                                        (James 4:1, 5)

Multiplicity and the War Within

If life is a puzzle, then you can sometimes find key pieces revealed in a single word -- words like compassion, or gratitude, or in my case, Raskolnikov.

In Dostoevsky's *Crime and Punishment*, Raskolnikov is the main character, a man who turns out to be an axe-murderer. The first time I read that book in college I was delighted to find him, which I'm sure says nothing good about me. From childhood, I have been intrigued by things that cut both ways: arrowheads in the hills of Kentucky, sharks' teeth along the beaches of Florida, and people everywhere with an edge, the ones who show up with a dual dimension to their personalities -- the ones like me.

Raskolnikov means "split skull" and it's the name of a man tormented by inner dialogue, driven to distraction and to destruction by the voices in his head. He is torn between right and wrong, between self-judgment and self-justification. When I was little, before I knew the word Raskolnikov, I made up my own name for the jumble going on inside my head. I called it *brain fever*. At night, I would lay awake in bed and listen to the voices within. Sometimes they were a big help. They helped me make sense out of the insensible. They helped me sort out my feelings and sift through my options. It was like having my own home team. But other nights, the noise in my head could drive me nuts. Some of these guys had pretty strong opinions. They were not shy, and they did not play nice. I would tune them out or shut them up, an approach that never seemed to work very well or very long. Sooner or later, they wormed their way back in and it would start all over again.

These guys are still at work in me, and when they get going, it looks something like this:

I say to myself, look, you are going to have to do something about this. You can't let this go on any longer… You're being treated unfairly. You're being taken advantage of, disrespected. You have to talk to them.

But I don't want to, another voice speaks up. They might get mad. What if they're mean to me? And what if I start to cry? That would be the worst, a direct violation of the Tough Girls Guide to Life.

I say to myself, maybe it's not so bad. Maybe you're being too sensitive, overreacting, making a mountain out of a molehill.

Then, dripping with contempt, another voice says, maybe you're just being a chicken, avoiding conflict… again… the way you always do. You're such a loser.

The debate rages on.

All of a sudden, I realize that I'm hungry, very hungry, starving. I hadn't noticed before, but now I see. I could use a little break. I need a little cake and I need it now. Chocolate cake. One…two…three pieces should just about do it.

I scold myself. Stay focused!

I rehearse exactly what I want to say. I make sure that I am being completely reasonable, logical and clear – beyond any possible misunderstanding or reproach. I prepare myself against counter-attack.

I get myself calm. I pray. I am ready.

I open my mouth but when I speak, it's as though I'm possessed. Some voice I don't recognize says something that I never meant to say: "What the hell is wrong with you?!"

From the bleachers, Jesus grins. Well, he says, it's not what I would do.

Yes, finding Raskolnikov was a big relief for me. I learned that I am not alone, that I am not the only one with a brain that works like this, even though it is a smallish comfort to find yourself in good company with an axe-murderer. Since then, I've learned that a lot of people work like this. It's like having the devil whisper in one ear while an angel whispers in the other. Though I gotta say, for me it feels more like a whole debate team has taken up residence inside my skull. The arguments go round and round until I drive myself nuts. I end up paralyzed and in despair. Sometimes I manage to break through the log-jam. I take some decisive action only to realize later that I have not come from an authentic spiritual center. Some other force has taken over and caused me to act in ways that are less than godly.

Apparently the Apostle Paul had this same problem. In his letter to the church at Rome he says, "I do not understand my own actions. For I do not do what I want, but I do the very thing I hate."

Like Paul, I hate it when this happens, and when it does, I go off on myself. How can I be so stupid? I should know better. I do know better. What's wrong with me?

I get so down on myself. It feels like I'm never going to get it right.

I do the things I hate, and I take this to mean that I'm dumb, a slow learner. Other people in this same situation interpret it differently. Some people see it as moral failure, a sure sign that they are lacking in faith, not as spiritually advanced or enlightened as they ought to be. *If only I had more faith*, they say, *I wouldn't be like this. I wouldn't act like this. I am a terrible person.*

It's true, when we are closely connected with God, we tend to say and do things that are more consistent with our faith. When we have the Spirit of Christ within, we live lives that are more congruent with the life that Jesus lived. I find it challenging. Tuning in to the Spirit is like tuning in to a radio station: the signal may be transmitted 24/7, but my reception is spotty. My connection is sometimes clear and at other times distorted with static. Sometimes I can't hear anything at all. I am not always attuned to God. Most of the time I live with a divided heart and a split brain. I can get it together for a little while, but then I find myself being torn apart from the inside out. It's Raskolnikov all over again.

What does Christian theology make of this inner divide? Paul attributes it to the presence of sin, which dwells within our flesh and is an inevitable part of the human condition. The Church Fathers account for it through the theological concepts of *Imago Dei* and *Original Sin*; we are made in the image of God but this image is corrupted through some kind of "genetic" spiritual mutation. Martin Luther described us as *corpus mundum*, mixed bodies with the capacity for both great good and great evil. Reformed theologians speak of *total depravity*, which despite how it sounds does not mean that we are totally depraved; it simply means that self-interest weaves its way into our efforts for good: our motives are always mixed.

James says that it's a divided heart which creates the divisions among us and that the disorder in our relationships flows from the disorder in our hearts: "Those conflicts and disputes among you, where do they come from? Do they not come from your cravings that are at war within you?"

Christian theology is well acquainted with internal divide, and in his clinical practice, Dick Schwartz kept seeing the same thing. He kept seeing clients like me, people suffering from inner conflict, people who were trying desperately and unsuccessfully to control or eliminate their inner voices, the parts of themselves that they hated. Not only did his clients suffer on the inside, these inner wars had a way of carrying over into external relationships. Instead of harmony, there was conflict. Instead of relationships characterized by unconditional love, clients practiced conditional approval. They judged and rejected others, even the ones they loved the most.

Psychologists know about this kind of inner turmoil, but for the most part they have considered it a form of pathology. Presuming a unitary mind, they have labeled it as a disorder of personality. Dick, on the other hand, found that this kind of internal dialogue is not the exception; it's the rule. It isn't specific to those who experience traumatic events or childhood neglect, nor is it unique to the realm of the mentally ill. Like generations of Christian theologians before him, Dick found it to be the norm in human makeup. It's not pathology; it's part of being human. It's who we are; it's how we come.

The first time I heard Dick talk about this, it was like reading Dostoevsky for the first time. I felt that same sense of relief. I am not the only one who works like this! Everyone works like this – axe-murderers and otherwise. And Dick gave me a new word. Multiplicity is a whole lot easier to spell than Raskolnikov.

Multiplicity in the model means that we carry within us multiple perspectives, a variety of parts which carry different memories, express different needs and desires, hold different beliefs and have different approaches to the life that we are trying to live. In the IFS model, these parts are not just my emotions gone amuck; they are multi-dimensional sub-personalities that are part and parcel of my make-up. I feel divided because I am. I can be furious with my mother, yet long for her approval and affection. I can be happy about some accomplishment, but in the next moment afraid that I will mess things up. I pray for overtime so Duke can pull out the win, but another part of me just wants the game to end so I can go to bed. I am happy when my friend is recognized, but I resent that my own achievement wasn't acknowledged. I can love my husband and I can hate him -- at the very same time. That's just the way it is. That's just the way I am. It's the way we come. Good to know.

There are multiple perspectives in every form of human community, on the inside and out. In our couple relationships, in our families, in our communities, in our country -- we have differing points of view and it is hard for us to make room for them all, much less honor and respect them all. It's as though our brains are too small. It's hard for us to take in a lot of information, especially when the information is contradictory or complex. We could try to expand our minds. Or, we could let go of our need to be master minds, our attempts to gain mastery and control over our environment. Instead of working with our own limitation, we usually try to make the world a smaller place and put things in their place. We synthesize and distill, reduce and refine, come up with formulas that help us govern the world. We integrate and whatever doesn't fit the schemata, we ignore or discount or reject outright.

Someone has to come out on top. Someone must be right. This is how we think, and this way of thinking makes us scrabble to establish our version of the Truth. People will fight over the one correct and authoritative version of any testament. This is true whether we're talking religion or science, politics or personal life. Myself, I used to spend a lot of time arguing with my oldest brother about the things that happened in our growing up. We never got anywhere at all until the time when we were right in the middle of an argument and I suddenly realized that he hadn't even been there when this particular event happened. My version of the truth was, in fact, the only version, which means, of course, I win! I also decided then and there that the whole enterprise was ridiculous, this arguing about what really happened when. Maybe it was time to give it up.

People rarely agree on The Truth because we come at things from different points of view, we have different experiences of the same event. We are like witnesses to a car accident; each one may see it a little differently, but none of us are wrong. It doesn't mean that the accident didn't happen; it just means that no one of us holds the whole picture. We are like blind people exploring the elephant; each one grasps a different piece. Each has some wisdom about the beast, but no one holds the whole truth about Elephant. No matter what size the gathering, we humans are diverse, and we have to make room for all, and harmony comes only when differing perspectives find shelter under one very big umbrella, or co-exist within a single skin.

At every level of organization, human systems are complex. I know I am. There are many pieces to my elephant. Some parts of me are competent and constructive, fun-loving and fair-minded. Other parts are mean and nasty, bent on destruction. Others are anxious and afraid, easily taken advantage of. The inner turmoil can be ferocious. At times, all of this gets in my way and in the way of what I have to do. I don't like it. I am just like the generations of theologians and psychologists who have gone before: I do not like the way I am. Parts of me I do not like; I do not like them here or there, I do not like them anywhere. And while this makes total sense, self-judgment is just the thing to make things worse.

When things go wrong, I get angry. I don't like this anger. It reflects poorly on my Christian character. Besides, I've been on the receiving end of someone else's anger and I don't like it very much. So I judge my anger. I blame myself for having it. I try to put it in its place. This does not help. My anger grows more intense. Now my attitude toward anger has become just as big a problem as whatever it was that made me mad in the first place. Buddhist monk Thich Nhat Hanh says:

"If we become angry at our anger, we will have two angers at the same time."

That's how I am with many of my parts. I get depressed but I don't like being depressed. I don't like the way it feels. I don't like how it behaves. I try to get rid of it, but I can't. Now I'm depressed about being depressed. Or anxious. I don't like anxiety – the things it does, the way it makes me feel. I try to beat it back, but I can't. Now I'm so worried about my anxiety that I begin to have panic attacks.

There's no doubt -- parts can be problematic, but they are still part of us and if we're are going to be made whole, then by definition, we need them all. No one can go missing. No parts locked away in the towers, hidden in the closets, or buried in the basements. Talk like this scares even me. What I usually want is to get rid of the troublemakers – the ones that cause me pain or create problems in my relationships. The simple-minded me has a simple approach. Let's get rid of the trouble-makers and find a way to make the split complete. But then I guess we'd be talking lobotomy, or some other form of amputation, and that doesn't seem like a very good idea either. It might be wise to find another approach. Maybe I could make room at the table for all these different parts. Maybe I could listen, learn, and lend a helping hand. Maybe I could make friends with my enemies before they bring me down. I think Jesus said something like that.

IFS helped me do this very thing. IFS taught me how to form new relationships with all the different parts in me. It helped me see them in a whole new light. These parts: they are the wounded ones in me. Many of them hold on to the hard-times and the traumas. They bear the brunt of so much pain. When things went wrong, they got left holding the bag. They got stuck with the past, got stuck in the past, while the rest of me moved on.

From time to time these burdened parts of mine act up, but hatred doesn't help. Condemnation doesn't help.

Abandonment doesn't help. They've had enough of that already. What helps is this: to be seen and heard, acknowledged and treated with respect. They want to be honored for whatever they hold and then what they really want is to be healed, so they don't have to hold on to these burdens anymore. Freed from the old roles, they can be transformed and take on new life. What they really need is the love of God, of God's own Self. Call it conversion, call it salvation, call it whatever you like, it is the power of Holy Spirit, and it turns out that here, within these troubled parts of me, within the very place of my greatest suffering, that God's even greater love is most revealed.

Multiplicity: it's the way that we are made, but it's not just a principle of our psychology. It's a fundamental paradigm in life. Once you start looking for it, you'll find it everywhere.

Nature is rife with multiplicity, outrageously so. God is flashy in this way, a divine creative energy that adorns the earth with diversity - over 20,000 species of butterflies and countless varieties of flowers, 34,000 kinds of spiders and 450 kinds of sharks, each with multiple sets of teeth.

Multiplicity is all over the scriptures. The Good Book itself is not really a book, it's a library, a compilation of many books that express multiple points of view. In Matthew 7, Jesus says, "Do not judge, so that you may not be judged." In Matthew 10, Jesus says, "If anyone will not welcome you or listen to your words, shake off the dust from your feet as you leave that house or town. Truly I tell you, it will be more tolerable for the land of Sodom and Gomorrah on the Day of Judgment than for that town." Jim Rand, Presbyterian pastor, says, "the Bible does not insist on uniformity or conformity. It sings praise and bears witness to God in a choir of voices, not a single melody line. It carries out an ongoing dialogue and conversation with itself – sometimes heatedly so – with truth emerging from its multiple perspectives."

Multiplicity is critical for a vibrant church life. We benefit from all the different perspectives, the different gifts, the different ministries, and in I Corinthians 12, Paul urges us to honor the multiplicity within our midst. "For just as the body is one and has many members, and all the members of the body, though many, are one body, so it is with Christ. For in the one Spirit we were all baptized into one body -- Jews or Greeks, slaves or free -- and we were all made to drink of one Spirit. Indeed, the body does not consist of one member but of many."

Jesus valued multiplicity. Talk about a man who liked the spice of life. He had followers from all over. There were Jewish fishermen and Syro-Phoenician women. There were tax collectors and other cultural outcasts – the sick and the strange. There were community leaders like Jairus, Nicodemus and Joseph of Arimathea. There was even a Roman centurion who found his faith at the foot of a cross.

Let's be frank. The original followers of Jesus were a diverse if not motley crew. Some of these people came with personal baggage and others came with cultural legacies of prejudice and hate. Some of them were lacking in social skills. A few of them were just plain weird. I'm guessing that some of them did *not* get along. Can you imagine what it would be like if any one of them had been put in charge of entrance exams or membership standards? This merry little band would have fallen apart at the start. The Christian movement would have collapsed before it ever got off the ground. But Jesus, he welcomed them all to his table, so what could they do? His followers had no choice. They had to learn how to live with each other. Even worse, they had to learn how to love each other. So do we.

Multiplicity – it's not just how we're made; it's what we know of God: the Triune God, the Three in One. Christians confess one God, but that God can be found in multiple forms. Divine multiplicity is expressed in the doctrine of the Trinity: God as Father, Son and Holy Ghost; God: the Creator, Christ and

24

Holy Spirit.   One substance; three persons, and so within God's own Self we find a multiplicity of spiritual relationship – Divine Self to Divine Self, Sacred Heart to Sacred Heart: Thou and Thou and Thou.

At times, I still long to be of one mind and pursue my goals with efficient focus.   But then I remember how many lives have been laid waste through the single-minded pursuit of a particular cause.   I think about all the different truffles at the candy counter and all the different kinds of kringle at the bakery, and how much my life is enriched through multiplicity. I go to church and find an amazing array of people with different personalities and different perspectives, all of whom share one faith and worship one God, and do it in very different ways.   Our world is rich in its complexity, and we humans are fearfully, wondrously made.

Now that I understand the principle and the value of multiplicity, I'm more accepting of the human condition, of my human condition. I'm more willing to work with who I am. I am forming new and trustworthy relationships with the different parts of me. IFS did that. It's a funny thing. I listen now to all those different voices. I do my best to welcome them and treat them with respect. I bring them in close, and when I do, they seem to settle down.   It's what I wanted in the first place -- a little peace and quiet, for goodness' sake.

I make room for all my parts and somehow this makes more room in me for God.

It's a paradox, a mystery; strange, but true. The Holy Spirit comes within and goes to work in me. My divided heart begins to heal at last. It's how I find shalom.

You are the light of the world… let your light shine before others,
so that they may see your good works and give glory to your Father
in heaven.

(Matthew 5:14-16)

Do you not know that you are God's temple
and that God's Spirit dwells in you?
(I Corinthians 3:16)

The Holy Canary

No matter what they say, the Holy Spirit is not a Dove; it's a Canary. It sings in you and it sings in me. I didn't learn that in seminary. I got this all on my own, but you can have it for free. The first time it happens, I am four. I'm in the cherub choir at church, but I'm not in the church exactly. I'm outside on the stone path which steps along the wall and dips down into the garden. I am singing one of the nursery songs. Forty-some years later, I still remember the words, but what I remember most is how it felt to be singing like that, with abandon -- full in my belly, strength in my chest, and with joy, as voice flows up through my body and enters the world. There's a song on my lips and it comes from my heart.

The morning star creeps over the hill,
While woods are dark and birds are still,
Children think of God's sweet care,
And they know his love is everywhere.

I am calm, but more than that, I am aware of the calm. A sturdy confidence fills me, flowing into every part of my little body and reaching into every fiber of my being. I know without knowing: I belong. I belong to the children's choir and I belong to this church, yes, but I belong to Something More. I am part of some greater chorus; I sing as part of some larger song.

Spirit sings in me, but from what I can tell, it comes to different people in different ways and it comes to us differently in different times of our life. We encounter Jesus in the scriptures, or in the sacraments, or in times of worship. Spirit flows through song and dance and finds expression in all manner of art. More coordinated friends assure me that the Spirit can even be found in athletic endeavors, moves as they move. Mathematicians even find God in the beauty of math. Go figure. Yes, some people see God in all things, look at a common thorn bush and find it aflame with the glory of God. Some people see Christ in everyone they meet.

Dick has come to see spiritual presence everywhere. This awareness came as a gradual unfolding. Working with clients, Dick followed their lead and listened with an open mind. He listened, and as he did, he began to hear the sound of Something More, a thread of transcendent something which his clients identified as "myself," and which Dick came to call the *Self*. This happened again and again until he came to understand Self as spiritual essence, a universal quality or capacity, inherent in us all.

It was quite the awakening and not anything that he ever expected, but there you have it. You never know when the Holy of Holies is going to show up. The Spirit is unpredictable. It blows where it will, Paul says, and this is all well and good, if you like surprises. Some of us do not like surprises. Some of us are not all that flexible. We want to know what's what and what you can count on in this life. Some of us would like God to be a little more predictable. I have tried to talk to Jesus about this, made a few helpful suggestions, but he's not all that interested. He says instead that I have made a god out of security. He says maybe I should take a good hard look at that, only I'm not interested, so there we are.

The first time Jesus shows up, I am just a child. In the years to come, there will be times when I lose the sense of him -- for days, or months, or more, but I will never forget. I know that God *is*, all the time, whether I can sense divine presence or not. This knowing helps, but not always. There are the bad times when I feel lost and alone. It's like playing Holy Hide and Seek, only I can't find Jesus, or God, or the Holy Spirit, or anything good at all. I get small and bitter. It seems like Jesus could be a good sport and show up a little, if only to help me out. Mostly, I blame God for this sense of absence, as if God's attendance is spotty, as if the disconnect that I feel comes from God's side of the equation.

I might be in the pit, but all around me, Spirit still moves. The earth still turns. The sun still shines, the rain still falls, and the God who is, is the God who will be, whether I can see it or not. God is not on hold, waiting around for me to get my act together. The world turns. Tell the truth, I'm not sure how I feel about this. When I hurt, I want everyone to sit up and take notice. Do I want the whole world to stop for me? Absolutely. But when I'm in a better frame of mind, I see how the Spirit keeps on stirring the waters, no matter what, and ultimately this gives me a greater hope. It's good to know that God is out there working on my behalf, whether I know it or not, whether I claim him or not. The love of Christ, it reaches out into all the world. I learned this from another song.

> *Jesus loves the little children, all the children of the world,*
> *Red and yellow, black and white, they are precious in his sight.*
> *Jesus loves the little children of the world.*

Jesus loves the little children, all the children of the world. There's no mystery in that. For me, the mystery is why some of God's children see him, and others don't? How is it that some people have the gift of Extra Spiritual Perception, while others seem tone-deaf to any sort of divine frequency?

Jesus showed up there on the garden path and my life changed forever. Having seen, I couldn't unsee. Having heard, I couldn't close my ears. I didn't want to. Having been with God, I longed for more. It's like being in love. You may not be in love at the moment, but you remember how it feels. You never forget what it's like to be in love. It's what you live for. We long for return.

I grew up with spiritual longing. It shaped my life and informed my path. In the 1980's, I was out looking for a career. Clinical psychology sounded pretty cool – academic challenge at acceptable reimbursement rates. I checked it out but what I found was a heavy emphasis on functioning. I wasn't so sure about that. I knew a lot of highly functioning people with hardened hearts and eroded ethics. I knew plenty of people who were successful according to the standards of this world, but they were walking around with unhealed wounds. Churches and corporations are full of people like this. I was one, and I had a sneaking suspicion that even higher levels of accomplishment weren't going to do the trick.

It turned out that few theorists actually believed in the possibility of healing, or held out any hope for wholeness. They were interested in drives and urges, cognition and chemistry, social constructs. Social science seemed heartless. Worse than that, it had no soul. If anything, there was a distinct bias against religion and a deep-seated suspicion about spirituality in general. I was looking for someone who knew about the connection between wholeness and holiness. Did anyone understand the power of sacred presence? What about the hope and healing which comes through a personal relationship with Jesus or an experience of divine grace? And what about the holiness of human spirit itself, and the way that Holy Spirit works within the human heart?

A Great Divide had opened up between psychology and

theology, between the secular and the sacred. It seemed so wrong to me -- the splitting unnatural, and the compartmentalization unhealthy, and it created a dilemma for people of any faith. The bias against religion made it hard for people to find counselors who were both spiritually fluent and clinically competent. When it began to feel like a choice between the standards of professional success and my own sense of Spirit, I gave up the search and entered seminary.

I made this choice because spiritual awareness matters. Spiritual presence has powerful impact. The Coyote Christ is a master of disguise and the Holy of Holies may catch me unaware, but when I have the eyes that see, everything is transformed. Everything in me is transformed. God shows up and I am strangely calm. My mind is still, my heart at rest. I trust, and this sudden loss of critical skepticism; it's so not me. It's like I have stepped into another world, and at the same time, I am fully present in this one. The boundaries of individual being melt away, yet I'm more at home in my body than ever. I am one with God. It isn't that I've lost my sense of self: it's more like Spirit has become concentrated and amplified within. Like Mary, the mother of Jesus, my soul seems to magnify the presence of God. That's how it is – a full on sensory experience. The Spirit comes within our Flesh; we bear God's grace within our bones, and after that, nothing is the same.

That's how it's been for me. This abiding sense of Holy Presence… this holy sense of Abiding Presence… it is held within my blood and bones. I am spirit, and I am flesh. I am body, and I am soul. I am connected in my every aspect of my being.

I learned this from my life; but I also learned it from the Christian scriptures. In the Bible, this critical connection between spirit and flesh is talked about in many different ways, and nowhere more graphically than in the creation account found in the second chapter of Genesis. God takes dirt from the ground, forms it into human figures and breathes this inert matter into being. Our material bodies are brought to life through the literal inspiration of God's own Spirit. This is quite a trick. If you've ever made mud pies or mud people, you know what I'm talking about.

In the New Testament, Jesus tells us that we can receive even more of this power for life. We can embody more of this spiritual energy: "I will pray the Father and he will give you another Counselor, to be with you for ever, even the Spirit of truth...you know him, for he dwells with you, and will be in you...you will know that I am in my Father, and you in me, and I in you." During Pentecost, the Holy Spirit is poured out on all the people gathered, a Spirit so alive and crackling that it is described as fire dancing through the crowd. Still later, Paul admonishes us, "Do you not know that you are God's temple and that God's Spirit dwells in you?"

Yes, we are people of spirit as well as flesh. When I need help, I look for people who get that. I look for those who know that the soul exists, even though spiritual presence isn't always obvious from the outside. Look at me and there's no guarantee that you will see Jesus. Talk about holy hide and seek! Most days it takes a little work to find him, buried as he is within my flesh. Some days, it takes a lot of work. Other days, you might as well just give up altogether and take it on faith. I want people in my life who get that, who understand that we are made in the image of God, no matter how ugly we look or how ugly we act. People who get this will treat you with honor and respect, whether they like you or not, whether you can pay or not, whether you deserve it or not. They do it for the love of God, because they can see the God in you, the presence of Christ in every one they meet.

When I need help, I look for people who are spiritually grounded, but I don't have any hard and fast rules about this. When it comes to service providers, I don't have a litmus test of belief. I don't require a Christian chimney sweep or a Presbyterian plumber, but when I'm in serious trouble, I do look for those who know about this treasure within. I trust the ones who trust in God. Don't get me wrong, I also want the best. I want professionals who are competent; it's just that I want people who see what they do as a form of service, who understand themselves as healers in the hands of an even greater Physician.

This is not a sign of spiritual enlightenment; it's more like enlightened self-interest. The way I see it, God works with those who work with God, and consciousness itself opens up avenues of divine possibility. Spiritual awareness opens me up so I can more fully receive the guidance and the grace of God, and if I'm in trouble, I want all the help that I can get.

It's amazing to me, but there are a lot of people out there who don't get this, who don't seem to know that we have a spiritual dimension. Of those who do, many don't seem to care. People do not approach their life from a spiritual perspective. People do not honor Christ as he comes to us in the form of another. This is hard for me. I am a person of bias and limited imagination, so I don't expect to find spirituality in the business world, in the arena of marketing and profit-making, but I do expect to find it in the helping and healing professions and in the church for sure. I'm a slow learner; I still get disappointed.

On the whole, we in the western world seem to be slow learners. It has taken a long time for us to reclaim spiritual perspective, to reconnect body with soul and regain a holistic approach to healing, and it would take a long time before I would find a valid psycho-spiritual approach to healing. In the early 80's, Dick was just developing the IFS model. He was busy with that, and I was busy as a pastor and chaplain. I took all kinds of classes and trainings and learned what I could of healing and pastoral care. I was pretty good at it, but my practice was largely intuitive. At church, I preached the principles of spiritual transformation but I didn't know how to apply these in a way that consistently helped my parishioners. All along, I was looking for a way to help people to develop their own faith so they wouldn't have to depend so much on me as their spiritual leader.

The first time I heard Dick present the model, it was something of a spiritual experience. Finally, here was someone who got it! Here was someone who understood the interconnection of psychology, systemic thinking and spirituality. And he's famous. Like... has credibility and everything. In one afternoon, all my trails converged and my fragmented life became a whole.

It's like that for a lot of people. We are introduced to the model and have a sense of instant recognition. IFS feels like something we always knew, but never named; something we sensed but didn't know how to put into words. Dick is the first to say that he has not created a new phenomenon. He did not create internal family systems, but rather developed a model that recognized these systems and gives us a way to work within them. He developed a new framework that fits with our inner experience -- a new model, a new language, a new way to work with what is. Here, finally, is a clinically sound model of psychotherapy which locates healing in the very place where people of faith have always found it -- in spiritual relationship, in the life-giving connection between the holy and the human. To my way of thinking, IFS has brains, but best of all, it has a Soul.

Dick didn't start out to be my hero. He didn't even set out to develop a spiritual model of psychotherapy. It just showed up. That Spirit blowing wherever it will. In the beginning, clients introduced him to the idea of parts and the principle of multiplicity. Before long they began to teach him about something else, about that Something More. As his clients began to separate from their extreme parts, they began to relate to themselves and others in a new way, from a different sort of place. They seemed to be more centered and grounded, and they embodied a presence which they identified simply as "my Self." In time, Dick made a connection between this "Self" and what others called the "Soul."   "It seems," says Dick, "that we all have qualities like curiosity, compassion, calmness, confidence, courage, clarity, creativity, and connectedness at our core. It's the soul that spiritual traditions talk about, but most psychotherapies don't know about."

In a 2004 Psychotherapy Networker article entitled "The Larger Self," Dick describes his growing spiritual awareness:

> Clients, once they've discovered the Self at the core of their being, show characteristics of insight, Self-understanding and acceptance, stability and personal growth… The more this happened, the more I felt confronted by what were in essence spiritual questions that simply couldn't be addressed in the terms of problem solving, symptom-focused, results-oriented, clinical technique. I began my own novice's exploration into the literature of spirituality and religion … Though they used different words, all the esoteric traditions within the major religions – Buddhism, Hinduism, Christianity, Judaism, Islam – emphasized the same core belief: we are sparks of the eternal flame, manifestations of the absolute ground of being. It turns out that the divine within – what the Christians call the soul or Christ Consciousness, Buddhists call Buddha Nature, the Hindus Atman, the Taoists Tao, the Sufis the Beloved, the Quakers the Inner Light – often doesn't take years of meditative practice to access because it exists in all of us, just below the surface of our extreme parts.

This understanding of "Self" makes the IFS model inherently spiritual, but the spirituality is generic, broad-based, and it comes with universal application. IFS is not identified with any particular path nor aligned with any particular religious orientation. People from all across the spiritual spectrum have adapted it and use it in their own particular practice. Dick describes Self as spiritual essence, a quality that exists within us and in the world around us. IFS is not a Christological model; it does not explicitly connect Self with the Christian understanding of Jesus as the Christ. It does not address the issue of salvation, at least not in the confessional way that we often describe in the Christian church. On the other hand, the model does facilitate a saving relationship with God; we develop a trusting, healing, transforming connection with the Holy Spirit. IFS is all about that.

As with the followers of any particular faith tradition, Christians bring a distinct identity to the model. It's not an exact fit and so we have to search out the places of continuity and discontinuity. We split all those theological hairs, build our own bridges, and for people of faith, this process is nothing new. Every day we look at the secular and perceive the sacred. Every day we look at the common and find a divine connection. As Christians, we view Self from the perspective of our faith and we offer our faith as a resource for understanding Self. When Paul came to Athens, he undertook this same kind of work, making a connection between what the Greeks worshipped as the "unknown God" and Jesus. What you worship as "unknown," he says, "we proclaim as God, the one who gives to all mortals life and breath…in him we live and move and have our being.'" In the same way, Christians can proclaim the presence of Christ as we find him embodied through the IFS model.

Of course, there is a great diversity within the Christian faith itself, and the bridge between IFS and Christianity will look different for different Christians. The conversation about Christian IFS takes place, not just between Christians and non-Christians; it takes place within the clan. There are probably as many variations of Christian IFS as there are Christians who use it. For some, the fit is close. For others, it is more of a stretch. For some, it is a bridge that goes too far and they may not benefit from the model. But for many Christians, the IFS model serves as a valuable spiritual resource and a means through which we grow in faith.

It's true that the IFS community contains a colorful assortment of spiritual seekers. We are a cornucopia of faith traditions and spiritual persuasions. At times, we might look more like an assortment of fruits and nuts, but that's OK with me. I know myself to be closer kin to people of *any* faith than I am to those who have *no* faith. I am more at home with people who practice any form of spirituality than I am with those who deny the Spirit which dwells within my flesh.

IFS has a fundamental spiritual orientation. Dick calls it Self and we call it Soul, or Spirit. Some people call it mindfulness, or heart awareness, or that of God within, but to me -- it's all God. It's the Spirit of Christ made manifest in a myriad of forms and expressed in a multiplicity of wonderful words and images. Language is a wonderful means of communication and I'm all in favor of it. Use your words. Speak your truth. But when it comes right down to it, words cannot convey the full essence of Spirit, or communicate the depth of spiritual encounter. We can't really define God, or pin down the Sacred; divine presence goes beyond words and in the end, it's not the words that matter the most, but the reality those words describe. It's not the precision with which we speak; it's the actual presence of God, the one who speaks without words and communes with us in the innermost regions of our being.

Despite the difference in our language and the difference in some of our theological orientation, IFS and Christianity share a common faith in the power of spiritual presence and understand spiritual relationship as the key ingredient in life well-lived.

In the IFS model, spiritual presence is the single most important element in facilitating a successful therapy session. Self-energy is key for any therapeutic intervention. In other words, things go better with God in the room. Stay in Self. In IFS, this is the closest thing that we have to a mantra, and most IFS practitioners embrace some form of spiritual grounding or attunement. We sense into the presence of Self. It can happen on the inside, in a matter of moments. It can happen on the outside as a time of shared meditation. It can be explicit or implicit. Like any spiritual practice, it gets easier and more fluid as you go along, and it's just the kind of thing that most pastors do when counseling parishioners or making a pastoral call or moderating a meeting. Christians sense into Self-energy all the time, only when we do it, we call it prayer. We, too, open ourselves to the presence of the Holy Spirit, seek its leading and its guidance. We set aside our own needs, our own desires, and our own designs in order to make way for God's unfolding. We have a mantra of our own: Your will, O Lord, not ours, be done.

In both approaches, spiritual energy is the active ingredient, leaven in the loaf. Divine presence is essential, and this is not a matter of metaphor. It's material. It's the real presence of God -- of the God who comes to us in whatever form and by whatever name that we are willing to receive, the God who comes alongside us in the service of a greater good. God, who makes us as one through the presence of Holy Spirit.

Spiritual presence is the key ingredient in the process of healing, so what we are looking for is a way to connect with this presence, a way to tap into the power of spiritual energy for personal and communal transformation. The IFS model gives us a way to do this. There is a methodology, but the model itself is not mechanistic. It's much more organic and flows from a family systems framework, which means that it adapts to the needs of a particular relationship. IFS can help people address specific behavioral issues and specific life problems, but these problems are considered in the light of relationship. The IFS model helps us address the spiritual issues that arise within the context of our human relationships. It helps us develop a personal and trusting relationship with the Self, and well-being in this relationship extends outward to promote healing in all other aspects of life.

A trusting relationship with the Self. The idea is familiar to many Christians, although again, we might describe it a little differently. We might talk about it as trust in the leading of Holy Spirit. We might refer it as a personal relationship with Jesus. We might picture it as a closer walk with God. Spiritual intimacy is a key part of our faith and we often think of it as the kind of relationship that two people might have with each other, as something which takes place in the space between ourselves and God. We're out there in the garden, walking and talking with Jesus. And we can do that. We can do just that. In this form of relationship, I am I and God is God, and we are two together.

There are other ways to picture spiritual relationship that take into account the principle of multiplicity. Instead of a unitary self, we might see ourselves in a more communal sense -- as a whole constellation of parts, an inner community that lives together in relationship with God, a corporate body of faith communing with the Divine Self. Jesus is there within our midst and Spirit takes the lead.

A lot of times it works just like that. We live with God, Christ dwells in us, and this is lovely.

And then there's this other thing that happens. Someone throws a coup. It's an inside job. Some part of me grabs the reins and grabs control, takes me for a ride. I may be consumed with anger. I might be overcome with despair. I find myself cleaning like crazy, organizing for all I'm worth. Round and round I go, on the merry-go-round that is my mind. Whatever part shows up, whatever the particular symptom might be, I am not centered. I am not grounded. I am not "in Self." Without spiritual leadership I am well on my way to being good and lost.

Sometimes I can see this, and awareness is all that it takes for me to regain my balance. Other times, I can see what I'm doing, but seeing is not enough. I see, but I can't seem to do a

38

darn thing about it.   At times like this, I need extra help. I go straight to God, God's own Self, the Real Deal.   I go directly to God and for me this is another form of what the model calls *direct access*.   I have direct access to God and God has direct access to all my parts.   God takes me as I am and hears me out. I get what I need, if not what I want and being in the presence of the Holy Spirit is enough.   My parts settle down and eventually I regain a position of spiritual leadership. I find my ground and off I go again, out into the world, body of Christ.

Our spiritual relationship can look like this.   There are other forms of spiritual relatedness and these take place in different ways, they happen in a different arena.   We can have connection with others in the world and we can have interrelationships within.

As individuals, we each live within a network of connection, a web of relationship.   We are part of larger communities and participate in a variety of human systems.   I am a physical entity connected with immediate family and extended family.   I live in my house on Harrington Drive and my house sits in my neighborhood and my neighborhood, in turn, is part of the north side of Racine, in the county of Racine, in the southeastern corner of Wisconsin, in the Midwest of the United States.   Call before you come.

In the same way, I am an individual soul, but spiritually, I am linked to a larger web of relationship, one that transcends time and space.   I am part of Covenant Presbyterian Church, an individual congregation that is part of the Presbytery of Milwaukee, which is part of the Presbyterian Church, USA, part of the Reformed tradition, part of the Christian tradition, part of the church universal, part of the human race, child of God.

And so it goes in every form of human being.   We participate in ever larger ecologies and ever expanding configurations of relationship.   We go "up the ladder," as it were.

The principles of IFS work at every level of human

organization. It facilitates spiritual leadership within the most secular of human systems and it fosters reconciliation within the arenas of world conflict. That's exciting all by itself. There's more. The IFS model brings something new to the field of systemic theory and it brings systemic theory into the realm of depth psychology. It offers an expanded range, a shift "down the ladder," as it were. Just as we can "zoom out" to view our relationships through a broad lens, we can "zoom in" and focus on our relationships as they exist on the inside of us, within our own internal family system. The micro view.

It's a little surprising the first time you think of yourself as having your own internal family, but once you get the hang of it, once you begin to see it in this way, you'll begin to make a lot more sense to yourself. Have you ever found yourself saying the same things your parents said? Doing the same things your parents did, even though you swore you never would? Have you ever found yourself in relationships that mimic old family patterns? Your parents may be dead and gone, but these dynamics are alive and well. That's because we have these parts in us, alive and well and doing just what they learned to do when you were little. They repeat old patterns because they are locked into old ways of thinking and feeling, hold on to old beliefs.

IFS is pretty hot stuff because it makes a connection between outer systems and inner systems, sees parallel process at work between our external families and our internal families. It brings systemic theory, relationship savvy and spiritual wisdom to our innermost workings and in this way, we can finally do something different. Self is the intervention that makes a difference. Spiritual attunement helps us facilitate reconciliation and healthy relationships among all members of our inner family. Through this process, we get reorganized on the inside and we open to Christ's leading in our lives.

IFS recognizes the presence of Spirit in our world and it acknowledges the power of Spirit within. The model helps me develop a more trusting relationship with God. It helps me embody the Spirit of Christ. IFS brings God a lot closer to home, because it allows for more of the Holy Spirit within my heart. Unlike most models of psychotherapy, IFS has it all: body and soul.

Spirit connects with every part of my flesh, and I can have a relationship with God in every part of my being. I know that this is good and true, but in some ways it is a hard truth, at least for me. If the Spirit of God is really within me, then I've got no good excuse. If I am a temple for Christ, then I will have to treat my body with respect. If Jesus lives within, then I must take him with me wherever I go. If I am truly a body for Christ, then I will have to let his Spirit lead in me. I will have to learn how to love at every level of relationship.

I don't know. That sounds like an awful lot of hard work. I'm not sure I'm up for all of that.

Jesus looks at me and shakes his head. It's not that hard, he says. It's simple. Just be your Self, and let my Spirit shine in you.

Some days, after I have given it my very best shot, when I have done everything I know to do and all my grown-up ways go south, I do just that. I stop working so hard, stop trying to make things happen, stop trying to figure things out, stop trying to gain control. I give up and the stopping is good. I stop talking about the Self and simply rest within the Self. This is so much better. Spirit settles down within my Flesh and as it does, I feel that old familiar feel, the welling up again, the cherished sense that I belong to Something More. Once again, song rises up from my heart and flows out into the world.

This little light of mine,
I'm going to let it shine,
Let it shine, let it shine, let it shine.

41

The Holy Canary.

It sings in you, just as it sings in me.   We're little lights, but how we shine!

We have this treasure in clay jars, so that it may be made clear that this extraordinary power belongs to God and does not come from us. ...so that the life of Jesus may be made visible in our mortal flesh.

(2 Cor. 4:1, 6-12)

Treasure in Clay Jars; IFS and Incarnation

I am in my late mid-40's. By any human standard, this suggests that I am middle-aged. Middle-age is nothing that I ever aspired to, but it's better than the alternatives: being dead, or being 50. Someday I will have to face the fact of growing old, but if all goes well, I still have time, time enough to get my life all straightened out. Being middle aged takes some of the pressure off, but growing old does not compute. How can I be growing old when I'm still growing up, still trying to figure out who I am and find my place in this world?

On the inside, it feels like I'm 25, and growing down. The books say that I am right on target, developmentally speaking. Apparently it is perfectly normal for a person of my advanced middle age to feel like an adolescent all over again. I may be right on target, but I have to tell you, knowing this doesn't make me feel much better. It seems like I should be farther along somehow – that I should be somewhere other than where I am. Better yet, I should be someone other than who I am.

I raised myself on books – the Brothers Grimm, and other tales of transformation – little girls in tower walls and ugly ducklings, a life lived in hope: the dream of turning into something different. The thorny bud blossoms into a rose, the creeping caterpillar changes into a beautiful butterfly. This is what we say to the children: *give it time, and you'll grow out of it. Don't worry; time heals all.*

43

Maybe it works that way for some people, but in my experience time is nothing more than the ticking of the clock. Time alone does not heal, and you can grow old without ever growing up. What I am learning in my ripe middle age is this: that it's time to come to terms with the equipment that I have been given. Transformation, if it comes at all, will have to come from the inside out.

I don't know how old the Apostle Paul was when he wrote his letter to the Corinthians -- old enough to have run up against himself, and hard. He hit his limitations full force. From what I can tell, Paul never did really come to terms with his humanity, and at times he despised his flesh outright. On the other hand, he does not traffic in the fairy tale hope that we will simply outgrow ourselves, or mature naturally into beautiful beings. Paul says something far more subversive. Paul says that we already have a beautiful being, an inner spiritual nature which he describes as treasure contained within our jars of clay.

The part about the clay makes sense to me. Our bodies are a lot like clay - - soft and supple when we're young, less pliable as we go along. As we age, our flesh is not as supple as it used to be and we grow lumps. Our bones become brittle and prone to breakage. We become more fragile and inclined to fracture, like pieces of dried out pottery. In the end, spirit leaves the flesh and what remains feels a lot like clay.

I don't know about you, but I don't really like thinking about this stuff. I don't like thinking about my clay and I certainly don't like the getting lumpy. It makes me nervous, like I should do something, get up and get to work -- mold my dough into something different, something better and stronger than ever before, while there's still time. Every now and then, I get on a fitness kick; try to whip my body into shape. I drive myself like a pair of mules. In the beginning I am kind and speak encouragingly. Then I turn on myself, lash out and threaten. After that, I try and bribe myself with treats. None of it works. In the end I usually feel worse, more embarrassed and

ashamed than when I started.   Mostly, I just try to ignore my
body. I am a good Christian girl and I don't think girls like me
are supposed to be thinking about flesh in the first place.

The fact is, I am spirit and I am flesh, and this may not
have been one of God's brightest ideas. It's certainly not what I
would do. Spirit should come in a prettier package, in some
glimmering, shimmering form -- a hologram or streams of pixie
dust. Gemstones are displayed in elegant settings; expensive
wines come in sleek bottles; beautiful women dress in designer
gowns. But what do we get? What do we end up with? Divine
treasure in earthen jars; Holy Spirit housed in mortal mud. It
seems like a misfit to me, but according to the scriptures, no
mistake. This is the way we come, with body and soul -- a
mismatch made in heaven.

Spirit joins with flesh. That's how the scriptures tell it.
In Genesis 2, God takes earth from the ground and shapes it into
the first human being; *Ā dām* (humankind) comes from *'adamah*
(ground). God breathes into this rough clay and invests us with
ruach. *Ruach* is a word multi-layered and rich with complexity of
meaning, synonymous with divine wind, life, breath, and spirit.
Multiple meanings are conveyed within a single word, and all of
them are understood as the nexus of sacred connection. A
similar process is reenacted at Pentecost.   The people are
inspired, literally in-spirited, as Holy Spirit is poured out upon
them. The Greek word used for this spirit is *pneuma*, and like
ruach, its Hebrew counterpart, it evokes multiple meanings of
divine wind, life, breath, and spirit.   It is the power for life, and
it comes from God.

We are material beings with bodies that are made up of
earthly elements, compounds, chemicals and the like. We are
governed by physical properties. But there is more to us than
meets the eye. Life force flows within us, and this energy comes
from God and is of God. Holy Spirit courses through our veins,
and so our material being, our matter, otherwise inert, comes
alive. Our clay comes fully alive, and this is more than a simple

animism or vitalism. This life that we have, it goes far beyond biology, beyond your basic physiologic process. It comes with awareness. It comes with self-consciousness. We humans come with transcendent capacities. We have a spiritual dimension and this makes it possible for us to transcend our own material being. We can achieve higher motivations and we can move beyond the needs of our flesh. We can align ourselves with a larger purpose and live our lives from a broader perspective. We can love with the love as of God.

The Spirit of Christ: it dwells within us, and the presence of this Spirit makes it possible for us to have spiritual as well as material connections. Through Spirit we commune with the Divine. The presence of Spirit within also means that we can have transcendent relationships with other people, relationships that go beyond physical need or desire. This spiritual dimension is not distinct from our human dust; it's infused throughout our flesh for as long as we live, as long as we still draw breath.

I'm not sure what it says about my spiritual maturity, but me, I'm a lousy breather. They say that breathing is an instinct, but it seems to me that my instinct runs the other way. I am one who holds my breath. I used to see this as a valuable skill, something worth getting good at. I would hold my breath and sink to the bottom of the pool with my brothers, competing to see who could hold out the longest, who could beat our basic need for air. It's just the kind of thing that we would do, and I must have gotten pretty good at it because now I find that it takes no thought whatsoever. The slightest ripple in my day, the smallest wave, and there I am, holding my breath, guarding against whatever is yet to come. My instinct is to mimic death. Like a bunny in the face of prey, I freeze. I freeze, and I've actually been known to faint like this, but it was so embarrassing that I had to give it up. There's one good thing about the fainting, though: it wakes you up. Falling breaks the spell.

Breathing is an automatic brain stem activity, but there's

more to it than that. Breathing is a biological function, but it also operates on a spiritual level. It links me back to God. In each moment of every day, I breathe, and as I do, I draw in that which sustains my life and renews my life. I breathe in oxygen and with it, the life-force that we know as Spirit. I am in-spirited. I am inspired. It's a process that gets repeated countless times each day. I breathe, but mostly unaware... which is fine, because I have a lot of other things to do. I can't be stopping to celebrate every breath or I'd never get anything done. On the other hand, when I do pay attention, I seem to settle down. I settle deeper into my body and experience a deeper connection with God, with life itself, and with all who share my air. Conscious breathing regrounds me in the Ground of All Being. A sense of well-being springs up from within. Breathing with awareness makes me aware of my being alive and aware of my fundamental connection with the Source of Life. No wonder so many spiritual practices focus us on our breath. It's a visceral experience of Holy Spirit: the divine wind, breath, spirit, life. It flows through my nose, my throat, my lungs, my chest. It pushes my belly out and then there's the release. I relax into the process, soften into the exhale. With every breath, I let my troubles go. The very breath of God: it touches me and it puts me in touch with the power of Holy Presence.

In much the same way, the IFS model is based on the direct, visceral experience of sacred presence, of what Dick calls Self and what I understand to be Holy Spirit. The Self, like Spirit, is always there supporting me, but for the most part this takes place out of my awareness. Out of sight, out of mind. Sometimes I forget that Self is there. I forget that God even exists. It's a form of temporary insanity. I go through my days thinking that everything is up to me, that I have to make do with what I've got and make the best of limited resources when, in fact, what I have is access to an unlimited supply of Self-energy. It's ridiculous. It's like receiving this great inheritance and then forgetting all about it. You come to think of yourself as poor, when, in fact, there is abundance. You are rich, but you don't even know. Instead you become more and more miserly, twisting slowly into Scrooge. What a waste of precious resources.

The IFS model proclaims the good news of spiritual abundance. It's like those public notices that they run in the paper every now and then, the ones that advertise unclaimed funds,the ones that say: you have money just sitting in the bank and you might not even know. It's like that.

The IFS model reminds us that we have a great spiritual resource: that heavenly treasure stored in our jars of clay. Our Self joins with our parts, meets them just as they are, right where they are; and where they are is in our flesh. It's the same with Jesus. Jesus meets us just as we are, right where we are; and where we are is in the flesh.

We are people of the skin and bone and because of this we come with basic human needs, needs that need to be met. There's the need for food and water and shelter and rest. There's the need for loving relationship. There's the need to be heard and respected, the need for intimacy and the need for independence. It goes on and on. So many needs. We're so darn needy. It's hard to take, not to mention humiliating, especially if you've been raised on the milk of independence. Needs are scary, especially if there's no way to get them met. Vulnerability isn't safe, not if the people you trust turn on you, betray you, take advantage of you.

When it comes down to vulnerability and your basic human need, Jesus is one of the kindest people that I know. When you're hungry, he doesn't tell you to stop being grumpy; he feeds you. When you're sick, he doesn't tell you to stop whining because others are much worse off; he heals you. When no one wants to be with you, he doesn't give you a lecture on social skills; he simply says, there's room at my table. And when you die, he doesn't say, don't worry, you're in a much better place; he raises you from the dead.

The IFS model takes this same kind of caring approach. It accepts the fact of human frailty and takes our need into account. In the model, each of our parts is viewed with compassion and treated with respect, even though these parts may be busy leading us astray. Instead of blaming or shaming these aspects of our person, instead of beating up on them or beating up on ourselves for having them in the first place, we learn a new way of relating with them. We learn how to love them, lumps and all.

It's a strange thing, but once we accept our basic, not to mention unavoidable, humanity, things begin to open up. Once we get over the humiliation of being human, we lose the need to hide. We stop hiding from ourselves and we stop hiding from God. All that hiding takes a lot of energy and when we stop, we are relieved. We take off the fig leaves and come out into the open, and when we do, we actually have a much better shot at getting our needs met. That's when we're met by God.

It helps to know your need. Take Thomas, for example. Doubting Thomas. He had needs. He wasn't about to believe in a resurrected Jesus until he saw it with his own two eyes. He wasn't going to take anyone's word for it; he needed to see it for himself. The guy has gotten a bad rap. If you ask me, Thomas was just like the rest of us, only more honest and brave. He spoke for his parts and when he did, the need was met. He was met by the risen Christ and not in some wispy ghost-like form either. Jesus appears in the flesh and blood. Touch me, he says, and know me for yourself.

Most of us have big skeptical parts, just like Thomas and all those people from Missouri, who are proud to live in a "show me" state of mind. Some people say that you shouldn't put Jesus to the test, but I do it all the time. I am all the time asking for a sign, looking for proof, needing endless amounts of reassurance, putting Jesus to the test. Maybe I shouldn't, but on the other hand, Jesus always seems to show up and so I get to see him, face-to-face. I get to know him for myself. I am needy for sure, but it's not all bad.

Jesus gets up close and personal with people; Self gets up close and personal with parts. Self shows up and it has this way of showing up within my flesh, within my flesh and within my bones, because that's where those little parts of mine happen to live. You know how it is… burdens that get expressed in the body; stress that translates into physical symptoms. Stomachs churn, jaws clench, muscles pinch, hearts flutter, heads ache. My fears and forgotten traumas, my unresolved conflicts and unexpressed grief, the betrayals and the false beliefs: any and all of these things can make me contract, brace, collapse, quiver, freeze, panic, contort, burn, grasp, gag and oh, so much more.

Parts express themselves in my body, use my very flesh as a means of communication. Parts work in wondrous ways. I didn't used to see it like that and I'm still not all that crazy about it… I mean, after all, it's not like it feels good. Symptoms show up in my body and it can be pretty uncomfortable. Sometimes I get scared and wonder where all of this will lead, but parts are nothing if not creative. I have to give them an "A" for effort. They will do whatever it takes to get the attention that they need. They are just like little kids, and from their point of view, negative attention is better than no attention at all.

Parts have all kinds of ways to get themselves heard. I used to not listen. I used to ignore my symptoms. Ignore them long enough, I thought, and they'll just go away. Well, some of them did, but others didn't. Some of them just got worse, louder and more intense until I reached the absurdly high threshold of my pain and cried "uncle." That's when I started to pay attention. I took up with IFS and learned to see physical and emotional pain as valuable forms of communication. Instead of killing the messengers, I learned how to listen with respect and how to decode the message. IFS helped me get in touch with my own flesh. It taught me how to relate to my whole self, even the parts that I didn't like. Especially the parts I didn't like. And, it

50

helped me deal with need.

Even now, I use the IFS model as a tool for continuing needs assessment. It's kind of like a spiritual MRI. I scan my body for hot spots or calcifications or contractions, for anything in me that feels alien or in need of attention. In the farthest reaches of my being and the most distant corners of my awareness, Self seeks out the lost and the lonely, the alien and abandoned, the dangerous and destructive. In Self, I can connect with all of these different parts of me and the way I relate to them looks very different from how it did before. I come now from the very heart of God. Instead of blaming or abusing them, I come to them with curiosity and compassion. In Self, I come to love them all. In Self, I seek healing for them all. Self supplies their every need, redeems and restores. Sounds a lot like Jesus: Holy Spirit tending to our flesh.

Spirit in the flesh: it's a special kind of connection. It's a spiritual relationship that takes place on the inside of me, and because of this, there is the potential for inner peace, no matter what's happening in the world around me. In the midst of chaos, I can still have peace of Christ at my core, and this is good, real good. Inner peace is important, because frankly there's not a lot of outer peace out there. I wish there was. If it were up to me, there'd be a lot more peace in the world, but you'd be surprised how many people don't consult with me. I don't always have control over what's happening around me. In fact, I rarely have control over what's happening around me. I rarely have control over my own life. Sometimes I can change my circumstances but other times I can't. Sometimes I can change my life, but other times I have to learn how to live with what is. But no matter what is, I can still dwell in the presence of the Lord. Wherever I go, I can still live in the Kingdom of God. I can have that inner peace.

What? Someone on the inside squawks. *What are you talking about? Inner peace?! And when does that*

51

show up?

Inner peace. I know it's a lot to claim, especially for someone like me -- someone who seems to live in the perpetual state of civil war. But I do have episodes of calm. I have moments of inner peace, sanctuary in the midst of storm.

It doesn't last forever. I am human and like everyone else, my clay comes with constraints. There are physical properties that come with the territory. Humans, for example, we don't fly, not on our own, anyway... although most of us as children give it a try -- jump and flap, jump and flap. All the Self leadership in the world isn't going to change that: isn't going to make me sprout wings and fly. I don't want you to get the wrong idea. My Spirit can soar all it wants, but trust me, my body isn't going airborne without a lot of borrowed horsepower.

Some human limitations are generic and others are situation-specific. We're born in a particular place and time, into particular families, of particular race, gender and culture. The circumstances of our life impact us and help define us. They establish a framework for who we are, and this framework establishes the context within which the Self will move. I am and always will be the youngest of three, only girl, born in 1961 to a Dutch father and an American mother. We moved all over the place and my mother died young. Those are the facts and nothing will change them. You can't undo the past. I can't change the facts of my life, but what I can do is change my relationship with them. I change the way that they affect me. I can heal and even find new meaning, holy ground in the same old tales. And there are new stories waiting to be told.

All of this is possible through spiritual presence and the process of transformation as it unfolds. It can happen through the IFS model. The Self works with who I am. Self deals with the reality of what is. It takes what has been and turns it into something even better. This is the power of Self-energy: to take the old and make me new; to accept the facts of my life and still set me free to live my life. It's the refiner's fire that Paul talks about. The chaff gets burned away and my impurities melt into the air. I am washed clean, baptized in the wellspring of eternal life. I shine like spun gold. Healing comes, and when it does, it will fit with the elements of my earthly existence and it will work within the frame of my particular life. At times, I long to trade it all in, trade me in, trade me up for a newer model, but that's not how it goes. God works with my raw material, with all my lumpy clay. Jesus had a human frame; I guess he values human form.

Frameworks are important and our bodies make up our basic human form. They serve as containers for all our human processes, and that's a pretty big job. I mean, think about it, our bodies hold it all -- our biological processes, our mental constructs, our historical references, our emotional life, the soul itself. In fact, here on earth, it's kind of hard to get around without one. And yet, so many spiritual paths and practices encourage us to leave our bodies behind, forsake our human form in order to achieve some "higher" level of spiritual experience. Some approaches are particularly harsh, even punitive. A strain of this runs through the Christian tradition. There are recurrent themes of renunciation and denial of flesh, the peculiar notion that any sensory experience might be somehow sinful and physical pleasure particularly suspect. H. L. Mencken once defined Puritanism as "the haunting fear that someone, somewhere, might be happy." But at the heart of Christian spirituality lies something very different. It's the idea of community, of intimacy and interconnection; the importance of relationship, including the one between our body and our soul. At the heart of Christian theology is this idea of incarnation, which means literally "in flesh," and it refers to the embodiment of Spirit: Christ's own Spirit held within our clay.

The Word became Flesh, John says, and lived among us full of grace and truth. Jesus took on human form and so was subject to human limitations, just like everyone else. In

53

Philippians, Paul says Jesus "emptied himself...being born in human likeness. And being found in human form, he humbled himself and became obedient to the point of death— even death on a cross." When it comes to flesh, Jesus was just like us. He got tired and hungry and irritated. His feelings got hurt and even he longed for a little down time. He enjoyed hanging out with his friends, and I'm pretty sure he fell in love, just like we do. He was vulnerable just like the rest of us, subject to the constraints of clay. He had parts. I like that about him. It makes him a little more human and more accessible, which, I do believe, was the whole point.

When it comes to Spirit in the flesh, Jesus was the ultimate, the big "I" incarnation, but we too are vessels for heavenly treasure. We are those containers of clay that Paul talks about. We hold Holy Spirit within, and this wine has a way of working itself into our flesh. It infiltrates our clay. That's how the holding really works. That's how it's supposed to work. Two dimensions co-exist in our one personhood. Spirit saturates our flesh, and this means that it can be found in every molecule in every part of our being. It's a working relationship. More than that, it's a loving relationship. We're meant to be together, and it's a terrible thing to try and separate us out, to keep the needs of flesh away from the benefits of the Spirit. It doesn't work and it's not what Jesus had in mind.

Our containers count. Whether we're talking about Jesus or your everyday average person, material being matters. The agency of Holy Spirit is the same and its thrust, if anything, is downward. It's not up, up and away; it's down to earth, as in Emmanuel: God with us. Martin Luther emphasized this downward movement. God, he says, humbles himself, "condescends" to be found in human form -- condescend, meaning literally: "down with" us. God came down to earth and when he did, the Divine did not choose to come in the most beautiful container of all, nor in the most powerful body of all. Instead, Spirit was willing to be found in the most vulnerable of all human conditions: in the form of an infant.   Talk about a statement.

We come in fragile human form and yet we too can serve as vessels for Holy Spirit. As Christians, we aspire to this very thing. We are wanting Christ to be found in us. As we grow in spiritual maturity, we seek to embody more and more of his Spirit. We seek guidance from above, even as our feet remain firmly planted on the ground.

I asked Jesus about this once, about his willingness to be vulnerable and about his choice of human form in particular.

If you really wanted to make a statement, I said, if you really wanted to do it right, why not come as a baby girl?

Not my fault, he said.

Girls are great, but it would have been a little too far off the map.   I had to work around the constraints of the prevailing culture. I needed access to the temple. I needed freedom, enough to move. I had to work with the frame.

Sexism and oppression... don't be putting that on me. That's human arrogance, not mine. In fact, I happen to find the female form particularly beautiful. I call it "good."

Well, I'm more comfortable with some parts of Jesus than others, so that pretty much put an end to the conversation, but I do think he had a point. When it comes to the human form, we are arrogant. We set up standards of physical perfection and then we compare ourselves with it, compare ourselves against others. We evaluate our bodies and rank them, pass judgment on them, revile them, reject them, abuse them. We are not the least bit compassionate toward our imperfections, our blemishes, or our weaknesses. We get rid of them if we can, and many of us would get rid of our bodies if we could, upgrade for a better model. Some people act as though the body is a "necessary evil," and all I can say is, that's not a very nice way to treat your life-long companion, and it's certainly no way to treat someone who works that hard on your behalf. Just think about all the things that our bodies do for us, every day. Where would I be without my body? Dead. Dead is where I'd be, and I don't think that's anything to rush into.

I am human. This means that I come with flesh and a whole lot of limitation. The question remains: what attitude am I going to take toward myself and the limitations of my frame? Could I move beyond the antagonism that I usually feel toward my jar of clay? Could I move beyond a begrudging acceptance? Could I dare to celebrate my body, flaws and all?

I don't think so. It sure doesn't sound like me. But still, it's worth considering. Maybe it's time for me to make friends with my flesh. That's what I'm thinking. Maybe we could learn to get along. After all, it's the flaws, they say, that make a diamond distinct. It's the misprint that makes a stamp valuable. Imperfection makes for that one-of-a-kind weaving. And the stories that inspire me the most are not the ones about perfect people with perfect bodies, living perfect lives; they're the ones about people who have overcome huge obstacles, who manage to move beyond the constraints of their human frame -- people whose spirit transcends their form.

All of us know someone like this, someone who should be a walking disaster area. They've gone through such horrible things that we would expect nothing from them except a wide-cut swath of heartache and destruction left in their tracks. And yet, these people not only manage to function, they flourish. They have not only found help for themselves, they reach out to others. They are living, breathing miracles, and in them, we see the hand of God at work.

Ted was that kind of person. As a child, he grew up in a violent, alcoholic family. He and his siblings were beaten on a regular basis and subjected to all kinds of verbal abuse. It was the kind of childhood that you'd expect to leave someone damaged -- permanently, irretrievably damaged, and it's true that Ted has endured many years of struggle with his own shame and rage. But he never gave up. He had a persistent hope for his own healing and a strong hunger for God. He was plenty angry at God, believe you me, but he knew that his hope and his hunger went together somehow. He followed wherever the Spirit led, and one of the places that Spirit led was to IFS. It has been amazing to see the power of Self at work in him.   I have served as witness to his journey and his journey has served as a powerful witness to me.

Christ's power is made all the more perfect in our weakness, Paul says.   Yes, in the very place of weakness, wonders are revealed.

That's how Dick sees it, too. He acknowledges his weakness even as he lives into his call as developer of the model. It's not me, he says. I didn't create the model. I developed it, but I didn't come up with it. It was given to me. A lot of it I learned from my clients; some of it just downloaded. I'm just the messenger. My job is to get it out there and not mess up. That's not easy for me, he says, because I make a lot of mistakes.

Yeah, Dick makes a lot of mistakes. I don't know if he makes more mistakes than your average bear. Maybe it's just that so much of his life gets played out in the limelight where everyone can see it. Dick is impossibly human, and that makes it hard for would-be disciples, for the parts in us that still seek perfection – the perfect father, the perfect friend, the perfect therapist, the perfect person… someone who is perfectly there for us.   Perfection -- it's what we ask of our leaders, but sooner or later, one way or another, they all come down off that pedestal… they fall off, they get knocked off, and they climb off. Leaders are just like the rest of us. We know this intellectually, but when their humanity is revealed or exposed, we still experience disillusionment. Disappointed though we may be, that very disillusionment is a vital part of our growth process; it opens us to an even greater possibility. It points us in a different direction. It turns us away from temporal leadership and toward the transcendent.

Dick does mess up, and when he does, his students are forced to look beyond Dick to the model that he brings. Practitioners of IFS eventually learn to stop emulating him and start embodying their own Self-energy. When they do, their use of the model becomes more authentic and Self-led. Authenticity is one hallmark of spiritual maturity. Instead of following after a great spiritual leader, we learn to exercise our own capacity for spiritual leadership.

So how much spiritual leadership does it take? How much spiritual presence do I need to enact the minor miracle of my own healing? How much Self will turn the tide? Pin Dick down and he'll say around thirty percent. Jesus is a little more cocky, if you can believe it. He says it only takes a tiny grain, a little leaven in the loaf.

Heavenly treasure is held within my clay. There's a little leaven in my loaf, and this means that my body can serve as a spiritual resource. The Spirit of Christ dwells within my flesh and this means that Christ himself can be found in me. It's taken me a really long time to learn to figure that out. I tried so hard to leave my flesh -- to abandon my body, to disconnect or beat it into submission. But here in middle age, I am finally beginning to get what incarnation is all about and to understand what it implies. If I want to embody Christ, then I have to embody my body. There is no other way.

Still, it's not easy for me. It's a pretty big shift. I just hope I've got enough breath left for me to truly take it in. It's another of life's little ironies. I spend the first half of life trying to escape from my body, and now in the second half, I'm trying hard to embrace it. I have this sneaking feeling that just when I finally get this lesson down, just when I learn to embody my flesh, and maybe even enjoy it... I'll be in my old age and there will be yet another lesson to learn. It'll be the time for the letting go.

But for now, I am spirit joined with flesh. Incarnation. It's not a new concept. As a pastor, I could talk about it and preach it from the pulpit and I could do a lot of things in the name of Christ, but to feel him right within my bones... not so much.

The first time I work with Dick, he says: Focus on the part. Find it somewhere in or around your body.

And I say, *What?*

I say *what* because I feel nothing in or around my body.

That's how I learn that I am numb. I never knew. I never saw it before. It's like a metal plate runs through my neck. My head seems to work just fine, but I don't have access to anything below the brain. The rest of me doesn't seem to factor in, except, of course, when it does. There are times when my feelings get the best of me. They well right up and burst right out. No more fingers in the dike. I find myself suddenly, inexplicably, taken over by anger, by grief, with fear or whatever it is that grabs me when my brain is being hijacked.

From Dick I learn how to reconnect with my flesh and reclaim the gift of my body. This is something new for me because I was taught to revile myself – to reject many different parts of who I am and to beat back the stirrings in my flesh. I don't blame the church in particular. I learned it just the same at home, at school and in the larger culture. What I now know is that I missed a lot of valuable information because I didn't know how to listen to myself. I didn't listen to the wisdom of my body. I was taught to override that sinking feeling in the pit of my stomach, ignore all those hairs going up on the back of my neck, the creepy sense that something's wrong. Other people talked me out of my truth and in time, I began to do the exact same thing. I talked me out of what I knew, ignored what my parts were trying to communicate through the medium of my flesh.

I start working with Dick and see all of this. I look back on my life and I'm intrigued, not to mention really, really pissed. No wonder I got to where I got. No wonder I went so far off track. I didn't listen to myself. There were so many road signs along the way, so many red flags and I missed them all. Ignored them all. I threw out my body with the bathwater.

But I am drawn now to what I see. I am so complex and interesting. Who knew? There is so much to me. I have many parts and each one has a place. Each one has a purpose, serves a function. Best of all, once I get to know them, I find that each one bears a hidden gift. It's like I'm all of a sudden one of those advent calendars where you get to open up the little windows and find a new picture on the inside. I find new parts and as they open up, I am surprised and delighted by what is revealed, by what I find inside. Let me tell you, therapy was never this fun before.

I also begin to see that IFS can serve as a means of spiritual discernment. We have Spirit in our Flesh, but how do we differentiate between the two? Which one is which? I kind of need to know. I don't need to separate them out, but if I want Spirit to take the lead, then I'd better know it when I see it. IFS helps me recognize spiritual presence so that I can approach my parts from the compassionate heart of Christ. This trusting relationship helps me to reorganize all my inner relationships. It reorders what Augustine calls our "disordered love." Reconciliation -- it can take place right here on earth, right here within my flesh, through the power of a Holy Spirit.

This is a radical shift for me, because I had my bags all packed and ready to go. Follow me, Jesus says, and there are times when I would gladly do it, leave my life and all these earthly cares behind. Just beam me up already. *Please!*

Jesus must have something very different in mind,

because every time I let the Spirit lead, it leads me right back into my life. God grounds me, right here on earth.

In John 17, Jesus is about to get beamed up, on the beams of a cross, which, by the way, is no one's favorite way to go. Still he takes the time to pray, and when he does, he prays that we would embody his Spirit in the world.

> *I am not asking you to take them out of the world, but I ask you to protect them from the evil one...As you have sent me into the world, so I have sent them into the world... I ask not only on behalf of these, but also on behalf of those who will believe in me through their word, that they may all be one...I in them and you in me, that they may become completely one, so that the world may know that you have sent me and have loved them even as you have loved me.*

Yes, we are to be Christ in the world, for the sake of the world, and this means that we have to be in our flesh. For all Dick's not being a Christian, this principle of incarnation is inherent in his model. He believes that we are here to embody Self energy and bring more Self energy to the world. From his perspective,

> We came to this world not to leave it as soon as we can, but instead to bring more Self to it – to create more connection both horizontally and vertically...If we fully embody the Self, by definition we are bringing more of it to this world... When our Self is more present it will elicit the selves of people around us, and so on. The potential is for exponential increases of Self leadership in this world, which, ultimately, will increase all of humanity's connection to the Self. Thus, to experience oneness with God, people don't have to rush out of this world, abandoning their parts and the people around them.

So how am I to think about myself? Who am I, really? My spirit is married to a flesh-and-blood body, till death do us part, and whether I like it or not, a life in Christ looks just like this. Christ's own life looked like this, so why do I wage war against myself? Clay was good enough for God. I guess it will have to do for me.

Just to be clear, I am still not completely reconciled to the idea. The Velveteen Rabbit never made my list of best-loved books. I do not like my well-rubbed flesh. I want my pixie-dust.

The Body of Christ, broken for you.
The Blood of Christ, shed for you.

It's Jesus again. He whispers in my ear and he is sneaky, that one, the Christ, because these are words I say myself and he knows it. I say them every time I celebrate the sacrament of communion. These words are part of the liturgy and I have said them hundreds of times myself.

Jesus shows me the bread and the cup. Jesus shows me the waters of baptism. He shows me these common elements, the stuff of daily life consecrated for a holy use. We experience the real presence of Christ somewhere in or around these material things. Jesus also shows me faces, the faces of so many people that I have loved even as I have served. They are coming up for the ashes, coming up for the bread and the wine. Some come with faces lined and worn, others come with eyes that shine, young and old, men and women; all of them coming, to touch and taste and experience for themselves the goodness of God. They come to receive Christ's grace and it comes to them by means of the material world. *God with Us.* It turns out that Jesus came, not as a human sacrifice, but as a human sacrament: the Spirit made flesh, for our sake, that we might see and touch and know for ourselves the grace of God.

Treasure in jars of clay. It was good enough for me, Jesus says. I think you'll be OK.

Our flesh and blood bodies. They are God's chosen medium for the miraculous. It seems ridiculous, but this is the raw material with which Jesus chooses to work. Ask Teresa of Avila and she will tell you it's the *only* way that Christ will work:

> Christ has no body but yours,
> No hands, no feet on earth but yours,
> Yours are the eyes with which he looks
> Compassion on this world,
> Yours are the feet with which he walks to do good,
> Yours are the hands, with which he blesses all the world.

We're not meant to leave our flesh, not so long as we're alive. We don't go running off with God until the day we die. Until then, it's the other way around. God moves in with us. Here in late middle-age, after all this time, IFS is helping me learn how to love my clay and to embody Christ – not to hold him for myself, not to try and keep me safe, but so that I can bear his light in me. I'm willing to be his hands and feet in the world, to let him breathe new life in me. After all this time, I guess it's time, time for me to come fully alive. Time for me to take my place and live within my flesh.

Jesus said to her, "Everyone who drinks of this water will be thirsty again, but those who drink of the water that I will give them will never be thirsty. The water that I will give will become in them a spring of water gushing up to eternal life."

(John 4:13-14)

Living Waters: Source of Self

I've spent a lot of time healing lately—four or five years, which is ridiculous since I only have these one or two little issues and practically nothing at all compared to the people I know who really need help.

Still, it takes as long as it takes and I've been doing whatever it takes to heal my heart and regain my soul. In the tradition of all spiritually enlightened people, I have surrendered to God. I have given my life over to the leading of the Holy Spirit. I have done this, sort of. It's more of a stop and go kind of thing.

Come, follow me, Jesus says. He's a broken record. No matter what I bring, no matter what I lay at his feet, he always says the same old thing: Seek ye first the Kingdom of God. Jesus is all the time quoting himself at me. It's a little pretentious and unbecoming, but what can you do? Follow me, he says, as if this is the answer to all my problems, and he says it with complete calm and confidence; I go a little nuts. Sometimes you just want to shake some sense into the man. Show me the money. That's what I say. Life is not that simple.

Like the other day. I'm lingering over a latte when my friend tells me that he's putting an end to our relationship. There's nothing wrong. I haven't done anything wrong, but coffee with me is complicating his life so now he's cutting me loose. I don't remember his exact words. I got enough to get the gist and then I took a little much-needed vacation from myself.

After a few days on autopilot, I crawled back into my skin, but let me tell you, this being present is not what they make it out to be. Showing up for your life means that you show up for all of it, including the hurt.

This man ended our friendship and anguish poured forth from me like blood. You'd think I had severed an artery or something. You'd think I'd wound up in a Monty Python skit. I mean: it hurt. But here's what really got to me. I thought I was making pretty good progress on that whole healing my heart thing. Layers of scar tissue had painstakingly removed, only now I find myself plunged into this fresh new hell, or rather a fresh new version of the same old hell: trust and betrayal.

Shortly before my friend stabs his knife into my back, he asks if Presbyterians believe that people are basically good or basically bad. Seriously, he asks me this... right before he becomes his own case study, before he offers himself up as the raw material from which I might derive an answer. And this guy knows about IFS and everything. What's up with that?! What happened to all that IFS grace? The whole thing doesn't feel very Self-led to me, but it's not enough to make me lose my faith in the model or anything. I've seen it before. It happens all the time. We aren't the people that we mean to be. We don't live up to our own expectations and we don't live up to God's invitation. Christians have been turning away from grace for a long time. Why should anyone in the IFS community or otherwise be any different? We all have burdened parts and no matter what part we play in this kind of encounter, whether we are on the giving or receiving end, experiences of hurt in relationship are part of what it is for us to be human.

My good friend has treated me badly and I am suffering for sure, but for all the pain I feel, I can't make him out to be a monster. I know him too well for that. He is just like the rest of us -- spirit and flesh, trying to make our way with who we are. We miss the mark. We mess up. We mess up a lot, but we are doing the best that we can, even when our best isn't nearly good enough. Even when our best is woefully inadequate, it may still be the best that we can do on any given day. My best is better on some days than others.

Are people basically good or basically bad? When it comes to human nature, Presbyterians are wary. We know that people have capacity for good, but then again, we do a lot of damage. We don't want to claim too much, don't want to go too far. We don't want to gloss over the reality of human suffering, particularly the suffering that comes at human hands, our own human hands. We worry about power and the potential abuse of power. We're anti-authority. We believe in checks and balances. Are you getting the picture? Presbyterians are a vigilant lot and these are *so* my people.

On the other hand, this vigilance itself is checked and balanced by a supreme faith in God -- in the sovereignty of God and in the power of Holy Spirit to work in all things for the good. Jesus has what it takes to right the wrongs and heal the hurts, to help God's Kingdom come. The grace of God is irresistible and divine love conquers all. People are a little iffy, but when we are connected with spiritual energy, a powerful force is unleashed into the universe. Jesus said, when two or more are gathered in my name, there I will be also. Jesus has this way of showing up and in the most unlikely people, and when he does, people are empowered. It makes me a little nervous.

In general, I prefer to play it safe, but for a little while there, I lost my religion. I lost my Presbyterian perspective. I forgot to be vigilant and so I placed too much trust in your basic human being. I got my feelings hurt and I am singing the blues, Janis Joplin style. Break another little piece of my heart now, baby.

Hearts get broken. I hate when that happens, but I haven't found any good way to get around it. I'm not willing to do what it would take. I'm careful, but I'm not willing to harden my heart any more than it already is. I'm not willing to completely wall myself off from other people. I'm not willing to cut myself off from the possibility of love. It's a fact of life: open your heart and sometimes you get hurt. It's the risk you take; the price you pay, and for the most part, it's worth it. It's worth it to be the kind of person I want to be, regardless of what the other person does.

I get hurt, and then I go to God. I pick up the pieces of my Humpty Dumpty heart, and I go knocking on God's door.

Hey, Buddy, I say, get a look at this! What's up with this?! And what are *you* going to do about it?

This is me, in my own little way, asking for help.

There are some who say that we don't need help. There are some who say that we can do it all on our own, that we have an innate capacity for healing and so we can heal ourselves.

IFS can sound a little like this. Dick describes the Internal Family Systems model as a "collaborative approach that relies on clients' intuitive wisdom." In his work with clients he discovered a universal characteristic. When their parts relaxed, all of them had "healing, creativity, and performance enhancing qualities. When my clients entered this Self state… they began to actively interact … in creative and healing ways."

Talk like this makes me sit up and take notice. Faster than a duck on a June bug, something in me comes full alert. Something in me begins to track and it goes along these lines. If I can take care of my own needs, then I won't need to depend on anyone else. If I can count on myself, then I won't have to count on you. If I can save my own soul, then I won't have to trust, not even in God. And think how wonderful that would be: never having to feel my own neediness… never having to get lost in the depth of my longing… never feeling vulnerable again. That is power and it has appeal.

Here's the thing: if I could have saved myself, I think I would have done it by now. If I could have healed myself, I would be whole. I have given it a pretty good shot. I made a point of being independent. I tried not to need anyone. I was

67

determined to be being self-reliant. I lived in a state of self-sufficiency for a long time but it turned out to be a pretty barren landscape. Autonomy is like a desert island—safe and secure, but in the end, stultifying. Jesus showed up from time to time, but even he got bored.

On the surface, the IFS model seems to promote a radical self-reliance. Dick's model has Soul, only he called it *Self*. He called it *Self* because that's how his clients referred to it, as "my Self." It makes sense, but from the Christian point of view, it was a huge mistake. For Christians and others, the *Self* is suspect. Self sounds so… well…selfish. It sounds like a "me first" kind of deal. Elaborate on the word *self* and things only get worse. There's self-interest, self-righteousness, self-centered, self-absorbed, self-satisfied, self-protective, self-serving -- on it goes, and none of it good. The word itself screams *Me, Me, Me!* It hints at all the things good Christians dread - the human heart curved inward on itself, the ego unleashed, the craving maw of endless need. Eeew.

But this is not the Self of which the model speaks; not the Self Dick has in mind. It is true that we can be self-focused and filled with self-protective behaviors, but this is part of what it means to be human; this is what comes from having burdened parts. But it is not the Self. In the IFS model, Self is something very different. Self is spiritual. Self, like the Soul, is the spiritual dimension of human being. It is both a quality and a capacity. It is a way of being present in the world. It is transcendent awareness, a kind of spiritual consciousness. It's when I have the mind of Christ. When I look out through his eyes, I see the world from his divine perspective. It's no longer about me, me, me. I see myself, I see my Self as part of Something More.

Self is who I am when I attuned with God and aware of that attunement, have the sense that we are one. Most days, life for me looks different. I try to do it all on my own, ego strength, full force. I use all my tools and all my skills; I bring all my striving parts to bear. I try to figure it out, whatever it is, whatever project is at hand. I try to force it, make it work, only it doesn't, or not enough. Not nearly enough. I try harder. I am still not satisfied with the results. I try harder. Still, not good enough. And so it goes. I put up a good fight. I throw myself into the fray again and again until I am bruised and bloody. Eventually I give up but only because I have to. Eventually I come to know my need of rest. I see the need for something different. I surrender. I lay it all down – my resentment and my rage, my fear and my failure, all my sweet control, and the will to power. I empty myself and lay me down. I say to God, oh, OK, I think I'm done. You might as well come in.

I scoot over and make room for Jesus. Ego steps aside. Tell the truth, I have dreaded this day, dreaded it and the experience of truly emptying myself. Who would I be without my ego? What would I find if all my parts get out of the way? I was afraid that if I really emptied myself that all I would find inside was nothing, the ultimate in Empty. Because, you know, there was this Void, a sense of Void in me. But now, here I am, face to face with Empty, and what I find is something altogether different than what I feared. In this vast expanse of Void, something stirs. From the bottomless pit of Empty, something arises. In hollows of my heart, something begins to fill and what I find is God. Spirit stirs, Spirit arises, Spirit fills. What I find is my Self.

I go into the heart of my darkness and it is not the Black Hole of my imagining. This is not the experience of annihilation. It is, instead, the experience of Something More, something larger than the wasteland within, something there that fills my Void. I understand it as the Divine Self, the Eternal Spirit, God: the essence of my life, when everything else is done and gone.

I have a soul, it's true, but I am not a completely separate Self; I do not stand alone. I am a Self that lives in life-giving relationship with God's own Self. I am nestled within a web of divine being, a particle in the wave of holy love. My individual spirit is sustained by the Holy Spirit; my life is lived within a Larger Life. I live within the heart of God. In him, as the Apostle Paul says, I live and move and have my being. This is my truest Self, and best.

I am still your basic human being. This means that I have my good days and my bad. I do good things and I do bad. There is good me, and there is bad me. I find it hard to sort me out. But all of it, my good and bad, all of me, my best and worst; God holds it all.

And at my core is this connection with Christ. Some people describe it as my Soul. Others understand it as the Spirit of Christ within. Some people know it as the Self. Whatever you call it, it is within me and it is power for good.

Tell the truth, I'm not sure why we spend so much time parsing human nature in the first place. However we understand the human condition, divine presence remains the significant player in the process of our healing and transformation. However we define our problem, spiritual intervention is a huge part of the solution. Whatever the disease, God is the remedy. When it comes right down to it, it's not about human nature so much as it is about divine nature. It's not all about *me, me, me.* Don't get me wrong. I'm not all that humble. I'm pretty big on me and think I really count. I am one of God's big time advisors. I offer advice all the time but I can't help it if God's not good with follow-through. But I am human and even I don't get it right all the time. I have found that I can't make it on my own. I'm just too poor in spirit, too overwhelmed or worn out. I can't find my Self to save my soul. I give up and go for help. I knock on heaven's door; someone's always home.

I go to God and this is like an oasis in the desert. I sit under the umbrella and simply breathe. I go back to my Source, and here at the well-spring of all that is, I drink and drink deeply. Spirit flows into all the dry and empty places of my being. I feel me suck it in. My spirit is renewed, revived and this feels good.

Those who drink of the water that I will give them will never be thirsty.

It's Jesus quoting himself at me again, but gentle now and kind.

The water that I give will become in them a spring of water gushing up to eternal life.

So why don't I go to this well more often?

And since we're asking, why don't I stop for gas? That's what my husband wants to know. He thinks you should fill up before that little indicator light goes on, but that little light doesn't mean a thing to me, unless, of course, he's in the car. To me, that light is an invitation to a game of gas tank chicken. How low can I go?

Let me just say, I have never run out of gas, automotively speaking. When it comes to life, well, that's a different story. I go and go, until I'm all give out. I hit the wall; I crash and burn.

From the wreckage, Jesus pulls me out.

I'm grateful, but I'm also getting a little too old for all the drama. I don't bounce back the way I used to.

I go to God more quickly now, before things get too bad. I ask for help. Every day I go, before my well runs dry, and I don't have to go all that far. Holy Spirit, stream of life, it gushes up in me. Well, it trickles anyway.

I soak in the waters of divine love and one way I do is through the IFS model. As a daily practice, the process helps me get in touch with God. It helps me feel him in my flesh. Holy love tingles and dances its way through my veins. I see myself in a new light. I resonate with another way of being.

God speaks his Word in me, and some people may call this intuitive wisdom. Others call it Self. Yet others call it Spirit or Soul. Whatever. By whatever name we call it, the experience of Holy Spirit remains the same and the grace of Christ is still revealed.

What most of us really want to know is this: how can you tell? How can you tell when you're in touch with God and when you're under the influence of something else altogether? How can you be sure it's Self and not just another part? It's a darn good question. Some of us have made mistakes before and we're a little wary. We don't want to be deceived or fooled again. After all, some of us are Presbyterian.

The good news is that you *can* tell, and here's how. For Christians, the experience of Self will be consistent with the person, promises and presence of Jesus. You can cross-reference your experience of Self with the person of Jesus as we find him in the scriptures. Check it out. You can also tell by how it plays out over the long term. Over time, authentic experiences of Self lead us to inner harmony and a deeper spiritual capacity. We bring more spiritual resource to our relationships. With God's help, even the ruptures can lead us into a deeper intimacy. Wherever we go, we embody more of the Holy Spirit and the difference is noticeable. In Galatians, Paul says "the fruit of the Spirit is love, joy, peace, patience, kindness, goodness, faithfulness, gentleness, self-control; against such things there is no law." If you're lucky, you know someone like this, someone who radiates the love of God in this way. And if you want it, you too can radiate the love of God in this way.

There is a way to gauge the amount of Self-energy present within us at any given time. It's the Self-o-Meter and you can get it on-line through the Center for Self Leadership. Nah, just kidding. There's no such thing. But there is a simple tool for spiritual assessment. You can detect the presence of Self by how it feels in your body. It's how it feels when we're with God. You experience the qualities of divine presence – qualities that Dick has put into a handy dandy format known as the eight "C"s of Self, or what I have come to call the eight "C"s of Christ. These are the qualities of calm, compassion, clarity, courage, curiosity, confidence, connection, and creativity. That's how you check for spiritual presence. When you have the Spirit of Christ within, you will experience some or all of these qualities.

It sounds simple, but it's not. For one thing, we have a lot of burdens and they keep us from tapping into these spiritual qualities. There's another problem. Many of us are not comfortable with feelings. We're not in touch with our own physical being and we're not fluent in the language of physical sensation. We don't know what we're experiencing so it can be hard to recognize the felt-sense of sacred presence. And as if all of this weren't enough, many of us have been taught that we are not to trust anything which takes place on the inside of us.

Anything that happens within is immediately suspect. Insecure about our spiritual abilities, we defer to the outside experts – the preachers and the priests, the theologians and the traditionalists. This kind of external authority seems safer somehow, more reliable. We think that we can depend on the people in charge. That's what we think. That's what we've been taught to think. Unfortunately, it's not always true. There are many good and faithful people serving in positions of church leadership, but position is no guarantee for spiritual presence. There are plenty of wolves running around in shepherd's garb; plenty of predators who run around in the guise of priest.

There are some people who sit on the opposite end of the scale. They don't have faith in anyone in the outer world. They don't trust any authority that exists outside themselves. For people like this, inner wisdom is the only way to go. It seems like the only safe and reliable option. I know what I need, I know me better than anyone else, or so they say. Unfortunately, that's not always true either. We have great spiritual capacity but we're also pretty good at pulling the wool over our own eyes. Personally, I happen to have a couple of pretty good Self-

73

like parts. They are remarkable. They walk like Self, they talk like Self, and it's really hard for me to see them as anything other than Self. Usually someone else has to point them out to me, help me see them for what they are: darn good imitation.

In the final analysis, it's not about location, location, location. God's leading may come to us from without, or it may rise up from within. Location all by itself is not a reliable indicator. Wherever it comes, whenever it comes, it's good to know when you're in the presence of genuine Self-energy. You have to discern, and this kind of discernment takes intentionality and it takes practice. Get as close as you can to Jesus, and to others who are experienced with spiritual matters. Study the scriptures, read theology, do your homework. Sing and dance and pray and do whatever you have to do in order to experience those mystical times of transcendent bliss. Make it a point to go where you find God and when you do, pay attention to how it feels. How does it feel when you're with God? What's the felt-sense of it in your body? Pay attention and your body will remember. Your cells will not forget.

And then this next thing is key for discernment: you have to know your parts. Get to know them well – their history and their hopes, their fears and their fantasies. Get to know them and then you'll know when they've decided to crash the party.

I've been getting to know my parts. I've been taking the time to look inside, and man, am I busy in there! I see so much. It's a little daunting. It helps to know that I am not the only one who has committed myself to a lifetime of seeking and discernment. It helps to know that I am not alone. Others walk this same path and many of them are glad to lend a hand.

And then there's help that comes from beyond.

So here I am, sitting at heaven's door, my broken heart in hand. From whence will my help come? It will come from the Lord. I know, I know. I'm just not sure how God will show. It pays to stay alert.

God works without.

God works within.

He lives in every single soul.

And if it's true that I get hurt, it's also true that I get by with a lot of help from my friends.

Speaking of friends... I have no real interest in forgiving mine, this one who hurt me so badly. I don't want to. I don't even want to want to. I don't want to forgive and I sure as heck don't want to forget. In fact, I kind of like my hurt. I like the way it feels. Being wronged, it somehow feels so right. It puts me in the right and I am feeling a little self-righteous. I think I'm going to keep my hurt around for a little longer, nurse it along, let it grow, feed it now and then. I've been mistreated and this makes me morally superior. Something like that. I'm not really sure how it all works, but I know how it feels inside. Injustice is a form of power and it tastes sweet.

All of this goes on inside of me. This attraction to power is a familiar part of my process and one of the things that clues me in and makes me begin to question myself. Could this be my parts at work? I stop and scan my body. I ask myself that question -- the one that checks for parts.

How do I feel toward my friend?

Not so good. Not one of the eight "C"s in sight. Darn.

The way I feel, it might make a kind of sense, but it's not all that hard to tell; even I can see: this is not of Self. The way I feel, it's not of God, and so I have to let it go.

I go back to my Source and let the waves of grace wash over me. I tend those wounded parts in me. Living Waters rise again and I rest me in this stream until I am refreshed, renewed, and reoriented. I regain my calm, my clarity and my compassion. That's three of the C's, at least, and good enough to go forward. I am back in touch with my spiritual Self. I feel the Self as it flows through me, and here in the presence of God, I feel something strange happen on the inside of me. Something tight has been released. Something caught is on the wing. I forgive my friend, and as I do, we're both set free.

A leper came to him begging him, and kneeling he said to him, "If you choose, you can make me clean." Moved with pity, Jesus stretched out his hand and touched him, and said to him, "I do choose. Be made clean!" Immediately the leprosy left him, and he was made clean.

(Mark 1:40-45)

The Leper Within; All Parts Welcome

It's late September and I am here in Panama City Beach, Florida, with Jean and Joan, two of my best friends in the whole wide world. We met in gym class, my very first day at Earl Warren High School in Downey, California. I was in the 9th grade; they were 10th. It's been a long time since we lived in the same town or shared the same state, but we've been friends now for over thirty years. This totally blows my mind. For one thing, I'm not old enough to have been friends with anyone for thirty years. Also, I'm a teensy bit insecure and thirty years seems like a long time to be hanging out with someone like me.

But Jean calls me up and she says, come on down -- down being a lovely little condo on the beach in Florida. She calls, and I am so there. I may live in Wisconsin, but I'm a beach girl, born and bred. We go for long walks. We pick over the broken shells. We sit and soak up the sun. I have died and gone to heaven.

We are there the three of us and we are there alone – no husbands, no children, no pets, no houseplants. It's a Moms Gone Wild Weekend, and we are cutting loose. Mostly this means that we do nothing, absolutely nothing. We don't cook, we don't clean, we don't drive the carpool. We sit around in the hot tub drinking fruit-flavored concoctions and belt out John Denver songs at the top of our lungs. We talk and we talk. It's beautiful, man, but it goes too fast and the Wisconsin winter

76

looms ahead. I stand at the ocean's edge trying to absorb as much as I can. I will my pores to open. I squirrel away warmth and light within my skin. I do what I can, but it's not enough. I know my need of more.

Jean and Joan are twins, identical. Tall and blond, they are California girls who love the beach like me. Also, they have tattoos. Jean has a sea turtle that swims around her right ankle. Joan has even more: two suns on her leg and a sprinkle of stars across her shoulder. It's mid-morning and I am free of all concoctions when I decide that it's time for me to get my own tattoo. I choose a fiery sun, a sun that will blaze even in the coldest, darkest day to come. Yes, I know that peace is an inside job, but give me a break; I'm not all that evolved. I need something to hold on to. I want something that I can see with my own two eyes, and when I lose myself in the endless gloom of slate grey skies, this sun will speak to me of warmth and light and love. For me, this is not a tattoo – it's an outer sign of inner grace, reminding me of what it is to be fully known and fully loved.

Did it hurt? That's what everybody wants to know. Well, let me just say that I have given birth twice without the benefit of narcotics. That has a way of recalibrating your scale. My friend says kidney stones have the same effect. So no, it didn't hurt, at least not in comparison. Besides, I knew what I was getting into, and for me the pain was worth it. It's a funny thing though, everyone asks if my tattoo hurt, but no one asks me what my tattoo means.

In my corner of the Midwest, tattoos come with stigma. The only people with tattoos are either Bikers or people with poor taste. When the rest of us get tattoos, we tend to keep them to ourselves, put them where the sun don't shine. They never see the light of day.

I chose my tattoo, but you don't always get a choice about the things in life that mark you. Sometimes you get born with them - physical deformities or features that set you apart from everyone else. Sometimes you get born into them – life circumstances that scar you on the inside, if not on the out. Either way, you get marked as different, and the middle school me knows this truth: different is not good. In many, if not all, human communities, different translates into defective and undesirable. Difference is met with discomfort, disrespect, and distance.

Apparently people have not changed all that much. It was the same thing two thousand years ago. The Gospel of Mark tells about a man who is marked by leprosy, leprosy being the catch-all term for any number of afflictions. Some of these skin things were highly contagious, not to mention gross. You couldn't tell which ones were which. You didn't know which ones were contagious, so what you did was shun them all.

Show up with sores on your skin and you are branded as a Leper. You become an immediate outcast. By law, you have to stay away from other people, 50 paces. Not only that, it's your job to warn them off. You tear your clothes. You stop washing your hair. Everything about you screams: *Reject*. People draw near, and when they do, you declare yourself: *Unclean*. As a leper, you aren't just a physical problem, you are a spiritual contaminant. You aren't just sick; you are the embodiment of sin.

This is not so good for self-esteem, but what can you do? You are a leper and you have no choice. Other people have their sicknesses and other people have their sin, but yours happens to be in plain sight. It's right out there where everyone can see it. You have nowhere to run and no way to hide.

It's kind of like having a zit turn up on prom night. OK, a zit comes nowhere close to having leprosy, but if you've ever had one on the night of your big date, you know what it is to be marked. Desperate, you try to cover up, but nothing seems to work. You fail and you are doomed. Everyone will talk about you. No one will get close to you, not even your date. Who would kiss someone like you? Your social life is over. You might as well curl up and die. That's how it feels anyway and you never forget the feel of it -- the threat of outcast.

We know a lot more about diseases now, but we still can't prevent them all or cure them all. Some of them are still contagious and we still isolate people, if only for their own safety. We put them in isolation rooms, and when I go to visit in the hospital, they make me take all the necessary precautions. I put on the paper gowns. Through rubber gloves, I hold hands. My lips move behind the mask. I find it hard to pray.

Diseases do have to be contained, but isolation for any reason is a powerful social phenomenon. A lot of the time it has less to do with a disease than it has to do with the level of our discomfort. Distancing doesn't reflect the substance of our faith nearly as much as it reveals the depth of our fear. People get this. At some level, we know just what's going on. We know the damage that comes from being shunned, so what we learn to do is hide. When something goes wrong, when something happens to us, we are often the ones to pull away first. We withdraw before anyone has a chance to find out what's really going on.

Jack is newly diagnosed with colon cancer, Stage IV. He doesn't have long to live, but he doesn't want to tell anyone, not even his closest friends. Once he shares the news, he knows what will happen. People will begin to see him differently, treat him differently. In a heartbeat, he will go from being seen as someone strong to being seen as someone who is sick. He will go from being fully alive to being half-way dead.

Linda has a different situation. She is in a marriage that isn't safe, not for her, not for her children. She needs to get out, but she is having a hard time doing what she needs to do. She knows what they will say at church. They will talk about vows and commitment and all the sacrifices that we have to make in order for the sake of the marriage. They will judge her. She has tried to be a good wife and a good mother, but now all of that is about to change. Linda is about to lose her marriage and with it her good name and her church.

Susan has a serious drinking problem, but she's not about to get help. She doesn't want anyone to know. She is full of shame and she knows how it is, that some people will interpret her drinking as a moral failure, as a sign of some permanent defect in her character. She can't just handle this on top of everything else. She'd rather lose herself in another drink.

John is gay. He's known since he was 12, but he hasn't told a single soul. He struggles with it, but he keeps the struggle to himself. If it ever gets out, he knows that he will be condemned for who he is. Some will call him unclean. He will not find welcome, not here in the small town where he lives, where he has lived for his whole life.

I can tell you story after story like this, stories about shunning as it exists in our day and age, but I don't need to tell you what it's like. Each of us has had experiences of rejection and shame, humiliation and hurt. We've been ridiculed. We've been despised. We've been outcast. It wasn't all that fun the first time. Yes, we've been there before and we're not going there again -- not if we can help it.

We develop protective systems, strategies that hide our vulnerability, and there are many ways to do this. Shift the focus; that's a good one. Point the finger at someone else. In systems theory, we call this "scapegoating" and it happens all the time in every configuration of human community. When things go wrong, you can always find someone to fault, always find someone else to blame. Usually a particular person or a particular group of people bears the brunt of it. When families come to therapy, they usually present with an identified patient. There's the problem child, the black sheep, the trouble maker, the malcontent, the one who started it, the one who won't get with the program... the root of all evil.

Most churches have one or two people who are known as

trouble-makers, always causing conflict. Communities and whole countries will trace their problems back to a particular group of people, the minorities, the ones who are different from the rest of us. We know who they are by the way they talk, the way they look, the way they worship God. Scapegoats are typically the more vulnerable members of a society, lowest on the totem pole, but scapegoats can also be the people who sit at the other end of the pole – on top of the world. When things go wrong, we can always blame our leaders, even though we are the ones who have empowered them. We can bring them down, run them off, behead a few. Get rid of them, we say, and everything will get better. Only it doesn't really work. Without awareness we don't really change; we simply move on to the next sacrificial lamb.

That's how it works. Hang out in an unhealthy system long enough and you will see the same things start to happen all over again, patterns that repeat. Hang around long enough and what you will learn is how to hide. You learn to hang out somewhere in the middle and lose yourself among the crowd. Keep your head down; keep your problems to yourself. Whatever you do, you don't differentiate and, above all, do not cause a fuss.

As a marriage and family therapist, Dick was familiar with these dynamics. In his work with families he observed these and other well-known sequences of human interaction, but then he noticed something else. The way that families related to one another on the outside seemed to replicate on the inside. The patterns that played out within a given family also played out within the psyche of individual family members. Just as different family members took on different roles, each person had different parts in them that took on these same roles. On the inside, parts formed alliances and polarizations that mimicked alliances and polarizations that you would see within the family itself.

The implications of this are huge, especially for therapists and pastors and leaders of community. It turns out that if we want to restore health and harmony to any human system, we have to work at every level of relationship. Trusting relationships need to be developed, on the inside and out. Healing has to take place, on the inside and out. Reorganization has to take place, inside and out. Positive roles need to be found, inside and out. Transformation, within as without.

When I came to IFS, I didn't know all that much about my inner family system. I guess I wasn't all that differentiated. Looking back, it's easy for me to see how I repeated relationship patterns that I learned in my family of origin. These patterns played out in my marriage and in my other relationships, in my work and in my play. I see now how those same patterns were also repeating on the inside. I had internalized ways of relating to myself that weren't very healthy. Wherever I went, I took my family system with me. In other words, I lived what I learned, as do we all, until we learn how to do something different.

I learned a lot from my family of origin. It was a tough school, but I learned a great deal, and one of the things I learned was how to be tough. I had parts that identified with the dominant culture. I had dominating parts. I didn't need anyone to oppress me any more, I could do it all by myself. I had my own enforcers now and these guys were experts in finger-pointing. They would scapegoat other people and bully the other parts of me, because deep down, I still had these other parts that were not the least bit tough. They were young and sensitive, easily hurt - the ones that hungered for a little kindness and a lot of love. With half a chance, these parts would gladly go outside myself and go looking to get love from someone else   They looked for love in all the wrong places, and this breach in personal security could not be tolerated by other parts, the ones in charge of protection. As a result, these tender ones in me didn't get out very often. They got pushed down and locked up. They became what Dick refers to as "the basement children" -- the parts of us that we bury away in the basements of our awareness. It's like I had my own little lepers, banished within.

That's how it goes: parallel process, all the way down, the same inside as without. My Dad, leader of our little pack, like a lot of parents, had some big-time protective parts. He tried to keep his children safe. By God, did he try. He tried to keep us locked down and under control. He had a few enforcers of his own, and if any of our unruly parts emerged, he would do whatever it took to reestablish order. We got grounded a lot. I hope it made him feel better, because he never accomplished what he set out to do though we did get really good at sneaking out of the house.

That's how it is with parts. Sooner or later, they find their way out. They sneak out or they bust out, but they do get out, and whatever they hold has a way of coming to the fore. Seems to me, we'd be a lot better off if we could acknowledge them and take care of them before things get too bad, deal with ourselves directly and in a timely fashion. But for most of us, this is a life lesson that we have to learn in our own time and own way, and that's why God granted me the miracle of childbirth.

I have two children and both of them were born early, which shouldn't have been a big deal for me because I'm one of those people who like to plan ahead, a regular Boy Scout, always prepared. I like to be prepared so that I can have everything under control. At least, that's how I used to be. That's how I was... before I had children.

The first signs of labor come. They are clear and unmistakable, as in my water broke. Hard to miss. But I am not quite ready. Yes, there's a little pain, but no big deal; nothing that I can't handle, because I am tough. I suppose some part of me might have been a little anxious, but if there is, I don't know it. Mostly, I'm annoyed. Things are not going according to plan. I am still working my way through a list. I have a shower to take and legs to shave, a little more laundry and the hospital bag to pack.

I focus on the things that I want to accomplish. I get everything all taken care of. Then and only then do I let my husband drive me to the hospital. At the hospital I am still trying to handle things on my own, tough it out. In the beginning I rely on my usual and preferred pain-killers: dissociation and hallucination. After awhile I come to my senses -- mostly because my body's message about impending childbirth has gotten so persistent that even I have to stop and listen. I've got parts in serious pain so I ask for the real deal. I want my meds and I want them now. But, no, the nurses tell me: it's too late for that. I have finally wised up and ask for help, but I have waited too long. There will be no drugs for me. There is no going back. The only way out is through, literally through a birth canal. My daughter is born.

Now, you'd think that I would have learned something from this experience. I should have learned, because it is not true that you forget about the pain once the baby is born. But still, I was trained up in the way that I should go. I was trained to be tough and self-reliant and the learning from childhood is very strong.

My second child announces his imminent arrival. Like his sister before him, he is ahead of schedule. Once again, I am not ready. Another list is not complete. There is that all-important shower to take and another bag to pack. Finally I stop and time the contractions. They are coming three minutes apart and the hospital is 45 minutes away. This time I hit the ER hard, demanding my drugs. But once again, I have waited too late. There are no drugs for me and the only way out is through. My son is born.

I stop having babies.

I thought I was being tough, but what I was, was stupid. I was nuts, but if I was crazy then at least my insanity made some kind of sense. It made sense in the context of my family system. IFS helped me understand about legacy burdens and about the beliefs that we take on from our families of origin. For my parents, children were not a part of the plan; marriage was not what they had in mind. For them, pregnancy was cause for great ambivalence and anxiety. On top of that, infants are helpless and needy, the embodiment of human vulnerability. There wasn't room for any of that in our home. As a child, I grew up quick and learned to hide my childlike parts away. I hid them well. Forgot I had them.

But now, here I am, giving birth, on a collision course with my own history. Children are literally pushing their way into my awareness. My biological children are about to confront me with my own inner children. Are they welcome, or aren't they?

Let the children come unto me, Jesus says.

He speaks and a wave of relief washes over me. Really? Children are welcome, all those little children, snotty nosed and all? And my own inner children, all those messy, needy ones inside? No wonder this is one of the most familiar and comforting passages in the whole Christian Bible. It makes me feel welcome, me and all my childlike parts.

But other scripture passages are far less welcoming, and scary.

If your right eye makes you stumble, tear it out and throw it from you.

When I was in preschool, I had this nightmare. At least, I hope it was a nightmare and not the vestige of a memory. A puzzle piece is missing and the teacher is standing at the front of the class. She holds up a pair of shears. She is threatening us with scissors, threatening to cut off our fingers if we lose any more pieces of the puzzle.

85

It is better for you to lose one of the parts of your body,
than for your whole body to be thrown into hell.

I'm not in preschool any more, so I look to Jesus for some kind of explanation.

At least he has the grace to look chagrined. All right, he says. I said it, but I was only trying to make a point. It's hyperbole! It's exaggeration! It's a literary device, for God's sake. I never meant for anyone to take it literally. I was just trying to get their attention. I was just trying to make a point; get them to take this whole enterprise seriously. Wake up! Do what it takes to turn your life around! Trust me, I'm not into self-mutilation.

In the Bible, Jesus speaks some pretty harsh words, and he does things that I find shocking. He turns over tables in the temple. He lets women wash his feet with their hair. He eats lunch with the unwashed masses. Jesus can be a little extreme. I don't agree with everything that he says and I don't like everything that he does, but ours is a working relationship. By that I mean we keep working on it. We keep working things out between us. Every thing is up for grabs; everything is open for discussion. All my parts, and all of his, are welcome.

In his day, Jesus not only welcomed the children, he welcomed all kinds of people, and that's pretty unusual, even in our day and age. He welcomed people who were rich and people who were poor, the oppressed and the oppressor, members of the dominant culture and people from the underclass. Some people say that Jesus exercises a preferential option for the poor. It is true that he reaches out to the poor and the exile and the outcast, but Jesus was far more radical in his approach. He included everyone : the wealthy and the privileged, the oppressors and the perpetrators. The invitation is open to all. Maybe it's just that the poor are more likely to respond -- the poor, and the poor in spirit. It's sad, but true, that many of us open to the Holy Spirit only when we have to – only when we are done with denial, when our defensive structures have been irreparably breached, when scapegoating no longer serves its purpose. The basement children have escaped and all hell has broken loose. That's when we know our need of help.

IFS makes room for all kinds of people and all kinds of parts. It's non-pathologizing and universal in its welcome, and so it is consistent with the ministry of Jesus. All parts, like all people, are welcome. Now that doesn't mean they get to do whatever they want. They can't just run amok. Sometimes we have to set limits on them, adjust their behavior, but in the IFS approach, we respect them and honor them, all of them, just as Jesus honored and respected all kinds of people. IFS helps us connect with our parts, just as Jesus connects with people.

Somebody once said that personal well-being depends on the state of our relationships. We are only as happy and healthy as our closest relationships are happy and healthy. That's true in our relationships with other people, but it is also true about the relationship that we have with ourselves.

So we begin to connect and establish healthy relationships, even with the littlest or the least likeable among us, and even with the littlest or least likeable within us. We make room for them and tend their needs, work toward our collective transformation. We welcome them into the family, our internal family and into the family of grace.

That leper in Mark's gospel, he was counted among the least and least welcome. Leprosy is painful and disfiguring. Add in the social isolation and you can see that this guy had a problem. The whole community had a problem. There's no doubt about that; you can't just let the lepers run loose. On the other hand, there are ways and there are ways. There are Self-led ways to relate with someone even while observing the necessary boundaries. In the first place, you treat them with respect, and that means you don't identify people with their disease. You don't reduce them to a diagnosis. There are no lepers, only people who suffer with leprosy. In the same way, we don't identify parts with the roles they take on; we don't mistake them for the burdens that they bear. We look for positive intent. We see beneath the surface. We know that there's a degree of Self in every single one of our parts.

This man had a disease. It was the disease, and not the man, which was a problem. It was the disease and not the person that needed to be contained. Physical separation may have been necessary, but the social shunning was inexcusable. Cutting people off, locking people up: it might be necessary, but we know that doesn't really solve the problem. It simply puts people on ice, freezes them in the context of a particular time and place.

The same thing happens when we shun our parts. We put them on ice. We stick them away and so they get stuck in the context of a particular time and place, and what this really means is that we are simply saving them for later. I'm listening to a song or watching a movie and suddenly tears stream down my face; I don't know why. I'm driving and someone cuts me off and rage erupts; the intensity of it takes me by surprise. At times like this I have to work backwards in order to find out what's really going on with me.

The man had leprosy. You could lock him away, contain his disease, but what he really needed was a cure. What this man needed was the healing of body and of soul. He needed help and he knew that he wasn't going to get it sitting around in any old leper colony. He could stay in his assigned place, but he knew that wasn't going to serve him very well. Everything in him agitated for health so he planned for his escape. He saw an opportunity and he took it. He got as close to Jesus as he could and then he asked for help.

Jesus took one look at him and that was enough to get the whole picture. He saw the disease and the disfiguration. He saw the greasy hair, the dirty clothes, the unwashed skin. Jesus took in the stigma and the shunning and the suffering. Jesus saw it all and he did not look away. He didn't try to deny or minimize or make it nice. He didn't send the man away. Jesus stood there and he was not repulsed. He was moved and then he moved beyond the established norm. Jesus reached out his hand and touched the leper.

What was he thinking?!

I mean, after all, he didn't have to do that. He didn't have to do it like that. He didn't have to touch the man in order to heal him. He's Jesus. He could have said a few words or waved a magic wand, and that would have done the trick. But no, Jesus has to go and touch him. Somehow Jesus knew that a personal touch was needed. Personal touch would reverse the decree of untouchable. Jesus touches him, and turns the whole world upside down. The man with leprosy is restored to society but now Jesus becomes the outcast. The leprosy is cured but now Jesus is contaminated. It's not just the disease. He has broken the rules and defied religious law. Jesus is now seen as a threat to the established order, and this makes him a leper in his own right. He withdraws from the city. He is contagious, and in more ways than one. Word of him spreads like wildfire. Jesus becomes known as a subversive element. He is one who touches the untouchable and brings hope to the hopeless. For different reasons, everyone wants a piece of him.

For Christians, the story of the leper is a story of hope. It's a story about welcome and the personal healing mediated through Jesus. It's a story in which fear-based rules give way before the coming kingdom of God. The historical Jesus has come and gone, but his Spirit still walks this earth. This divine presence is alive and well and his invitation into the realm of sacred relationship remains -- in this world, in this day and in our age.

Christians have faith in the power of Holy Spirit. Dick has this same kind of faith in the power of Self and shares the good news of Self-energy with anyone who will listen. Dick is not Jesus, but he has his own mission and his own ministry, with stories to tell, words of assurance to share, and the invitation, always, into spiritual relationship and the healing that is possible through spiritual presence. The Self, like Spirit, is always there, and so there's always hope, even for the despised and outcast, the most hopeless among us.

The potential for restoration is always there, but something is required of us. The invitation is issued, but we have to respond. Like the leper, we have to want it. We have to know our need and acknowledge our parts, even the ones that we would shun and push away out of our awareness. We have to bring them out of the closets, empty the basements... and bring them into light. We have to take the risk, reach out and allow ourselves to be touched by holy love.

After the encounter with Jesus, this once hopeless leper himself became a gospel messenger. He just couldn't help it. He told everyone about Jesus and about the amazing day when he was healed. But after awhile, people got tired of hearing about it. His kids began to roll their eyes. You know how it is. Yeah, Dad, you've told us that story a billion zillion times before. Eventually the old guy learned to keep it to himself. Being different was still difficult.

And in the years to come, this one-time leper would still have his days of gloom and dark, just like the rest of us. Life goes on, just as it did before. Amid the endless stream of slate grey skies, he reaches for his fruit-flavored concoction or for his wife, and as he does, he catches a glimpse of his hand. His skin: it's still smooth and supple, free from any mark. Looking at it, he remembers that day, the day he decided that he would no longer live in exile, the day that he decided to reach out and ask for help, the day he took the risk and took himself to Jesus.

That leper still embodies hope. There's no sun tattooed on his ankle, but then again, he doesn't need one. His skin, old as it is, remains fresh and luminous. For him, it is an outer sign of inner grace, reminding him of what it is to be fully known and fully loved. The old man smiles and he gives thanks to God, for all is well.

So Ananias went and entered the house. He laid his hands on Saul and said, "Brother Saul, the Lord Jesus, who appeared to you on your way here, has sent me so that you may regain your sight and be filled with the Holy Spirit." And immediately something like scales fell from his eyes, and his sight was restored. Then he got up and was baptized, and ...he began to proclaim Jesus in the synagogues, saying, "He is the Son of God."

(Acts 9:1-19)

Trusting In Divine Transformation; No Bad Parts

For Christians, the Bible serves as the unique and authoritative witness to Jesus Christ, but the way some people talk, it makes you wonder if they've ever read the thing. Or maybe they still read from a children's version, cut down and cleaned up, fit now for human consumption. The Bible has parts that are for mature audiences only. Even then, it contains a lot of dangerous material and you wouldn't want it falling into the wrong hands, into the hands of people who would take the written Word for a weapon when God intended it for good.

In the Bible, we find God revealed. We get a good look at God, but we also get a good look at human nature. We get to see how humans try to co-opt the Holy. It isn't a pretty sight.

In Psalm 137, one of God's people lusts for revenge. He expects God to side with him against his enemies. Happy shall they be, he says, who take your little ones and dash them against the rock.

In Genesis 19, Lot is willing to sacrifice his virgin daughters to an angry mob in exchange for the safety of his visitors.

In Ephesians 6, slaves are instructed to obey their human masters with fear and trembling, and in sincerity of the heart, as though to Christ.

91

What?!

This is what I'm saying. Even Jesus, who is such a nice guy in general, says things that I find shocking.

Truly, he says, just as you did not do it to one of the least of these, you did not do it to me. And these will go away into eternal punishment, but the righteous into eternal life.

I am all for ethics, but I'm not keen on the idea of permanent penalties. This is not my preferred Jesus and when he talks like this, I don't know what to make of him. Is this Jesus being weird or doing what he can to wake us up? Is this Jesus, full of the Spirit, or Jesus, speaking from his parts? Either way, it makes me squirm. I am supremely interested in the matter of my survival and I mean long-term... like forever.

Threats of condemnation: they are so compelling, and so distracting. Just try and have a decent conversation with someone about Christianity and it always goes right there to the issue of judgment. You just can't get around it. Everyone gets so fired up about it and I guess you can't really blame them. Condemnation has this way of making people defensive. Apparently people don't like it when you damn them to hell.

If you're a Christian using IFS in a Christian setting, then maybe you don't have to deal with the issue of salvation as it relates to a confession of Jesus as Lord and Savior. We could assume that everyone is already on the same page. On the other hand, we're multiple by nature and this means that our parts are rarely all on the same page of anything. Even in the most committed of Christians, you'll find parts that don't believe and do not trust, parts that want to rebel and rail against religious rules. You'll find parts that have been relegated to the outer darkness by the other parts in us that pass judgment and condemn.

The IFS model takes into account these inner experiences of dissent. It allows for differing perspectives, within the larger body of the Christian church and within our individual Christian bodies. Multiplicity means that we don't all think alike. We won't all think alike. And yet, it is still possible for us to live together in peaceful, purposeful community. This approach may offend the more orthodox among us, but it gives other parts a little room to breathe. The model makes room for our doubt and disbelief and disappointment, and it gives us a way to work with our doubt and disbelief and disappointment, even as we profess our faith. In the long run, this makes for a more authentic faith.

Christianity is by definition Christocentric. Christ is at the center and because of this some non-Christians do not trust the Christian practice of IFS. They fear a secret campaign of conversion. Other people find the Christian practice of IFS suspect for the exact opposite reason: it doesn't proclaim the lordship of Jesus. They prefer counseling that is explicitly Christian. There's an easy answer for this dilemma. Address these issues up front, at the very start of a counseling relationship. Whatever your spiritual preferences, it's always a good thing to know who you're working with – where they stand and what they believe, where you stand and what you believe.

The IFS model is not based on a particular faith tradition, but it does include some basic beliefs. One of them is this: no bad parts. Parts may do bad things, but they are not inherently bad. They are not evil. Quite the contrary. All our parts are valuable and necessary, contain talents and qualities that can enrich our lives. They all have the potential to serve as contributing members of our inner family. Burdened parts may act in hurtful ways, but they do it, not because they are bad, but because of the burdens that they bear. Burdens twist our parts and turn them from their inherent potential for good.

There are no bad parts in the IFS world, but it would be a mistake to see IFS as a model that advocates moral relativity. On the contrary, the IFS model is a path toward healing. It unburdens parts and helps them find new roles. Once destructive, they're now constructive. Once negative, they become positive. They add to the inner family and to the world community. IFS actually equips us to live a life more congruent with ethical imperatives of the Christian faith and do it gladly.

Parts that act in cruel and destructive ways need spiritual relationship just as much or more than our more socially acceptable parts. In some ways, it's a matter of approach — what works and what doesn't, what helps and what hurts. We are quick to judge, but when it comes right down to it, judgment is not effective strategy. It is not a successful means of motivation. Judgment may coerce behavior change and it may force some of our parts further underground, but this is not the same as true transformation. Blame, shame, criticism, contempt, ridicule, condemnation -- all variant forms of judgment, ultimately all of them prove counterproductive. They tear down, rather than build up, reject rather than reconcile, and in the IFS model, as in the Christian walk, we are called instead to ministries of reconciliation and restoration.

Christians, like everyone else, are big on judgment. Read the scriptures and you will find judgment, but look a little deeper and things get more complex. We find God, but we also find that God's ways are not our ways. God doesn't do things the way that we would and God doesn't discard people the way that we do. God takes a murderer and makes him leader of the liberation: Moses. God takes a swindler and puts him in charge of a chosen people: Jacob. Jesus puts together a dream team, but when he does, he doesn't choose from the best and the brightest; no, he goes for the underclass, a group of tax collectors, fishermen and the like. In the scriptures, we come face to face with Jesus, but we also come face-to-face with our own assumptions and our own arrogance.

No, the Bible is not all sweetness and light, which is one of the reasons that makes me think it's worth reading. It has bite. It gets me all riled up. It makes me take a good look at me. When it comes to humankind, the Bible is unflinchingly honest. The good, the bad, and the ugly – you can find us all right here

94

in one big book, and if the Bible doesn't offend you, it should. In it you'll find ethnocentrism, nationalism, homophobia, misogyny and genocide, not to mention random acts of cruelty. Women are attacked, children are sacrificed and tribes of people wiped out wholesale. There are threats of judgment which frighten us and calls for moral authenticity which challenge us. And just when we are about to rise up in righteous indignation, Jesus tells us not to pass judgment on others, but instead to love them all.

There's no doubt that the Bible can be offensive, but for many, the most offensive thing about the Bible, the most outrageous notion in the whole book is the unconditional love and grace that it offers. Everyone is welcome at the table. Everyone gets an invitation to the party. Everyone is given another chance. It doesn't matter who we are or what we've done, we can be forgiven... forgiven and redeemed, reconciled and welcomed back into relationship.

This is so wrong.

In theory, I am all for grace. In reality, I think that God could be a little more discriminating. I'm like the woman in my Bible study who said: all this grace is well and good, but let me tell you, I don't want to get to heaven and find Hitler there. Well, that shut me up for a full five seconds. I had to admit... me too. Hitler in heaven; it just doesn't sit well. Forget what Jesus says. I want to see Hitler in hell. Him, and a few others on my short list.

When it comes to grace, I find it hard to go along. I know what Paul says about justification by faith alone but the truth is: I believe in meritocracy. I want to be rewarded for my hard work. I want everything that I have earned and I want everyone else to get what they deserve. Like that guy who's been tailing me for the last ten minutes, riding up my backside. Forget grace. I don't want him to get the benefit of the doubt. I don't want any excuses about being late for a meeting or about how badly he has to go to the bathroom or how he has this unresolved rage because he was treated rotten by his parents. What I want is for him to get a ticket. I want to see those lovely blue and red lights flashing as they pull this guy over. I want to drive by and give a little smile, with a bit of wave, on the inside.

So maybe I'm coming from a part. Yeah, I'm pretty sure that this is just a part of me speaking, but I think that it's a pretty common part, and not mine alone. Take the story of the prodigal son, also known as the story of the big brother who got messed over. Day in and day out, that elder son is out there working his tail off on the family farm. He is the embodiment of respect, responsibility and doing the right thing. Meanwhile, baby brother is out there living it up, wining and dining and spending down the family dollar. Worst of all, he's breaking their father's heart. Big brother is helpless to do anything but stand by and watch, watch as the estate dwindles and his beloved father withers away. Then the troublemaker has the nerve to show up again, and now the older brother has to watch as his father welcomes this black sheep back into the fold, watch as he is greeted with open arms and the best in fatted calf. Big brother is enflamed with resentment. No duh.

Jesus tells a similar story about day laborers hired to work in a field. Workers come throughout the day and begin working at different times, but in the evening when the landowner settles up, all workers get paid the same wage. Guess how well this goes over? The ones who have been working since dawn were outraged. And who wouldn't be?! They lodged a complaint against the landowner. These last, they said, worked only one hour and yet you have made them equal to us who have borne the burden of the day and the scorching heat.

Are you envious because I am generous? The landowner asks.

Well, yes.

And then, and *then*... that father says to the elder brother: we have to celebrate and rejoice, because this brother of yours was dead and now has come to life; he once was lost and now has been found.

Yes, it's amazing grace. And yes, I know that I'm supposed to be OK with this. I know that I'm supposed to celebrate the profligate love of a generous God and to have in myself this same openness of heart and generosity of spirit. But it's not like that, not for the parts in me that work so hard to be responsible, to play by the rules and do the right thing. These ones, they make snippy little comments about "enabling," and "rewarding bad behavior." Parts like this want every one to get what they deserve, and they feel entitled to the grace that they have earned.

I know… you don't earn grace, but you just try and explain that to these guys. They know how the world is supposed to work and they like it to run right. In the IFS model, parts like this are known as "managers" and they are a subset within a larger protective system. Protective parts are there, you guessed it, to protect—to keep us safe from any threat, past or present, real or imagined. That's their job. You can recognize them by their role; you will find them at work in any human system. Managers manage. They try to manage other parts of us and they try to manage the world around us. Managers look ahead. They like to nip trouble in the bud. An ounce of prevention is worth a pound of cure: that's a manager motto for sure. Managers anticipate; they scan for threat and strategize to influence potential outcomes. These hard-working, responsible parts keep things running decently and in order, and most of us wouldn't get very far in life without them. They are the list-makers, the time managers and the financial planners. They are the organizers who understand that firm structure conveys a certain amount of security. Managers oversee our appearance and they govern our behavior. They keep us from doing anything that might prove to be embarrassing. They restrict our emotions and discourage us from taking any unnecessary risk. At least they try. Look at a chaotic life or church in perpetual chaos or a family that is often out of control and you're likely to find a system without sufficient managers.

Here's the thing about managers. They mean well, but they often come with their own baggage, burdens derived from previous experience of chaos. Manager parts are high risk for burnout and resentment. It's possible for them to relax, but not very often, only if everyone else is following the rules or if some other competent managerial type takes charge. Managers can take their sense of responsibility to the extreme. In the war against chaos, they can become rigid and downright controlling, lapse into dogmatism and dictatorship. The manager parts are usually sanctioned in our society and so they often claim the right of moral superiority. They will rule by force, if need be. They may command respect but they're not a very happy lot. What they really want is appreciation, a little love, and a very long nap.

Managers are good, but what good are they without something to manage? Fortunately, there are other players in the protective system that we refer to as "Firefighters." We call them firefighters because they jump in to douse the flames of inner pain. They numb and distract, and they give managers a run for their money. Firefighters often show up in what we refer to as "bad habits," and whatever they do, they can do to excess. They will drink, smoke, gamble, eat, engage in retail therapy, watch TV, work, exercise, daydream, abuse sex, and engage in any number of activities that aren't necessarily bad in and of themselves, but can be harmful when taken to extreme. Firefighters can take any delight and make it destructive, take your average pleasure and turn it into an addiction.

Firefighters are a fun-loving group, but like the managers, they are fueled by their own inner desperation and the need to protect our vulnerable parts from any more pain. Managers are more cognitive and tend to think about the long term consequences. Managers form our first lines of defense, but when the front line is breached and our security is compromised, it's the firefighters who react. They spring into action, the first responders in a crisis. They help us fight or flee or freeze. They drown our sorrows, numb our hurt, quench our thirst, fill in the emptiness, disconnect, distract, and do whatever it takes to put out the fire and contain our pain. Firefighters live in the moment and they don't give a rodent's behind about consequences. They are very effective in the short term, but in the long run, an abundance of firefighter activity will lead us into lives of chronic crisis and chaos.

The managers and firefighters don't get along very well, but they combine to make up our protective system. They share a common goal and serve a common purpose: namely they try to protect us from any more pain. In terms of approach, these guys are polar opposites and their differences often create inner conflict. They're like partners who come at life from different perspectives. They're like parents who can't agree on how to raise the kids. One drinks and the other tries to control the drinking. One under-functions and the other over-functions. One is permissive and the other punitive. In family systems, polarizations like these play out all the time. Wherever we go, it's the same old dynamic but in the end, we end up hurting the young and the vulnerable, the very ones that we were trying to protect in the first place.

Like birds of a feather, parts flock to other like-minded parts and they will lead us to like-minded people. People who are dominated by their managers tend to congregate, well, in congregations -- in religious communities and schools and clubs, in bigger businesses and political action groups and the military. They naturally gravitate toward institutions because institutions organize around a common good and they promote some kind of social order. And managers naturally gravitate toward the management positions waiting to be had within those organizations. Firefighters, on the other hand, know better than to be found in the company of managers. They know where they're not welcome. They prefer to hang out with others of their ilk, with people and parts who engage in the same kinds of activity. You'll find them in bars, or on-line chat rooms, at the all-you-can-eat buffets. Managers try to manage the firefighters but firefighters have their own ways to deal with manager energy and they are very good at it. They lie, manipulate, steal, avoid, deny, lash out and do whatever it takes to keep on doing what they do. They can be sneaky, but when it comes to commitment, firefighters are right up there with the managers. They will do what it takes to put off the flames of inner pain.

Is one of these roles better than the other? Well, yes, of course. The managers are better. Everyone knows that. At least, that's what my managers say, and God knows, I have plenty of them. You can imagine what the firefighters have to say in response. You will have to imagine because the firefighters, being what they are, are a lot more colorful in their use of language than what my mangers will allow on the written page. When we're in our protective mode, there's a lot of judgment and it goes both ways.

Who's the best? What parts do we prefer? Which is the Father's favorite? Parts are like that. They compare and compete, just as people compare and compete, just as the disciples engaged in this kind of dispute. When it comes to hanging with Jesus, the disciples made it into the top twelve, but even that wasn't good enough. They still argued amongst themselves. Jesus, Jesus, on the wall, who is the greatest of us all?

It's ridiculous, and right up my alley -- the comparison, the competition, the jealousy, the judgment, the need to achieve, the need to be affirmed, the need for reassurance, the need to prove that I am good enough: my Father's favorite. I pile up the accomplishments, but they don't last, don't seem to do the trick. There's never enough and there will never be enough, not so long as I labor under the same old burdens. I end up with the same old polarization, one that likes to present itself in terms of good and bad, best and worst, right and wrong.   Managers judge the firefighters and firefighters judge the managers. Round and round we go, and while it's all very compelling, in the end, I get nowhere at all.

Managers and firefighters not only fight with each other, they will turn on their own kind. Firefighters will pass judgment on each other.   Maybe I spend too much time at work, they say, but at least I'm not out there spending money on a bunch of stuff that we don't need.   Maybe I drink a little too much but I don't do drugs.   So what if I spend a lot of time on the computer; it's not like I'm out at the bar meeting other women like the other guys I know.

And if you want to see a real fight, put a couple of big time managers on the same project.   Put two people in charge of one committee. Go to a presbytery meeting and watch your brothers and sisters argue over every letter in the law or, more likely, every punctuation mark in the motion.   Church people have a lot of managers. We will do whatever it takes to keep things under control, even if we have to nail Jesus to his cross in order to keep the lid on.   Sometimes I froth quietly at the mouth. Jesus talks me down.

Judge not, he says, *that you might not be judged.*

Judge not, Jesus says, and I just seethe inside. I hate his compassion and his whole "turn the other cheek" philosophy because in this moment, I am filled with judgment. I say, let's blow the whole thing up, and be done with it. I'm not just talking about the meeting... I mean the whole world.   Like Jonah, I can't abide the grace of God:

> O Lord! Is not this what I said while I was still
> in my own country? That is why I fled to Tar Shish at
> the beginning; for I knew that you are a gracious God
> and merciful, slow to anger, and abounding in steadfast

love, and ready to relent from punishing. And now, O
Lord, please take my life from me, for it is better for me
to die than to live.

When someone hurts me, I find it hard to be spiritually
present. Pain gets in the way of my compassion. Why be kind
when others are mean? Forget turning the other cheek; I want to
hit back. Who doesn't want to hit back? I'd rather stay mad.
I'd rather walk away. I'd rather hold on to hate, thank you very
much, and I am not the only one. You want to make someone
really mad ? Tell them that they need to forgive. See how well
that goes over.

Many of us would rather die than see the good in our
enemies. We would rather watch them burn in hell than see
them saved by grace. We feel this way and it makes a kind of
emotional sense, but I don't think you can expect God to go
along with it. This is more the devil's work. The word Satan
has its roots in a Hebrew word which means: *to accuse.* It
makes me wonder, when we make an accusation against
someone, do we then become the accuser, the Satan? When our
parts pass judgment on other parts or other people, are we
operating in satanic mode? Could be. Worth considering.

Now, when I feel myself being overcome with judgment,
I try to look a little deeper. Henry Wadsworth Longfellow said,
"If we could read the secret history of our enemies, we should
find in each man's life sorrow and suffering enough to disarm all
hostility." "Be kind," wrote Philo of Alexandria, "for everyone
you meet is fighting a great battle."

And Jesus, who is the ultimate in Divine Presence, has
this little thing to say about loving my enemies and praying for
the people who persecute me. Paul jumps right in on the
bandwagon. "Do not be overcome by evil," he says, "but
overcome evil with good."

It's easy to write people off, but before you do, you might
want to consider their secret history and you might want to look
beneath the surface.

My Dad and I, for example; we don't get along. He's

dead now, so it's going a lot better than it used to. I have a lot of stories about the ways in which my Dad done me wrong. They are some of my favorites, but since he's dead and all, I'm trying to give him a break.

For the first 55 years of his life, my Dad was a traditional male, so he came into parenting with a bit of a handicap. My mother died young, leaving him to raise three children. He felt overwhelmed and inadequate, and he responded as all such fathers do: he was defensive and controlling. I responded as all oppressed people and teenagers do -- with overt resistance and covert retaliation.

Do you know what scares fathers of teenage girls the most? If you don't, ask teenage girls; they know. It's teenage boys. Teenage boys – that's the way to get to dear old Dad. Just hint that I might be ever so slightly interested in boys, at some point, in the distant future, and that was enough to send him over the edge. That's what I did and maybe it wasn't very nice, but I gotta tell you, it was sweet.

I used to think of my Dad as the personification of evil, and in some ways, he was, but it took a long time before I figured out that he probably felt the same way about me. Ours was a difficult relationship and the fallout followed me for a long time, until I began to do some inner work. I started with IFS and got some pretty good clarity. A minor miracle occurred. I felt compassion, for the both of us. Family life may have been ugly at times. It may have strayed into the demonic, but even at our worst, we weren't evil people. We were good people in a bad situation. We found ourselves trapped in roles that we didn't want, with no way out and what we did was all that we knew how to do. We did the best that we could do, even though I have to admit that that best wasn't very good. Just make it through. Sometimes that's as good as it gets.

My Dad and I, we're not the only ones who work like this. It happens all the time in families and other human systems. People get labeled. They find themselves stuck in a particular role. It happens by chance, and it happens by choice. It may come to us through gender or birth order, and there are so many parts for us to play. There's the hero and the martyr, the anxious one, the funny one, the black sheep, the peacemaker, the lost child and the devil himself. Maybe you like your role and maybe you don't, but still you play your part and the drama unfolds.

People get polarized. Life gets ugly. We behave badly. We even hurt the ones we love. Don't pretend that you don't know what I'm talking about. Don't you know how to get to your wife or your husband, your parents or your children? Don't you know just the right thing to say or the right tone to use, the eye roll or the look guaranteed to drive the other person wild? Some of us do even worse and we do it on purpose. We have it in us. There's capacity for bad even in someone who is really, really nice, like me.

Shortly after my daughter was born, I was snuggling with her, breathing in that clean-baby smell. I was filled with a powerful, irrational love. Seconds later I was flooded with an equally powerful, irrational hate -- a surge of protective energy born of imagined threat. I discovered another part of me. I knew that I would kill anything or anyone that might harm my daughter. Until that moment, I didn't know that I had it in me, the capacity to kill. But I did, and I still do, and I thought I'd mention it -- for the sake of anyone who might be interested in my daughter.

In general, I am not an advocate of homicidal tendencies, but in myself I can see a positive intent. I will protect my children at all cost. If you're a mother or a father, it's good to have a part like that because children are vulnerable. They need protection. I am there for my kids, and if I had to, I would kill to keep them safe, even though killing is contrary to 99.9% of what I believe, and if it ever came to that, in the end, I would know this truth: I had a good part that got stuck with a bad role.

Parts have positive intent. They can be mistaken and

misguided, mean and nasty, but to their limited way of thinking, they are contributing to the cause, doing what they can to help me out. IFS helped me understand this about myself and it was such a relief, because I was finding me pretty confusing. It seemed to me that I showed up in different ways at different times, even when I was the only one in the room. At the time, I didn't know about multiplicity and parts so I didn't know what to make of me. I kept trying to get a handle on myself but I wasn't getting anywhere. I just kept going in different directions all at once.

Was I a good person, or wasn't I? Was I a good Christian, or wasn't I? I behaved badly at times and I had fantasies of worse, but in my heart, I knew that I wasn't all bad. Not only that, there were things in me that other people didn't like, but I knew for a fact that they had worked for my good. Rage, for example, it's not one of your most popular parts. It was never voted Homecoming Queen, and in Christian circles, even your average anger is not all that welcome. I was fairly confident that my rage was a) not nice, b) not Christian, c) scary, and d) pushed others away. But I knew another side to rage. When I was a lonely adolescent lost in the pit of depression, when I was about to lose myself in razor blade meditation, rage stepped in and took me out. It moved me out of my despair. Anger saved my life, but everyone I knew, including me, wanted to get rid of it. I didn't know what to make of this. I was supposed to get rid of my anger, and yet I knew a hidden truth. Rage helped me survive, and underneath I had good reason for the anger that I held.

Parker Palmer faced a similar dilemma in his relationship with depression. After years of fighting with it, fighting against it, he finally came to see that his depression served an important purpose. It had a positive intent:

> I developed my own image of the "befriending
> impulse" behind my depression. Imagine that from

early in my life, a friendly figure, standing a block away, was trying to get my attention by shouting my name, wanting to teach me some hard but healing truths about myself. But I …ignored the shouts and walked away.

So this figure, still with friendly intent, came closer and shouted more loudly, but I kept walking. Ever closer it came, close enough to tap me on the shoulder, but I walked on. Frustrated by my unresponsiveness, the figure threw stones at my back, then struck me with a stick, still wanting simply to get my attention. But despite the pain, I kept walking away.

Over the years, the befriending intent of this figure never disappeared but became obscured by the frustration caused by my refusal to turn around…When I was finally able to make that turn – and start to absorb and act on the Self-knowledge that then became available to me – I began to get well.

That's how it is. That's how it works. We have problematic parts and so we blame all of our problems on them. We finger them for being at fault. We don't see the ways in which we are scapegoating them, but we are, in fact, blaming the victims of our own inner system. These parts bear the brunt of our life's pain and they get left holding the bag. We fail to see their positive intent. We forget that they in fact hold the key to our ultimate healing.

We want to get rid of our parts, because we see this as a viable solution to our problems. We would be wrong. Jesus says something very different. Jesus says: make friends with your enemies, be reconciled with your neighbor and live peaceably with all. The same process holds true on the inside. We are to be agents of reconciliation for our own inner relationships. We listen to all our parts. We hear the complaints. We acknowledge the pain. We negotiate truce. We work toward peace. We come to our parts with the courage and compassion of Christ. In Self, we come to care about them and care for them. Holy Spirit steps in to assume its rightful position of leadership, and when it does, our parts are finally relieved of their impossible roles and released from unrealistic responsibilities. Good parts get liberated from their extreme roles.

Good parts do get stuck in bad roles. Once you understand this way about yourself, it will make a big difference. Things begin to make sense. You begin to make sense. I developed a whole new attitude toward my parts. I found a new appreciation for them and a greater compassion for their predicament. I no longer blamed or judged them. I wanted to help them. It was a big change. Even more significant, Dick says, is the reaction of parts when they finally feel understood:

It was as if they had been trying to tell their stories all these years and couldn't get through. All they seemed to need was for the person's Self to understand what happened and appreciate how bad it was. Once that was complete, many of these parts immediately transformed. Clients reported that their image and experience of the part changed. It was as if a part had released a burden that, like a computer chip or curse, had been governing its existence. Many parts became joyful, as if liberated from bondage, like the flying monkeys in the Wizard of Oz after the Wicked Witch melted. After being unburdened, many parts just wanted to play or dance or rest. Surprisingly, others took on a role opposite to the one they had been in. For example, Diane's critic wanted to become a supportive cheerleader, encouraging her to do her best.

107

The Holy Spirit is infused throughout our flesh; even our parts contain the spiritual essence that we call Self. If we are willing to listen, our parts, though burdened, often have words of wisdom to share. They bring things into our awareness and communicate messages of support and encouragement, love and affection. Protective parts alert us to areas of potential harm and childlike parts can be spontaneous and playful, fill us with wonder and zest for life. Parts can be spiritually profound.

My son, preschool age, asks me where God is, and I say, Matt, where do you think God is? He points to the sky, up there, and then he points to his heart: in there. And I marvel. How many papers have I written, how many sermons have I crafted, how many words has it taken me to say that exact same thing?

A little child will lead them, says Isaiah, and in the wilderness of our inner landscape, parts prepare a pathway for our God.

In other words, it doesn't do to disrespect our parts.

Parts are good, but don't get me wrong, and don't get Dick wrong either. The IFS model does not endorse immorality or accommodate injustice or sanction unethical behavior. On the contrary, the Self includes important spiritual qualities like clarity, confidence and courage, and these qualities give us the ability to speak out. It's just like Jesus, who embodied the ultimate in spiritual leadership. Jesus had clarity and the courage of his convictions; he was confident enough to confront others when necessary. Grace is not another way to say, "Anything goes."

If anything, the IFS model makes it easier for us to discern the pull of our burdened parts and differentiate the prompting of the Holy Spirit, to determine the direction in which God is truly leading. The Self still holds people accountable for their actions. We still speak up but when we do, we do it from Self and not from any of the parts in us that would blame, shame, judge, and condemn. In fact, when we are in

108

Self, we are more likely to speak the truth in love because we are spiritually centered; we have the Spirit of Christ within. We speak the truth in love, showing forth love for all of God's people, with all of their parts.

No bad parts. It's an essential tenet of the IFS faith and it's just the kind of thing to make a Christian queasy. We are well steeped in the theology of original sin. Born bad, that's what many of us believe to be the truth about our human nature. Born bad, or at very least, ambiguous. I don't remember my birth and I don't feel qualified to offer a definitive opinion. For the most part, I think the point is moot. I may not have been born sinful, but I don't think it took me very long to get there.

People ask the same kind of question using the IFS language. People want to know if we're born with burdens or not. I don't know for sure. It seems like the answer should be no. On the other hand, some of us do seem to come with burdens from the very beginning -- develop them in utero, depending on what was happening with the mother or in the prenatal environment. Other people seem to come with what we call legacy burdens, issues that have been handed down to them from their family's history or from the general soup of prejudice and persecution that stews in the larger culture. Burdens can be derived from our parents' past or taken on from their dreams for our future, and all of that can be in place before we're ever even born.

Are we born good or bad? Are we good through and through, or are we inherently flawed and sinful? It's another one of those darned polarizations, and it seems to me a dead-end debate. Frankly, I don't care how we come. I'm much more interested in the process of our becoming. It's not so much about my birth; it's about the process of my rebirth. I am born again and again and again. Unburdened, part after part after part. Whatever it takes, as long as it takes, to make me whole, and what matters most is the possibility of goodness, my own goodness. I may be stuck in the past, but I don't have to stay there forever, and my future is not determined by it, not by the things that I have done nor by the things that were done unto me. I can't be held in the prisons of any pathology and I am not bound, not even by the powers of a prevailing pessimism.

You can believe in original sin and still make good use of the model, but you have to set aside your judgment, and you have to believe in the possibility of goodness, in the power of divine presence in the work of spiritual transformation. Some people may see this as a return to our original state of goodness. Others may understand it as conversion to a completely new way of being. In the IFS model, there is hope for every part, no matter how badly it's behaved or how heavily burdened it may be. In the Christian tradition, we hold out that same hope for all God's children. No one falls outside the embrace of God's arms and no one lives beyond the scope of Christ's compassion. Hope: this is the faith we share; the common ground on which we stand.

At times, Dick has described himself as a "hope merchant," and not to be comparing him with Jesus or anything, but Jesus offers this same hope and he offers it to everyone. Jesus doesn't just preach the good news, he *is* the good news. With him it wasn't pie in the sky by and by, it was come and eat, let's party now. Take up your mat and walk. Wash in the waters and be cleansed. Come on down and lay those burdens down. Repent and receive. The Son of God waits for you behind doors #1, 2 and 3. Open any little door; you just can't lose.

When it comes to people, Jesus offers his hand to anyone who will take it. He is so cheap.

As Anne Lamott writes:

> His love and mercy fall equally upon us all.
> This is so deeply not me. I know the world is
> loved by God, as are all its people, but it is much
> easier to believe that God hates or disapproves
> of or punishes the same people I do, because

110

these thoughts are what is going on inside me
much of the time....

This drives me crazy, that God seems to have no
taste, and no standards. Yet on most days, this
is what gives some of us hope.

Hope for all. It's too good to be true. Even those in the
inside track find it hard to believe. John the Baptist asks, are
you the one we're looking for?

Don't take my word for it, Jesus says. See it for yourself.
It's an evidence-based approach. The blind receive their sight,
the lame walk, the lepers are cleansed, the deaf hear, the dead
are raised; the poor have good news brought to them. And
blessed is anyone who takes no offence at me, he says.

Grace offends. I guess he knew.

And still, he keeps on with the offer. He welcomes the
good, the bad and the ugly. He may hate the sin, as they say, but
he loves the sinner and that includes me. Jesus looks at the
worst in me and what he sees is the potential for good. He
looks at my mess and what he sees is a mission field.

Yes, Jesus gets really excited about that kind of thing - the
seeking of lost lambs, the finding of lost coins, and the return
from exile - all those prodigal sons who finally make their way
back home. When it comes to grace, Jesus is a pusher, and if I
find it offensive, it's because I have a big Big Brother part, full of
resentment. I can easily become one of those righteous who slip
into the self-righteous. Like Pilate, I would wash my hands and
walk away; but Jesus never walks away. He just keeps pushing
hope. For him, no one is a lost cause. No one is too far gone.
No one is damaged beyond repair.

Look at Saul and you will see. Now there was a man
who did some serious bad, a manager run amok if ever there
was one. Saul was a killer of Christians. He methodically and
mercilessly tracked them down. It was religious cleansing and

111

the Christians hated him with a passion. But Jesus looked at Saul and when he did, he saw something different. Jesus saw the possibility of good. Jesus, by the way, is already dead, but he isn't one to let a thing like that get in his way. He comes to Saul and through that encounter with divine presence, Saul is changed. Saul has a change of heart and a change of name; Saul becomes Paul. The disciples are not amused. They find it hard to believe. They are, in fact, downright offended. They don't want to see Saul saved; they want to see him burn in hell.

It takes them a little while to get over it. In the meantime, Saul not only takes on a new name, he takes on a new role. Instead of persecuting Christians, he now carries the good news of Jesus Christ into the gentile world. If the Holy Spirit can do that with someone like Saul, just think what it can do with you and the worst of your parts.

God did not send the Son into the world to condemn the world, but in order that the world might be saved through him. Jesus says, "Love your enemies, do good, and … your reward will be great, and you will be children of the Most High; for he is kind to the ungrateful and the wicked. Be merciful, just as your Father is merciful."

Jesus cares about everyone, even the ones who hurt me, and I don't like it, not one bit. On the other hand, I know the hurt that I have caused, and if there's hope for them, there's hope for me.

Jesus reaches out his hand to me, and even though I am still burning full with judgment, I decide to take it. It gives me something to hold on to. It's a start anyway. Who knows, maybe one day I'll become more like Jesus and see the world through the eyes of his grace. Who knows, maybe one day I might find enough of Christ in me to love my brothers and forgive my enemies? I'm not quite there yet. In the meantime, I'm trying to reserve judgment. I still work hard for my grace, but I am leaning more toward the possibility of goodness -- God's goodness and also my own.

We must no longer be children, tossed to and fro and blown about by every wind of doctrine, by people's trickery, by their craftiness in deceitful scheming. But speaking the truth in love, we must grow up in every way into him who is the head, into Christ, from whom the whole body, joined and knitted together by every ligament with which it is equipped, as each part is working properly, promotes the body's growth in building itself up in love.

(Ephesians 4:14-16)

Courageous Love; Life Learned in Relationship

Growing up in the 60's, I spent my days under the more or less supervision of my mother, who would take me along with her on the endless running of errands. We'd go to the super market, the post office, the fabric shop... wherever it is that grown-up women go to ruin a perfectly good day. My mother, I think, liked the company, but mostly I was bored out of my gourd. I dragged along after her, kicking at the sidewalk and wearing my very best bored face. The only bright spot was the J.C. Penney. There, in the ladies department, you could find round clothing racks, large metallic rings hung full of dresses and slacks, but with enough room on the inside for a kid to climb in and get lost. Department stores had another thing going for them: magic mirrors -- rows and rows of angled glass like at the carnival funhouse. Jump into the center and there I am: a dozen "Me"s, or more – fragments, fractals, mirror images of the Multiple Me; each one identical. Center stage, I jump and twist and twirl. I do my best to take them by surprise, catch them out – just one of them out of step, off a beat. I never do. Never once do they fall out of line. At least, not while I'm looking. Guess they were well rehearsed.

I was a child then, and curious, intrigued by me. Do I

really look like that? What happens if I do this? Or this? Can I see my butt?

The old people did not share my love of mirrors. They had walls covered with old family photographs and dresser tops crammed with snapshots, but to find a mirror, you had to go into the bathroom. It seemed like they had this great love of photos, but just try and take a picture of them. Boy, that'd get them going. They didn't want any pictures taken, not of them as they are now, in other words: old. At the time, I was impatient and annoyed. But I love you, I said. I love you, just the way you are. I love you, on the inside and out.

I'm older now, so I know better. Me and the mirror: we're no longer friends. We didn't have a falling out exactly; we just kind of grew apart. We don't look at things the same way. You see, on the inside, I picture me as more like 24 years old...well, maybe more like 18. Whatever. A part of me is stuck in my past, and I'm just fine with that. In my mind's eye, I look a lot like Kate Jackson, and while this may be an illusion, I am totally OK with it. It's just that my mirror has a different point of view, sees me differently. I'll be going right along, minding my own business when I suddenly catch a glimpse of myself in the mirror and what I see is shocking. It's Oma! How the heck did she get in there? I look in the mirror and what I see is someone else. It's so strange – this sense of me in someone else's aging skin. I'm my own horror movie and all my little parts get scared. I snuggle them in and hold them tight. I know, I say, in my most soothing voice. That was bad. I saw it too. Don't worry, I'm here. I'll take care of you. I'll take care of it... I'll get rid of all the mirrors.

Late at night, when they are safely tucked in bed, I slip down to the bathroom. In this mirror, there's only one of me, and that's enough. I pull at my face. I lift my lids and tuck my chin. Now I get it. For the first time ever, cosmetic surgery makes sense. That's what I need: outside help.

Tell the truth, I'm already getting outside help. A lot of

it.   When I get to feeling ugly or old, or stupid, or insecure, I go
running to my friends and family for a little reassurance.   I'm
discreet, but still, it goes like this: tell me what you think. How
does this sound to you? Am I making sense?   I'm right, right? I
mean, I'm not wrong, am I?

I have my pride, so I don't come right out and ask, but
still, I have my ways. What I really want is for someone to tell
me that I'm good and that I'm beautiful, inside and out. Tell me
I'm OK.   Tell me that you really, really love me and that you
always will, no matter what, so help you God. Pinky swear.

What I want is someone who will help me feel all better,
safe and secure. I want someone who can make me feel
complete, complete and whole, and that's a big job. It seems like
a lot to ask. Not that I haven't tried. I have looked to others,
hoping they could help me with the void I feel inside. And I, in
turn, have tried to love others into wholeness, giving and giving
until there was nothing left to give.   It works for a little while,
but not very well.   It's like trying to serve soup when the hungry
push faster than you can ladle. It's like trying to fill up a bathtub
with the drain still open.

Run like this, relationships are hard work. Makes me
want to toss in the towel, that or throw my ladle at someone.
Relationships are difficult and disappointment comes with the
territory. I know that, and yet, when it does, I am absolutely
convinced that something has gone wrong.   There *must* be
something wrong – wrong with me, with the other person, with
the relationship, something wrong with the world... wrong with
God.   It's not supposed to be like this, I say. Love isn't
supposed to be this hard. Only maybe it is.

Relationships are how we learn. If nothing else, trouble
in relationship paradise has a way of bringing us back down to
earth, moving us away from our fantasies about the ideal and
back into the land of the real. More than that, broken hearts
open us to the possibility of an even greater love. Barbara
Brown Taylor says, "I am here to tell you that disillusionment is

not a bad thing. Disillusionment is, literally, the loss of an illusion – about ourselves, about the world, about God – and while it is almost always a painful thing, it is never a bad thing, to lose the lies we have mistaken for the truth."

I sometimes get disappointed in relationships because I expect more than is humanly possible. I want perfection, the perfect partner, meaning perfect for me, someone who will be there for me, in just the way that I need them, every moment of every day -- someone who lives to make me happy. Does that seem like too much to ask?

I'm guessing that most of us end up with some degree of disappointment in our relationships, with partners who turn out to be something other than what we had imagined, or partners who turn out to be different from what was, in fact, promised. Once we come down off the hormone high of the honeymoon phase, we go into makeover mode. We try to make our chosen one over in the image of a perfect partner, into the image that we have engraved upon our hearts of the perfect soul mate. We fall in love, but when that love stops flowing, even for a moment, we get in touch with the inner dark, with the monsters that lurk in our murky depths. We get scared and then we do what we do. We go to work on what Dick describes as one of three projects:

> In the first project we try to force our partner back into that loving redeemer role; we plead, criticize, demand, negotiate, seduce, withhold, and shame. In the second project we try to figure out what our partner doesn't like about us and then try to sculpt ourselves into what we think he or she wants, even if that is a far cry from our true nature. The final project kicks in once we give up on getting the love we crave from our partner. At that point, we begin to close our hearts. We either search for another partner, or numb and distract ourselves from the pain so that we can stay in the relationship, or alternatively, live alone.

116

We are looking for true love, and the search can take us many places…few of them good. We search, but we end up walking around in circles. Partners change but we end up in the same kind of relationship. Different voices speak, but they begin to sound alike. New people; same old problem. It's the same old thing all over again, again, and again, and again, until we begin to notice something. We have these different relationships with one common denominator. *We* are the common denominator. An unsettling thought worms its way in: maybe the problem isn't them; maybe it's *me*.

Boy, do I hate when that happens. It's sobering. One minute, there I am full of outrage and aflame with injustice. In the next moment, I am sober -- stone, cold sober. I see myself in a whole new light, and when I do, I wake up to find sticks and stones clenched in my fists, sticks and stones that I meant to throw, and the haunting sense of others launched, launched and landed, hit the mark. I am looking at myself, and the person that I see is not anyone that I ever meant to be. This is not my best Self. This is me, gone mad. This is me waging war against the ones I love. It's so disappointing. I am disappointed in my partner, but I'm even more disappointed in myself. It's a sobering moment, and it's essential -- especially if you want to end your domestic violence and learn how to love the ones you love.

We stop and take a good hard look at ourselves, at ourselves and what we're bringing to the party. Things begin to shift. We stop pointing fingers at others. We loosen the stranglehold. We blame less and assume more responsibility for our actions and for our emotional well-being. Dick's got a nifty phrase for this little about-face. He calls it the "U turn," and it's a critical turning point in the treatment of any relationship. Let me tell you, therapists all over the world heave a big sigh of relief when it happens. This U turn doesn't deny or minimize the damage that has been done. It doesn't absolve anyone of anything, but it does mean that we acknowledge our own parts and we take responsibility for the role that we have played. We begin to release the other person from our impossible expectations.

As for me, I came to couples therapy brimming with desperation and resentment. I wasn't all that interested in a U-turn, but I definitely wanted someone to help me with my husband. I wanted someone to get him turned around, turned around and straightened out. Yes, I wanted what all wives want: someone to fix my husband. I can't tell you what turned it around, turned me around. Well, yeah, IFS turned me around, but I can't pinpoint the exact moment. At some point, something in me switched and my understanding of resentment changed. Until then, I had seen my resentment as the end result of all the wrongs that my husband had done unto me, a sign that he needed to do something different. After that U-turn I saw things from a new perspective. Now I understood resentment as the end result of all the things that *I* had not done for myself. Resentment was a sign that *I* needed to do something different... so I did. I stopped blaming David for my unhappiness. Instead I simply started doing the things that made me happy. I stopped blaming him for ruining my life and started living my life.

It was big change, and it shook things up for the both of us. It was hard, but it got better. Ask David and he says that my shift shifted our relationship. In the face of my anger and resentment, he had found it hard to show up with anything other than fear and defensiveness. I guess I might have been a little difficult. He was so busy contending with my protectors that he didn't have time to deal with his own. Given enough space and support, it turned out that he could be with both his parts and mine. That was a nice surprise. I remember the exact moment *he* made *his* U-turn, mostly because I was watching for it like a hawk. One day he stopped explaining and justifying and started asking me questions, asking out of a genuine curiosity.   One day he asked me about my experience of something that had happened in our marriage.   Oh yeah, I played it cool, but inside, I was falling off my chair.

Me and my honey, we've learned a lot from each other over the years.

That's how it's supposed to be, Dick says. Your partner is there to help you learn. Your partner serves as your tor-mentor; they mentor you in your life lessons.

Oh yeah, I say, I got the whole torment idea, I just didn't know that I was supposed to be happy about it. I didn't realize that it's supposed to be a good thing.

It's not the most popular approach, Dick concedes, but generally speaking, what your partner provokes in you is the very thing that you need to heal.

In other words, I say, my husband is just like all those mirrors. He helps me see my butt.

Yep, Dick says. It takes courage to love someone and it takes even more courage to let someone love you, the whole of you.   But once your parts feel accepted and embraced, once you feel the support of the other person's Self and you've tasted that kind of love… you won't want to give it up. It's worth the work.

Disappointment in marriage meant that I had to come to terms with the truth about myself.   It focused my attention on the baggage that I was dragging with me into this relationship and into many other relationships.   It served as what Dick calls a "trailhead," the starting place on a path that would eventually lead me into deeper healing within myself and within the relationship.

Disappointment in marriage also meant that I had to come to terms with the truth about all human relationships. They're not perfect. They're just not.   At least not according to my definition, by which I mean: perfect connection – the bliss of being one all the time: Cloud Nine.   But if you're in this life to grow, relationships are a pretty good way to do it. We have all manner of relationships and they give us plenty of fodder as we move through a continuing process of romance, rupture and reconciliation. In all our relationships, we are in the process of breaking up or making up, deepening or distancing, a little at a time, all the time, and this perpetual motion will put you in touch with a lot of parts. All those ups and downs, all that falling in and out of resonance -- you get to know the other person really well, and you get to know yourself really well. For richer and for poorer, in sickness and in health, in the good times and bad; through it all... no, because of it all, we get the chance to grow in love.

Love over the long haul. It's not for sissies. Commitment helps. We commit to the other person. We commit to the relationship. But most of all, we commit to the journey itself. We are here to grow spiritually. Viewed from this perspective, we no longer see human relationships primarily as a way to get our needs met. We don't use love as a way to lose ourselves or escape from our problems into the bliss of being one. We do get needs met and we can enjoy the full depth of our connection, but we also see the field of human relationship as a rich and fertile ground, a playground, a learning lab in which we get to experiment and practice, a place in which we can both embody and receive the kind of love that is of God. We promise to walk alongside each other, to companion one another as mentor and tormentor, lover and learner. We promise to be present, as best we can, for all parts of a common life and for all the parts that come up for us in the living of a shared life. We promise to partner.

Ask someone to define marriage, and they will often define it in terms of commitment. Marriage is the commitment to stay with each other no matter what. I hear this all the time, especially from someone struggling to stay in relationship, even when their partners have become controlling or violent or have turned away into any number of addictions, even with partners who are driving the family into financial ruin or driving everyone around them crazy. People will put up with all kinds

120

of destructive behavior, because, they say: I took a vow.

Commitment also falls easily off the lips of those who are desperate to keep their partners and to keep them in place. But, they say, you *promised*. You promised to stay with me, no matter what. You promised, they say, and when they say it, it has the ring of accusation and coercion.

Ah yes, those marriage vows. Beautiful as they are, they can be co-opted and forced to serve as an all-purpose recipe for relationship abuse. Not that there's anything wrong with those vows, mind you. I love those vows. They are so moving, the one place in a marriage ceremony practically guaranteed to make you cry. In the face of such love declared, how can we help but weep for the sheer beauty of it, for the courage and the innocence, not to mention the insanity of it all. Vows are lovely. They speak to our heart's desire and they resonate with all the parts in us that long for true love, a soul mate. Many people need this kind of commitment in order to feel secure, safe enough to love without fear, safe enough to open into the deepest levels of intimacy. These vows can provide a bedrock for family, a sturdy foundation for the building a life together, and this is a good thing. But for others, these same vows seem to serve as license, giving them permission to act without consequence, an arena in which to test for limits over and over again, until they finally find some.

Commitment is important, but when it comes to any human relationship, it's good for us to know what it is that we're looking for and why. What parts might be at work? What assumptions do we bring, what contracts do we make? Do we make our commitment out of a mature understanding, or is it a way for us to cling and control? Are we in a loving marriage or are we in love with the idea of marriage? When things get tricky, we often turn back to our vows, but it turns out that we can be more committed to the idea of commitment itself than we are to our actual partner or to addressing the issues that undermine true love. Commitment becomes more a form of rationalization rather than a reason to courageously address issues in the relationship. Being faithful is important, but keeping a vow to the vow does not a marriage make.

Commitment starts with the letter "C" but you won't find it on Dick's list of spiritual qualities. That's because the essential element in a relationship is not the fact of our commitment; it's the nature of our connection. It's the bond between us. There's a definitely parts-led aspect to our human love. We might want someone to depend on or someone who will depend on us. We might want someone to lift us up or settle us down. There's sexual chemistry and we like how it feels. My parts like your parts. And that's OK. We like the particularity of another person, the particular constellation of their parts. It's you I like. And if you like me, what more do we need to know?

Well, what we need to know is how we can also have a Self-led kind of relationship. We need to know how to hold onto our Self, even when we are head over heels in love. We need to know that we can care for ourselves, even though we have this blissful, boundary-blurring connection with another person. We need the ability to stay spiritually grounded, remembering that our primary relationship is the one that we have with God. If we can do all of that, then we're good to go.

And since very little of that is going to happen any time soon, courageous love means that I'm going to love you anyway, and I will have to learn as I go along. I am willing to engage the process because this *is* the process. This is how it works. We learn of love, as we learn of life, only by living it.

Courageous love is a principle, but it is not a rule, hard and fast. It looks different at different times. Sometimes courageous love means that I will put the needs of my partner first. At other times, courageous love means having the courage to stand up for myself, even though my partner isn't going to like it. Sometimes it will take courage for me to be present and simply listen when my partner has a complaint to share.

Courageous love means that I give up my old escape routes and reengage my partner from a place of Self.

Let the Spirit lead and we will grow in love as we go along. We will experience more Self to Self connection at every level of our being. We won't have to force ourselves to act in loving ways; that kind of love flows naturally from a Spirit-filled heart. Dick describes this as a Selfless kind of love, a love in which you freely put the growth of another above your own need for security. Jesus says the same kind of thing: that you can lay down your life for the sake of your friend.

When I am in Self, I will work toward the highest good, and I can do this because I am secure in my spiritual relationship. I can do it because the Spirit of Christ is in me. I work toward this way of being because, when it comes down to it, I don't want to live with a lesser love. As individuals, as couples, as a community of faith, we practice courageous love together so that we can all grow up and grow up together. We grow closer together. We grow up in every way, as Paul says, into him who is the head, in whom all parts are joined.

Dick says we do the hard work because it's worth it:

A Self-to-Self relationship based on courageous love is so fulfilling that if you were to taste it, you wouldn't be inclined to leave it. To have all of your parts feel accepted and embraced; to have the freedom to explore and express all of them so that your liveliness doesn't have to vanish; to experience abiding encouragement to follow your trailheads and learn your lessons; to know that the loving support of the other's Self is always there, no matter how life hurts you and no matter how the parts of each of you interfere; to feel the sacred "coming home" sense of connection to the divine in each other – for most of us, that is our heart's desire.

123

The sacred "coming home." The sense of divine connection. We can experience it in our human relationships and, at other times, the very limits of those human relationships will turn us back to our relationship with the Self, with God. Disappointment in my marriage turned me back to the ultimate in spiritual connection. It helped me remember that my primary relationship is not the one between me and my sweetie. It's not even the one between me and my kids. It's surely not the one between me and my chocolate. My primary spiritual relationship is the one that I have with the Holy Spirit. My primary spiritual connection is the one that I have with Jesus… with God, the wonderful and amazing Divine Self: transcendent, yet immanent; other, yet inner; reliable and yet wildly unpredictable; extravagant in grace; and always, always available… there when I am there, when I come home to God.

I like knowing that God is here, here as the eternal light; alpha and omega, my beginning and my end, both within me and beyond me. My very being is nestled in God's greater being. All around me are the Everlasting Arms. This awareness helps me on a daily basis. In this life, I may suffer all kinds of loss and I may lose my way, but the *"I"* of who I am is never lost. It's the ultimate in safety. This is spiritual confidence, and when I am secure, my inner survivalists disarm. My thrashing, grasping parts settle down, and as they do, serenity wells up from within. Peace spreads throughout the inner landscape. Battle-weary troops relax into a welcome rest. At long last, here is the redemptive love that I've been looking for. It's love in just the right place and here, in this ultimate spiritual connection, I find the saving grace I seek.

> Jesus slips into the seat across from mine. He helps
> himself to a sip of my coffee and smiles his quirky
> little smile. Redemptive love? Saving grace?
> Really? You're going to go there? That's awfully

Christian of you.

My response is not particularly Christian.

So, he asks, are you going for any particular theory
of atonement? Christus Victor? Substitutionary?
Moral influence?

It's Church History 101; Professor Steinmetz all over
again. Jesus is so irritating. It's no wonder, I say,
they killed you. I'd do it myself if I thought it would
do any good.

No, really, he says. I want to know. What are you
going to say? Are you going to talk theology, or are
you going to talk about divine love? Are you going
to tell them that you love me?

I don't even tell *you* that I love you, so why would I
tell them?

    My comeback is quick and snappy, but in a flash, I am
caught. I hear my own words and see: he has backed me into a
corner. He is quicker than me, that Jesus, and not one to miss an
opportunity. Jesus confronts me with the truth of myself. Gone,
as they say, from preaching to meddling.
    I begin to whine. You already know I love you. I don't
see why I have to say it.
    Jesus waits, but in the end, he is disappointed.
    I can't. I won't. I don't, although I do come up with
what looks to me as a reasonable compromise. I offer to write
those three little words on my napkin and pass it over. No
thanks, he says. He'd rather wait for the real deal.
    I am disappointed too, disappointed in myself because I
thought I was farther along than this. It's not like I haven't been

here before.

Years ago and thousands of miles away in the south of Holland, my father is in the hospital where he is recovering from a major heart attack. I call to see how he is doing. He is fine, but tired. Thank you for calling, he says, but could you please not call for a couple of days. He needs to rest. He is so tired.

In an instant, my heart fills with dread. We will never speak again. I don't know how I know, but I know, and I know that now, if ever, is the time for me to speak up and tell my father that I love him. If I have ever told him this before, I can't recall. I summon the words. For a full three and eternal seconds... one hippopotamus... two hippopotamus...three hippopotamus. I will the words to come, but they don't. I can't. I won't. I don't.

Two nights later, sirens scream through my sleep. In a minute, the phone will ring, but I have the news already: my father is dead. His ashes are long since scattered, skated away on the canals of his boyhood, but my love for him lies buried still within my heart.

The sad truth is this. I can talk about love. I can write whole sermons about love, but to let that love flow freely, and from my heart... not so much.

I get pretty discouraged, but Jesus is nice about it. It's OK, he's says. It's just another trailhead. That's all. Love is hard and you still have parts that need help, the ones that keep you from trusting and from loving fully, even me. But don't worry, I'm not going anywhere, and love, love is never lost.

Jesus knows just what to say and, unlike me, he says it. Bathed in grace, my heart begins to soften. I guess that's what a little Self-energy will do for you. It melts my heart and it helps me to be more compassionate with myself and with others, with all of us here on earth who are learning the ways of love.

For people like me, love is challenging and risky -- a dizzying, disorienting roller coaster ride of romance, rupture and reconciliation. It's a Tilt-a-Whirl way of being in the world that shows you the truth about yourself and helps you find your butt, whether you want to or not. But if that moment of U-turn is sobering, then the moment of Re-turn is equally amazing. Defenses soften, walls crumble, and the scales fall from my eyes.

Now I see. I look at those I love; only I see them now for who they really are. I see my husband, my children, my friends, my Jesus, myself, the unwashed masses, and in this moment of clarity, I wonder, how could I have ever been so blind? How could I ever have forgotten the truth about us, about who we are, all of us, at heart? I see again the Self, the Holy Spirit as it dances such an intricate and lovely dance, weaving its way within us and among us, drawing us into swirling patterns of interconnection. Through this love, a Self-led love, our broken bonds can be re-membered. We are knit together into one spiritual community. We partner courageously and gladly, for the growing up in faith and the building up of love.

On that day you will know that I am in my Father, and you in me, and I in you… those who love me will be loved by my Father, and I will love them and reveal myself to them.

(John 14:20-21)

The Spirit-Led Life: A Priesthood of Believers

I am a new mother when I see the card. It's drawn in the comic style of Roy Lichtenstein. A woman, blond and elegant, looks up from her pillow in shock and alarm. "Oh my God!' she exclaims, "I left the baby on the bus!"

For me, motherhood is like this: the lightning bolt of panic. Oh my God, I say, how did *this* happen? Never mind that I know how it happened, but how did it *happen*? How did I end up someone's *mother!* How did I come to be responsible for some little person's life? And what if I leave my baby on the bus?

Some days are like this: the sudden jolt of awakening. One day we look up to find that we are not in Kansas any more. Oh no, not us. We are in a strange new land or in some a foreign state of mind. Life takes us by surprise. OMG, as the youngsters text, am I finished with college already?! What, I have a mortgage?! A woman in her 90's says, "How did I get to be so old? It went so fast."

I am visiting at the senior center. As I go in, a woman and her friends are going out the door. I'm going out to celebrate my birthday, she says. How old, another resident asks? Eighty, she replies, and the second woman says, wistfully, voice full with longing and nostalgia: oh, I remember when I turned eighty! How does *that* happen? Since when does turning eighty look good?

We wake up married or divorced, back at home or far from home, widowed at 30 or dating at 60, bankrupt or wealthy, employed or not, addicts or church elders, even both. So many

128

things make up a life, and many of them we never thought to call our own.

The other day someone asked me, "How did you decide to be a minister?"   Well, I have been ordained for over 20 years and   believe me, I've been asked this question before. Every time my inner blonde looks up in shock and alarm. "Oh my God, you mean, I'm a *pastor*! How did *that* happen?"

I never meant to be a minister. It's what I'm doing while I wait for my other life to show up.

Ministry was never part of the plan, at least not part of my plan. When it comes to life, that's my biggest complaint; it doesn't go according to plan.   Come to think of it, I never really got a plan. I never got the map.   Some people seem so focused. Some people seem to know exactly what they're about. Their call, their vocation seems clear.   But for me, life has never looked like this, and the spiritual journey for sure has never looked like this.   It's always been more about taking the next step, whatever that next step was, even though at times it looked like I was walking out into thin air, stepping out into nothing; or like driving in the fog with your headlights on and seeing just enough to move ahead, one car length at a time.

The things I do, they don't make sense. I don't think I have ever made a smart career move. I have left positions that paid me well and left people who loved me well. I've never been able to explain it to anyone's satisfaction and certainly not my own.   I've never been able to explain myself except to say that the Holy Spirit is leading me somewhere, that God has something else in mind. I'm just trying to follow Jesus.   That's what I say, like that makes any sense.

I'm following Jesus. That's what I say and it's only a little better than the old cliché: I'm going to find myself. Although as it turns out, following Jesus and finding my Self turns out to be the exact same thing.

Following Jesus and finding my Self: it's what I have tried to do, but for all of that, I'm not so easily led. I balk. I dig in my heels. I go galloping off into exile, where I am free to wander in the wilderness and worship all my golden calves. I will gladly sit in the belly of the whale and stew in my own juices until I stink. Then, and often only then -- when I've finally had enough of me, I do something different. I turn to God. It's not the most sophisticated spiritual dynamic, but it seems to take me where I'm meant to go.

I am trying to follow the Lord Jesus, and you would think that this would be explanation enough, especially for other Christians, but even in the church most of us prefer a more rational approach to faith. We like it when religion and reason track in the same direction. I prefer it that way myself, but that's not how it worked out. Mystery has something else in mind and Holy Spirit has a mind of its own.

I know this, but I still find it hard to adjust. I don't know why I have to be such a difficult disciple. I don't know why I have to go kicking and screaming all the time. Following Jesus might be a challenge, but my life only gets worse when I don't. I suffer even more. I can plug my ears and turn away, but when I do, I disconnect from God. I can close my mind and shut my heart, but when I do, I am depriving me of my Source, the well-spring of my life. Spiritually speaking, I starve myself. It's what I do. It's where I go, and why on earth would I want to go and do a thing like that?

I don't know. I can't seem to help myself. It's all those pesky parts. That's what they do. That's how they work. Some of them, I know for a fact, do it on purpose. They don't want anything to do with God. They have, as we say... *issues.* They're mad at me and reject the whole idea of Self. *What good are you? Where were you when we really needed you?* That's what they want to know.

Other parts take me away from God, but unlike the first group, they don't do it on purpose. They're just too busy. They've got a lot to do and they're just too busy to take time out for all this introspection. They're not anti-God, they just don't have enough time in their day for God.

And after all this time, I still have parts that don't believe in Self and they sure don't believe in parts. They think IFS is ridiculous. After all these years of IFS training and IFS therapy! Even Dick finds it a little hard to believe, but that's what I'm saying… I'm difficult.

Parts separate me from my sense of Spirit. They disconnect me from Self and they do it not because they're bad, but because they are burdened. They are still carrying their own cross. According to the IFS model, these burdens show up in the form of extreme beliefs, emotions, sensations, and behaviors. They skew our perceptions. They distort our cognitions. They blind us to the truth about spiritual presence. They interfere in our relationship with Self and they keep us from accessing the transforming power of Self-energy. They keep us from fully embodying Holy Spirit. In traditional Christian terms, these burdens function in the same way as sin. Sin separates us from God, and that for sure is what these burdens do.

This separation can happen in many different ways. There's my sense of guilt, for example, and the corresponding image of God as angry, vengeful, and punishing. There's my sense of neglect and my corresponding belief that God is uninterested, unavailable and apathetic. None of this draws me closer to the Divine or makes me want to cozy up with Christ.

Sometimes I get flooded with feeling, overwhelmed by emotion, a state in which there is no *think*, only *do*; there's no real ability to function, although there is an awful lot of flailing about.

When it comes to my relationship with God, pain can be a problem. Physical and psychological pain make it hard to be anything but consumed with my own suffering. And then there are the debilitating messages that we take in from our families and the larger culture, burdens about skin color, gender, sexual orientation, nationality, religion, ethnicity and so on.

All of these this can separate me from God, from you,

and from my innermost being, from every form of spiritual relationship, and this truly is sin at every level.

Whatever is going on in the circumstance of my life, separation from Self only makes it worse. Spiritual alienation deprives my life of meaning and renders my suffering senseless. This kind of separation from God – that's just suffering heaped on top of suffering; it is a living hell. I keep my visits short.

Like that prodigal son, I do eventually come to my senses, return to my Self. I find my way back home. Lucky for me, God leaves a light on. It doesn't seem to matter how long it takes, or what I did while I was gone. It doesn't seem to matter how many times I lose myself or lose my way; the Spirit remains steadfast. Jesus waits on the porch to welcome me with open arms, comes racing down the road to greet me, just like my golden retriever. Talk about unreasonable and irrational. God's love unwavering is ridiculous. It's also really, really nice. Love like that is worth waking up for. It's worth coming home to. It's heaven on earth. I'm right at home, with parts and all, and that's when I see: the soul that's saved - it is me.

From what I can tell, life looks like this for a lot of folk. It's the cycle of turn and return. It's a popular path. We turn away from God. We forget about the Self. And while we're gone, the Spirit waits. The invitation remains open and the lights remain lit. Inquiries are made and divine search parties are sent. Behold, Jesus says, I stand at the door and knock. Then, one day, something happens and we become more open. Something cracks us open. Hardened hearts break open. We become open to our spiritual dimension. We reconnect with Spirit. We do it in our own way and in our own time, but this process of healing and unburdening and embodying more Self, this is not a process that leads us into life; this is life itself. This is what our life is all about.

The Spirit moves and sometimes it is hard for us to get the Big Picture. Isolate a single moment in time, a single point in space, and it might not make a lick of sense. In fact, it might feel as though we have just landed in Kansas all over again. But put that moment in a larger context and the overall pattern is exquisite. Put it all together and you'll find that we are part of one great dance. Everyone is invited to this ball. You don't have to be an expert in spirituality. You don't have to be a religious professional. Priests come in handy, but even then, they're not essential equipment.

Maybe it's just my Reformed perspective talking, but there's no big deal about clergy. Most of them are nice enough, I guess, but I don't really like the way they look. For one thing, they wear those funny clothes – robes and all, dog collars and those silly looking hats. It seems to me that they go out of their way to look special, different. They may look different on the outside, but underneath, my sources say, they look just like me. Well, some of them anyway.

In some denominations, the clergy are truly seen as something different, as somehow the Special Ones of God, but I am on the inside track and so I beg to differ. I am clergy. I know me well, and from what I can tell, I'm not all that different, or if I am, it's only in the designation of a role. I may graze through different pastures, but I am just like any other lost lamb. I may have dedicated my life to Jesus, but I am as wayward as any other disciple. And when I'm in need of help, I can go directly to God, just like the rest of you. You can go to the church or you can go in your room, as Jesus says, and pray. We all have direct access to the Divine. We call this the priesthood of all believers.

Dick says the same thing about the Self. Self is spiritual essence, and as with the Holy Spirit, we can find it everywhere, both in and around us. You might find it concentrated in a particular person, but each one of us has a Self. Spirit is housed within us and so it's right there, wherever we go, accessible to us all, 24/7.

Don't get me wrong. It is still good to have communities of faith. Healthy spiritual communities support our growth.

They support our spiritual relationships. They uphold the vision, know the journey and will do what they can to walk with us along the way. This is true for Christian community and it is true of the IFS community. There are texts; it helps to study. There are others with more experience, people who can tutor us and help us learn. There are gatherings that strengthen us and make us glad.

It's all good, but when it comes right down to it, a certain amount of this is up to you, between you and your God, between your parts and your Self. Holy Spirit is accessible. Self is everywhere, and while this sounds all well and good, it also means that you can't pass the buck. No one else can do it for you – not even the priest. Not even Dick Schwartz, the great Guru of IFS. You have to work on your own relationship with Spirit as you understand it. You have to reconnect with your own Self. You have to develop your own spiritual capacity and grow in spiritual maturity. Spiritual leadership is not my job alone. I just happen to get paid for it.

You can follow me if you want to. I can be your spiritual leader. I'm pretty good at it, but there are a few things that you should know upfront. I usually know where I am, but I don't know where I'm going. In spite of some mighty fine managers and some strong spiritual connection, I make my share of mistakes. They don't work out all that well, and they aren't all that fun, and I wonder sometimes, why would anyone want to follow me? Why would anyone want to make my mistakes? Why wouldn't you just make your own?

Spiritual leaders are all well and good, but you can only follow them so far, up to a certain point, and then it's up to you. You learn what you can, and then you take off the training wheels. You take those teachings out for a test drive. You take the model and make it your own. You step out in faith. Instead of listening so much to others, you listen now much more to God. Instead of following others, you follow the leading of the Holy Spirit. Let the God games begin.

Whether we share a common faith in Christianity or IFS or anything else, our individual paths still look different. We are different people living different lives, and the real joy of parts lies in the particularity of our personality. Holy Spirit has consistent spiritual qualities and Self comes with certain universal characteristics, but parts… oh my, those parts! They are the things that make me Me. My parts make me unique. Oh, these little guys, they are my own, and they come with a wonderful array of gifts and talents, quirks and questions. I love them as I love my own children. They are so interesting and wise and you never know just what they'll do. I love them, if for no other reason than they are my own and given in trust to me, for me to love and lead – to help me to learn how to love and how to lead. They are me, and we are me, and we are one together. We are family.

I am glad, of course, for your company. No doubt you are interesting and wise and full of your own surprises, but it just might be that God is leading you in a different direction altogether. You might go a different route. It's funny how we share the same Spirit, and yet we end up in completely different places. I'm glad to share what I have learned, but you're not me. You have your own lessons to learn, your own life to live, and I think when it comes right down to it: you're meant to be your own unique embodiment of Self. You are the You God has in mind.

Hassidic sage Rabbi Zusya, another great spiritual leader, once remarked, "When I reach the next world, God will not ask me, 'Why were you not Moses?' Instead, he will ask me, 'Why were you not Zusya?'"

Why not be yourself?

Which begs the question, what is it that leads in you? Is it Self, or is it parts? There are times when I feel completely at one with the Spirit and other times when I am completely dominated by my parts, but most of the time we live on a parts/Self continuum. It's a shading of degrees, a fluid process as I move back and forth across the scale. Sometimes I am more parts-led and other times, more Self-led.

If you want to develop your capacity for spiritual leadership, it helps to know about parts.

Follow the leader. Maybe, like me, you played that game when you were young. I loved that game, but I must confess: I loved it the most when I got to lead. In my college drama class I learned a slightly different version. It was even better than the first. In this version everyone gets to lead, all at the same time, and we lead with different parts. Did you know that we lead with different parts of our body? Some people come into the room forehead first -- the neo-cortex brings them in. Others let their bosoms lead. I think we all know a few people like that. There are others who slink in belly first, or groin first, or even the odd few who lead from the knee. Try, they said, just try and lead from a different part. Parts in the lead! Who knew?! And here I thought I was just walking.

I forgot about that game for years. Then I caught up with IFS and I learned it all over again in a slightly different form. I learned about parts that lead on the inside! Who knew?! And here I thought I was just living. Once I started paying attention though, I found a lot of parts, and not just when I walked. Different parts can have their way with me, step up and run my life. There's a part that wants to prove that I'm a good person so it has me do good deeds. There's a part that feels responsible for, well, everything, and so I try to fix, well, everything. There's a part of me that likes to win, so I work hard to stay on top of the game. I'm a busy girl.

When it comes to questions of leadership, it helps to know your parts. Luckily for me, my strongest parts have the sense to be socially acceptable, even sanctioned. They get rewarded and reinforced. They make for success according to the standards of our world. These are the parts that people see. Other parts are not so nice and not as smart. They want what they want, and they don't care what they have to do in order to get it. They can intimidate or manipulate, bully and blame. They don't like feeling empty, so they stuff in me whatever they can get their hands on. They don't like feeling anxious, so they look for things to make them safe. They look for love in all the wrong places. I try to leave these guys at home. As far as I'm concerned, they're grounded -- for the rest of their life, and mine.

At church, they say, everyone is welcome. In Jesus' name, we welcome all. That's what we say, but even at church, some parts are more welcome than others.   Mostly, we like those Managers. For one thing, they know the importance of a good financial pledge. They pledge *and* they like to get things done. God knows churches are a lot of work. Someone has to keep up the building, keep track of the bills, run the Sunday School, and ride herd on wayward pastors.

You can find a lot of Managers at church, but you can find them somewhere else. They tend to hang out in our minds, in the neo-cortex. A Manager tends to be your more cognitive type.   They think a lot. They like to figure things out. God bless 'em, every one. Here in the western world, we are in love with our intellectual parts. Reason, it seems, is reason enough for our very existence.   I think, therefore I am. That's what Descartes said, and that's what many of us seem to believe: that we are our minds. That's what we think, but then again, isn't that just what a thinking part would think?!   Isn't that how a reasoning part would reason? Logic likes to think of itself as Self; it's a Self-like part.

In Western Christianity our love affair with the brain goes even further. We have come to identify it with our very soul.   Augustine considered cognition to be a definitive characteristic of the soul which he defined as "a substance endowed with reason and fitted to rule the body." He defines the human being as a "rational soul using a mortal and material body."

Don't get me wrong. I love a beautiful mind as much as the next girl; maybe even more. Remember the last time you had a good idea? Don't you just love it how your brain lights up on the inside, the way it flashes like a pinball machine and explodes across the inner landscape like fireworks in the dark?! Don't you just love the sparking sensation of electrodes as they leap-frog through your synapses?! It's a beautiful thing, baby.

I have a good brain, but that doesn't mean I totally trust it. I don't confuse it with my Self. It is not the seat of my Spirit. I love the myriad of cognitive parts that occupy my mind, but they are not as reliable as they would like me to think. They mean well, but tell no one, sometimes they make things up. They interpret. In lieu of any real information, they will make up little stories about what's going on in the outside world, or better yet, about what's going on in someone else's mind. They make things up to make things fit. They rationalize. They justify. They will "forget" important pieces of information and bury other parts altogether.

It's good to think things through, and in the spiritual scheme of things, reason has an important place. But the mind is not the soul and reason is not the rightful ruler of our internal systems. Reason has a place and it comes right after the experience of revelation. We have an experience of divine presence and then we reflect on that experience. Mystery manifests, and then I try to figure out what it all means. The Spirit shows, and then I try to make sense of it. God is big, but my brain is small and the Coyote Christ has this way of messing with my mind. I'm pretty sure that he does it on purpose, but what I've learned is this: there's no way for me to wrap my mind around the whole of God. Not that I haven't tried. I've been through this cycle a number of times, and now when the Holy of Holies is revealed, I simply try to take it in. Soak it up. There will be plenty of time to think it through later.

People with good minds often make good leaders, but these are not the only ones who like to lead. There are plenty of people out there with strong wills and loud voices. Others whine to get their way. We all have ways to get our way. On the inside, it's not much different. I'm my own little power struggle. My parts have lots of different ideas about what I should do. They elbow and shove and do what they can to sway me. Everyone makes a grab for the wheel. We don't get very far, but every now and then I do finagle a spectacular crash.

There was the time I yelled at someone for not being compassionate enough. That was parts-led.

There was the time when someone yelled at me for no good reason, and I just stood there and took it. In fact, I'm pretty sure that I even agreed. That was parts-led.

The lack of paycheck was getting to me, so I interviewed for a job that I didn't really want. I liked hearing the "yes," right before I realized that I had to say "no." I'm pretty sure that this was parts-led too.

In the parts-led way of life you might do the right things, but you do them with the wrong spirit.

In the late 1970's I attend my first honest-to-god demonstration. I am in L.A. to walk for peace, but a lot of other people have came for something different – sex and drugs and rock 'n roll and every cause under the sun. We are a colorful crew. We pour into the streets; hundreds, and I am one. Powerful energy surges through the crowd. Fists pump the air and we have an awesome chant: "Hell no, we won't go, fight no war for Texaco." I ride this wave and ride it high, but after awhile I hear how the voices have become strident, how the rhetoric has turned ugly. Chaos rumbles right beneath the surface of this churning crowd. Claustrophobia kicks in and I have to *get out*. It's all I can do to keep me from pushing other people out of the way, and it dawns on me: for this being a peace protest and all, it isn't very peaceful.

In the parts-led way of life contradictions like this are common: hate-filled pacifists, corrupt law enforcement officers, pro-life activists who murder, and preachers who preach unconditional love while spewing hatred and condemnation.

Oh those parts. They mean well but they can be

misinformed and misguided. What really makes for a good leader? You can read a hundred zillion books on the topic. They offer a complete manager makeover. They will teach you different skills and techniques. You'll learn how to influence friends and manipulate others. You'll learn how to run the maze and strategically position your cheese. But for the most part, these books don't really teach you how to lead; they teach you how to win. They teach you how to get what you want, but that's not even close to what Jesus had in mind. Come follow me. That is what he says. It's funny, all these books on how to lead and so few on how to follow.

All these things actually encourage the kind of leadership that comes from our parts. Spiritual leadership is something different and it doesn't necessarily mean that you are in charge of other people or take the role of leader in a group. For people of Spirit, authentic leadership is not derived from positions of authority. It comes instead from an inner authority. It's not about being the leader or following the leader -- it's about the thing that leads in you. IFS is spiritually empowering; it helps to free us from an inappropriate dependence on Designated Spiritual Authority and into a trusting relationship with God. We come to depend upon the authority of the Holy Spirit. In a Spirit-led Life we are guided by the Spirit of Christ as it moves within and we resonate with that same Spirit as it manifests in other people. In a Self-led Life, Self serves as the leader of our internal systems and our external systems. It's the role of Soul to lead at every level of relationship and in every configuration of human community.

The Self-led world looks very different from what you get with parts. There's less conflict and more collaboration. There's less haranguing and more harmony. There's less contradiction and a lot more congruence. The experience of Self leadership, of course, is rarely pure. We still have parts and there are still times of struggle, but the process of deliberation is much shorter and the quality of conversation is more considerate. We work toward consensus and the decisions reached are more in keeping with the heart of Christ, with the presence of Self.

Holy Spirit works through process and it leads largely through influence and invitation. Our life plays out, and as it does we are invited to see the hand of God at work, experience the presence of God nearby. The opportunities for greater awareness come to us again and again. God is so patient. Most of us would have given up on ourselves and on this world a long time ago, destroyed it even if only for the sake of a better kingdom yet to come. But not God. God never gives up, and this is one quality of spiritual leadership, one of the four that Dick has outlined in what he calls the "Four P's" of a therapist. In relationships with other people and in relationship with themselves, people who embody spiritual leadership show forth patience, persistence, perspective and presence. The Self is patient, taking as much time as it takes in order to build a trusting relationship with parts. Self is persistent, tenacious even, in its commitment to healing. Self comes with timeless perspective, able to ride the ups and downs of our daily turmoil, and it is not deterred by the intensity of our parts in anguish. Through it all, and to it all, Self remains present; Holy Spirit abides.

How do we know when we're in Self? How do you know when you're with the Divine? I don't think we really teach people how to discern the presence of Holy Spirit and yet we all seem to have some internalized sense of what God looks like. Nine out of ten Sunday Schoolers surveyed will tell you that he's a very old white man with a long, white beard. He looks a lot like Dumbledore or Gandalf, and he speaks with a deep voice as if from the inside of an echo chamber. I don't know where they get this stuff. Probably from the same place I got it. Images of God: they get in your head and then it's hard to get them out again.

Sometimes it's hard for me to recognize the presence of

141

God, especially when he shows up in a whole new disguise, and it's really hard when he shows up in the disguise of me. Seems to me, I'm pretty murky. I see things through a mirror dimly. I get Spirit filtered through the lens of me, and this means that I only get God in degrees. That's how it is: I'm Spirit in the Flesh. Self comes to me in Parts. And while I'm not altogether happy with it, I guess it is enough. It has to be; I'm all I've got, at least for now.

In my own eyes, I am only a little hovel, a hut too dim to house the Holy. But Jesus, having no standards at all, has moved on in. He's taken up residence in my heart and he's home to stay. I'm learning to live with it. I'm learning to live with him, and this means that I am learning how to listen. More than that, I'm learning how to live with Love, to live with Love in me.

How can I discern divine presence? How do I know when I am following the lead of Spirit instead of my parts? When the Beloved is at home in me, when the Self has room enough to flourish, there is the felt sense of spiritual attunement. I experience what Dick describes as the 8 C's of Self and what I call the 8 C's of Christ. They are spiritual qualities, key characteristics of the divine presence. There's compassion and connection, confidence and courage, clarity and creativity. I feel calm and strangely curious. When I am trying to differentiate between my Self and parts, when I am assessing my capacity for spiritual leadership, those eight "C"s make for a handy dandy checklist. There's also my corresponding list of "anti-C's" – qualities that indicate something other than spiritual leading. This list includes things like being closed or cut-off, cautious or cowardly, confused or controlling, cruel or conceited, chaotic or complacent.

I've gotten a lot better at discernment and IFS gets a lot of the credit. IFS taught me how to more fully embody the Spirit of Christ so that I could bring spiritual presence to my parts and be more spiritually present to other people. That's a pretty big plus. Now I know what it's like to be in Self, how it is when I'm with God.

Not only that: things get weird. Life gets weird. I need something and it shows up. People seem to speak the very words that I need to hear. Paths cross, stars align, pieces fall into place. I see signs of Holy Presence everywhere and Jesus shines in all the people that I meet. I see the same old things in a whole new way.

There's another thing, a new weirdness right in me. I know the words that I should speak, and I speak them. I know the things that I should do, and I do them. I stay present, even in the face of things that scare me. I speak for my parts and do it from my Self. I love my enemies, even while they persecute me. OK, well not that so much. I can hardly love the ones I love, but I would say that I'm much more open to the possibility of loving my enemies. And at times, there is even the experience of supreme peace, a peace that surpasses all my understanding.

I owe it all to IFS.

Well, not really. I get a little over-excited. I am an evangelist for IFS and Jesus is tolerant. He just takes another sip on his brewsky and shakes his head. I don't know what you're getting all excited about, he says. It's right there in the Gospel. It's what I've been telling you all along. I don't know why you needed Dick to tell you what you already know. Do you have any idea how much time and money you could have saved? I guess it's true, he sighs, what they say…how a prophet is without honor in his own hovel.

Meanwhile, I'm in party mood. I put on some tunes and start to dance. Come on, I say to Jesus. Come on and dance. Don't you want to dance? Tell you what, I'll even let you lead.

Jesus laughs. He knows me better than that. But still, we share the same flesh and we move in the same circles. We dance the same dance. I don't know exactly where the Spirit is leading me, but I do know this: I have a beautiful life and one day the work that God has begun in me will be complete.   The glory of the Lord will be revealed.   Then as now, my heart will be full -- with wonder and with awe. Wonder and awe. They don't start with the letter "C," but close enough. Wonder and awe: that's how it is when I come into the presence of Holy Spirit, when I wake to find the Self in me.

Jesus rebuked him, saying "Be silent, and come out of him." When the demon had thrown him down before them, he came out of him without having done him any harm. They were all amazed and kept saying to one another, "What kind of utterance is this? For with authority and power he commands the unclean spirits, and out they come!"

(Luke 4:35-36)

Therefore, since we are surrounded by so great a cloud of witnesses, let us also lay aside every weight and the sin that clings so closely, and let us run with perseverance the race that is set before us.

(Hebrews 12:1)

Others Among Us: Critters and Guides

For some of us, the Esalen Institute is as close to Eden as it gets. Even in January, even in the deadest darkest day of winter, everything here is alive. Vegetables grow in the garden: kale and chard and artichokes. Flowers blossom: roses, and morning glories, and California poppies. Chickens scratch for bugs and the smell of fresh turned soil is moist, earthy and shamelessly fecund. En route to Mexico, monarch butterflies stop to adore the eucalyptus, and in the ocean water right off the coast, the whales breach and blow as they too head south.

I have my own journey to make. It looks to be a pilgrimage, though the feast, as Hemingway says, is moveable. At the moment I am fleeing the brutal, bitter dry-ice chill of Wisconsin winter. That and the cold which shelters in my heart. I have come here to attend Dick's workshop. I arrive in this unbelievably lush place; I think that I have died and gone to heaven.

I wander the grounds and shed my coat, shed my sweater, shed my gloves, layer after layer of winter armament until I find my skin. My pores newly bare, gasp for life and breathe again. Check-in time is at two so I make my way to the little office store. The room is packed, but for the moment, Claustrophobia and I am getting along just fine. People come and people go. The door opens; the door closes. The door opens again and in walks Evil.

Swear to God. It's like every nightmare movie you have ever seen, the ones I never watch. The room is chill. Though light, it's dark, and joy is sucked from every single soul. It happens in a flash. Evil has entered this room and it came with a thinnish man who looks to be perfectly normal. I know different, but no one else seems to notice. They talk and they laugh, and I have to get out. Forget my hard-won place in line; I slip out through the crowd and out the door. I pray… no, I plead… please, please, please, *please* do not let this man be in my workshop.

Ha. Ha. Ha.

I'm upset so I don't really hear it at the time, but I'm pretty sure Jesus is laughing. I won't get the joke until much later and even then, you have to have an appreciation for divine irony.

That evening, I go to the assigned room and sure enough, the man is there. Of course, he's there. I mean, really! Does everyone's world work like this? Does every life serve up just the thing you need, even if it's the last thing you want? You run, but you can't hide.

I ask Jesus. Is it just me, or are you obnoxious in this way to everyone?

He looks at me evenly. That depends, he says. Would you rather be special, or would you rather be just like everyone else?

It has the ring of trick question, but I don't have the time.

146

I've got to keep an eye on this guy.

In this workshop, as with most IFS trainings, demonstrations are a key part of the learning process. Demonstrations not only model the model, they give lucky participants a chance to work with the master. So guess who wins the lottery? No, not me... the other guy. The Man and Dick begin to work. It's a good session, I suppose. They find parts and they seek Self. Yeah, yeah, yeah. It's a fine session, but I am skittish and jumpy. I can hardly stay in the room. I jab a thumbnail into the palm of my hand again and again. Pain helps. It distracts, diverts. It feels like I am going crazy but this information is not something that I want to share. Why advertise?

Then all of a sudden, everything comes to a stop. Dick calls a time out. He begins to talk to us, not about Self or Parts, but something altogether different, something he calls *Critters*. You don't have to believe in this stuff, he says. In fact, I'm not sure that I do. I don't know if it's real or not, I'm just reporting on what a number of clients have described and what seems to work. It's not part of the model and some IFS therapists never run into this phenomenon, but many others do. Either way, it's good to know how to work with it if it shows up in your clients.

Some people show up with something that doesn't seem to belong to their inner system. It comes in from the outside. Critters, he says. They don't belong to us. They are foreign entities. Negative energy, maybe. Free-floating, unattached burdens, maybe.

Demons, maybe... is what I'm thinking.

Someone asks him about this, about demons like in the Bible, and he says, yeah, maybe, but I don't like to call them that. You don't want to give these guys too much power. They can't hurt you if you're not afraid of them. That's the important thing, not to be afraid and to help your clients not be afraid. If you stay in Self, if you have enough Self-energy, you can send them out and this really helps people, helps the whole process of

147

unburdening.

Dick talks, and my body gets very still. Alert. Until then, I had never met anyone who knew about this kind of thing. In fact, I had an aversion to people who see evil everywhere and find the devil at work in all things. Still, I had had some pretty strange experiences and a few intuitions of my own. It wasn't anything that I was willing to talk about or even admit fully into my awareness, but as Dick spoke, every word rang true. Looking back, I'm guessing this was not a good sign.

At the hour's end, I am still freaked, but the man is doing a whole lot better than he was before. You can tell. His presence is different. His energy is different. Even his face looks different, relaxed and calm.

As a rule, I don't talk about demons and such. I am way too sophisticated for that kind of stuff. I have a lot of education. I don't believe in a Devil, and I certainly don't believe in demons.

Jesus, apparently, did. In the Bible, Jesus often comes up against what the scriptures call *demons* and when he does, he casts them out. In the Bible, the casting out of demons and healing often go together; a blind man sees, a mute man speaks, a young girl is freed from torment and a boy cured from seizures. Jesus helps those who are described as being *under the power of the devil*, and his disciples do the same. Too bad they didn't get a chance to work with the rulers of our nations or the top executives in some of our corporations; I don't believe in demons but I'm pretty sure that some of them are possessed.

Jesus dealt with these entities, but as it turns out, in the Bible, you didn't have to be on a first-name basis with Jesus in order to send these critters out. Other people did it too. The disciples didn't like this very much. They pushed for a department of licensing and regulation, but Jesus was cool. Let it be, he said. Whoever is not against us is for us.

Jesus may have believed in demons, but what I believed about Jesus was this: that he was simple-minded and naïve. At least in this one regard. Not naïve even -- more like primitive, the product of his age... uneducated. You couldn't really hold it against him. That's how I thought about it. And when the Bible referred to *demons*, I viewed this more in terms of cultural context, the understandable attempt to explain things for which there was no scientific explanation. We, having the benefit of modern science, know better. There are no real demons, only the processes of mental illness. The devil does not exist, except as the projection of our fear. That's my take on the matter. In sophisticated systems like mine, demons are exiled. If only they would stay there, right where they belong.

I did not believe, did not want to believe, and this mindset affected my vision, determined what I would allow into awareness. That's how it works. The human mind tracks on a particular target. We see what we want to see or expect to see and so we sometimes miss that which lies outside the parameters that we ourselves have set. We live inside the box.

In my box, I have to say, it's lovely and kind. I like it here. In my box, everyone bears the image of Christ; everyone has a Self.   Here in the land of sweetness and light, evil does not exist. People might be naughty, but they don't really mean it. Sometimes they hurt me; they hurt me bad, but this is just their own little way of asking for help. And I am here to help, because that's what Jesus would do. That's what Jesus wants me to do. In fact, this is the Jesus Box.

Jesus objects. Don't call it that! It's not my box. I
don't believe in boxes any more than I believe in tombs,
and I sure as heck know a viper when I see one.

OK, I say. How about this? I'll call it *my* Jesus box. *My*
box... it just happens to have your name all over it.

Yes, my Jesus box is a beautiful thing, inscribed with my favorite scriptures about peace and justice. It's decorated with scenes from God's own Kingdom come: people from the north and south, the east and west, at one table eating turkey. The lamb and the lion are napping together and boy, are they cute as they sack out on the same rug. All my best friends and Bono are there and it's a lovely place.

There's nothing wrong with my Jesus box and my Jesus box is not wrong. It does depict deep spiritual truth, but it's still a box and doesn't encompass the whole world in which I live. It's my own little garden, a sanctuary designed to keep me safe, only it doesn't. Truth is: I miss things. I excuse things. I minimize things. I fail to see the Shadow. I don't always recognize emotional risk until it runs right over me. The good that I envision, it's all true, and yet in its own way, the box itself can be a trap. I don't get the whole picture. I don't see the world that lies beyond my four perceptual walls, and this means that I'm not really safe at all. I deny, and this means that I don't deal with the harsh reality that unfolds outside my box.

Jesus Boxes come in all shapes and sizes. You can get them anywhere. In some versions the walls are papered with the Ten Commandments and various Holiness Codes; angels hover on the ceiling and the caverns of hell gape beneath our feet. There are other boxes filled with the social gospel, depicting all kinds of good works and the good news of liberation here on earth as it is in heaven. Other Jesus boxes look a lot like soup kitchens or classrooms, concert halls or courthouses, hospitals, jails and street missions and conference centers -- just about anywhere that we might find the Holy Spirit hard at work. Each box has something to offer, but take any one of them alone and you have just one piece of the Jesus pie, and in isolation, any single perspective can turn into a trap.

As for me, I'm still left with whatever is happening in that room with Dick, the man, and the critter. I am curious and drawn to the topic, but at the same time, still upset. The session finally comes to an end and I escape gratefully out into the garden where it is easy to believe in God and in all things bright and beautiful. All I have to do is look around and see it for myself. With the feel of sun and the sound of surf, my heart slows into a steady and reliable rhythm. I relax and things loosen up on the inside. I am free, free and full of hope and more alive than I have been in a long time. It feels good. This, I think, this way of being, this kind of inner spaciousness... it's where I want to be, it's how I want to feel, all the time.

Next day though, we're back in the workshop, just doing a little experiential exercise, just a little practice session among friends, when *they* show up. No one else can see them. Heck, I don't see them so much as sense them: two bouncy ball-shaped things that whiz around my head, jabbing and poking, and all the while singsong taunting: You're gonna get it! You're gonna get it! Really, it's like being back on the playground of my elementary school. It's utterly juvenile and it makes no sense at all to be scared, except that I am. I am scared. No, I'm terrified. It is completely ridiculous and yet I'm completely convinced: I am in big trouble.

Here's the thing, that's how these critters work. They're so convincing. They're insidious and worm their way in with grains of truth, with bits and pieces from our past experience. They prey on our false beliefs and like heat-seeking missiles, hone in on the very point of our vulnerability. Why would I get in trouble? What is this terrible thing that I have done? I've put myself first, my own needs first. I am being selfish. I have left everything behind, my work, my husband, my kids... all of it, to enter this garden of delight. I am about my own liberation and the journey has just begun. That's the trouble. At least, that's what some parts are telling me. I am being selfish and selfish people get punished. That is the truth they know, the belief they hold, and just as a virus enters my body through a weak spot in my immune system, this oppression is taking advantage of this weak spot in my spiritual system.

So now I am afraid. I'm being punished for what I've

151

already done and for what I still intend to do. I *am* going get it.
I know I am. I'm shaking.

Dick comes over. They can't hurt you if you're not
afraid, he says.

Yeah, and that helps me how? I *am* afraid and the fear
feels primal. I am afraid and I need help. Dick is there and he
seems to know what he's doing. I'm glad he does.

With this sense of oppression, when this kind of fear
turns up me, I like to get a little help. When it turns up in our
practice, in our clients, it's good to know how we can be of help,
whether we believe in this stuff or not. The phenomenon,
whatever we call it, has been part of the human experience and
part of human cosmologies for a very long time. Spiritual
healers have developed ways to work with it.   Some people call
it cleansing or "clearing." Some people call it "sending it out."
Traditionally, the Christian church has called it "exorcism" or
simply, healing.

I'm no expert, except what I know from my own
experience and a limited survey of the subject, but it seems to me
that the Christian approach and Dick's approach are pretty
similar and their process relies on spiritual presence, spiritual
presence and spiritual confidence. We trust in the power of
Spirit and this faith overcomes all fear.

In one respect, Dick's approach is different from most
other forms of healing whether it is Christian or New Age or
ancient, and this distinction is one worth noting. The healing is
not performed by someone else, not by a priest or a practitioner.
It's not a ritual, not something that is done to me or enacted
upon me; it comes more as the Holy Spirit abides in me and
moves through me.   Others may serve as guide or coach, but the
effective agent is Holy Spirit at work within me.   A fuller
embodiment of Self, that's the real issue at hand, because perfect
love casts out all fear. Filled with spiritual presence, full with
Self-energy, there is no longer room in me for fear, no room for
anything other than the goodness of God.

Dick is there to do just that, help me regain my spiritual grounding. He stays right with me. His calm and confidence is contagious. He doesn't do the work for me, but he does coach me. He helps me take care of all my tormented parts until they finally trust and relax and make more room for Spirit. I find at last that I am no longer afraid. Jesus is in the room. God is within me and through the Holy Spirit empowering me. Now the work that I have to do seems simple. I send these critters off.

So now you think I'm nuts and I don't blame you one bit. I know… it's crazy!! Totally and completely crazy. Unbelievable. I completely agree. But let me tell you, in that moment of release I am *so* relieved that I don't even care. So what if I'm crazy. It's over. Thank God, that's what I am thinking. Thank God, that's over and done with.

This is what I say to myself, but even then, somewhere in the back of my mind, there is the lurking suspicion that this is not over. This is not the end of it. These are just the little guys, minions of some greater power. This will come again.

Three years later, the appointment is met. I am back at Esalen attending another of Dick's workshops. Apparently I just don't have the smarts to stay away. Each morning in this garden of delight, I wake up miserable and for no good reason that I can tell. I am being oppressed in the core of my very being. I am being tortured and tormented, beaten up on the inside. All those horrible Hieronymus Bosch depictions of hell --- he got it right, only it turns out, you don't have to die to get there. There is a living hell and it happens within. Don't ask me to explain it; I don't know how it works. The science of it eludes me and it certainly doesn't fit inside my box. I only know that it is happening and I am miserable.

For days I try to get myself out of this place. I am desperate to win one of those demos with Dick and time is running out. I'm not sleeping, which means I have a lot of extra time to pray. I go to the healing arts offerings – the movement classes and the various meditations. One night late, I join the

153

didgeridoo meditation. The tone of this ancient Australian horn reverberates in this room, flows up and out into the starry night. It echoes within my chest. All around me people are praying in all the different ways that people pray. The Divine is here. Jesus is here. Come to find, for the first time in days, I am not afraid. What I am is ready -- calm, curious even. I let the critter thing come.

How did you get here? I ask. How did you get to be in me?

An image comes. I see myself. I see me standing in my bedroom, the one with the pink shag rug, a middle school me, mother dead; miserable at school and miserable in my own home. I see me teased, tormented, and full of hate and rage. I want to hurt the ones who hurt me. I want revenge. I want to punish. I want Power and I want it now.

It sounds melodramatic, but if you've ever been there, you know that moments like this can be a matter of life and death. This is a crucible for destruction, the kind of suffering that lays the groundwork for another Columbine or for the suicide of countless teens who see no other way out. I see me sell my soul – not in any dramatic, Faustian kind of deal, but I open my heart just a little and that's all it takes. This dark energy, it slips right in. It's easy, trust me. All you have to do is ask -- not even ask; just relent.

Tell the truth, power does help. I *am* stronger, strong enough to stick up for myself and stand up to my enemies; strong enough to keep myself alive, and power like this will carry me along for a long time. This kind of power helps, but in the end, as it always does, it turns on me. I can see this now.

Why do you keep on doing this? I ask.

Because I can, it says, and I like to.

I feel it begin to manifest in my skin. My lip gets all twitchy and my body starts to jerk a little. I have never seen *The Exorcist* but I have heard enough to know that I'm not about to go there. I have had enough. Just as once I opened my heart to darkness, I open now to Light. I invite in the Light, God's light, light of Christ. I feel it shine in me. In every fiber of my being, I am Light. Jesus is light and in him there is no darkness at all. The Spirit is fully within me and this means that there is no room in me for dark. I don't even have to send this darkness out; it goes. It cannot co-exist. I am clear and clean and free.

That's just how it is, Dick says. That's how people describe it and you work with this just as you would any other belief system. You treat it with respect. Sometimes people say that they invited these critters in because they were feeling powerless, and these are often people who have experienced some kind of trauma or abuse. A lot of times there are stories about revenge, desire for revenge or acts of revenge. Critters come in because the Self is not in the body. Self can be pushed out through traumatic experiences or through extreme drug use, and without the protective presence of Self, the body is vulnerable and these guys just get in.

That's how it seems to work anyway, and no matter how they come, he says, the way you treat them is the same. You have to stay in Self. The important thing is not to be afraid. Just stay in Self and let the Self-energy send them out, out into the Light. I've even found, he says, that you can feel compassion for these guys. A lot of times they don't like what they're doing. They just don't know how to get out of it and they're scared too. So you can help them, even if they don't think they want it. You can send them out or over to the other side, off into the light. In fact, it's better to help them be healed and transformed in this way rather than set them loose back out in the world. Again, he says, you don't have to believe in any of this stuff and I only teach it as it shows up or as people want to know about it. It's not really part of the model but people seem to find it helpful.

Everything that Dick says makes sense to me. I begin to look for other healers; people who know how to do this kind of work. I find them. They are out there. Some of them have a practice which is based on the church's history and experience in

155

such matters. Other people draw on the ancient wisdom of indigenous peoples and spiritual practices that I once would have considered "primitive." There are other practitioners who do this work: energy workers and body workers and people of the healing arts.

Some of this fits closely with Christian tradition and some of it doesn't.   The process that Dick describes corresponds with how such healing is described in the scriptures. Be not afraid, Jesus said. Fear not. He says it a lot so I guess that must count for something.

Is it possible to deal with these whatever-you-call-thems on your own? Sometimes. The important thing is the degree of spiritual presence. If you've got a lot of Jesus in the room, then you can do it on your own; but then, you aren't really on your own, are you?   Most of us need a little help. We can help others, but we can't get enough separation from our own fear, can't hold enough spiritual energy. Most of us need someone else there, someone who keeps the faith and embodies Jesus, someone who can come alongside of us and coach us. For this we can rely on others in our spiritual community.

Well, that's where it gets a little tricky, at least for me. I go where I can to learn what I can about this stuff, but I'm not telling the folks back home. For many Christians, this stuff is way outside the Jesus box and outside the mainstream of the church to which I belong. I don't talk about it.

They would be afraid. This is what I say to myself. And it's true, maybe some of my parishioners would be.   But mostly, it's my own projection. I am afraid.   It's not that I'm afraid of the critter things.   I'm afraid of my own people. I'm afraid of all those stones waiting to be thrown, afraid of ending up outside the fold, afraid of losing my precious credibility, afraid of tarnishing my reputation. I am afraid of losing the earthly powers which, frankly, I still enjoy.

Meanwhile, I have been writing about my journey and what I have learned of my faith through the lens of IFS. I have a perfectly good, practically complete draft of the book when Dick says, are you going to talk about what's not in here yet?   You didn't say anything about critters.   Are you going to talk about that?

Oh yes, I say.   Earnestly, I say, I should do that.

I say yes, but mostly because I am compliant and I don't want to look like a weenie in front of him. Also, I'm ashamed of my power-hungry, security-seeking parts.   I am scrambling to get back into my Jesus box – the one in which no evil exists for me to write about, and the one where no one throws any stones, especially not at me.   I am my best three-year-old me, hands over my ears, and my eyes squinched tight.   My eyes are closed: I can't see you. My ears are closed: I can't hear you.   Make it go away.

Later that night I consult with Jesus, which is a big mistake. He always seems to side with Dick.   In my heart I know that these guys have my back, that, in fact, we all side together.   They will help me with any stones, but still... I drag my feet.

If I do this, I say to Jesus, you know what will happen; they will come.   If I start talking about critters and the like, you know what's gonna show up in my office.

That's right, he says. They will come and when they do, you'll be there. People need someone who can handle this kind of thing, who can let them talk about their experience of evil and not freak out. I don't care what they call it or how they picture it, people need help with their experience of darkness. They need help to overcome the powers of darkness and that includes the darkness within. You can help them with that. If you stop and think about it, you'll find that it's already happening, and you are doing just fine.

Jesus is right. On a regular basis, clients talk to me about evil – about relationship evils and personal evils and systemic evils. Some of them talk about critters too, though they usually call it something else. They describe it as a darkness or a crushing weight, a force, a malice, the inner experience of oppression or torment, a demon or even the devil. Most of them know what it is. Many of them know when it came, and why. They seem to know what belongs to their inner system and what does not. Few of them know what to do about it. I coach them until they have a strong sense of spiritual presence, until they are no longer afraid. Spirit-filled, full with Self, people begin to experience this energy in a different way, see these things in a different light. They become strong enough to set the boundaries that they need. And in the face of such concentrated spiritual energy, these things themselves often transform. They may become small and timid. They may scramble and try to puff themselves up, or try to hold on, burrow their way back into our human host. Sometimes they appear as lost and lonely souls looking for company – wandering ones who have not yet found their way to God. Whatever it is, divine presence is the answer and so we send these ones on their way, we point them back toward Holy Spirit. We stand firm, entrust them to the greater wisdom and care of God.

But for all the evil that walks through my door, people also come with spirits that work for good. Many of them describe strong experiences of a particular spiritual presence. Sometimes they can identify the person. There's God and Jesus, of course, but also Mary and any number of the saints. Sometimes it is someone who has left this material realm -- parents or grandparents, spouses or children, cherished friends. Sometimes it comes simply as a light or a shape or a felt sense. These ones are spirit, though we sense them through our flesh -- we see them or smell them, hear them and feel them. We know that they are there, and however it is they come, there's no question of their intent. They come for the good, and when they do, we experience those eight C's of Self, the spiritual qualities of Christ. We know we're in good hands.

Paul says that we are surrounded by a great cloud of witnesses who cheer us on so that we can run with endurance the course that is set before us. For me, these are familiar words, a favorite encouragement at funerals and standard fare on All Saint's Day. At times I have thought of these witnesses as *the Dead*: people who are no longer with us, except as their lives live on in history, who serve as examples for us to emulate. At other times I think of them more as a heavenly host, sidelined souls who watch from the bleachers of the afterlife, stuck behind plexiglass barriers like they have at the hockey game: *The Dead*, separate from us, unable to help. Sometimes I have thought of them as observers who look over my shoulder, waiting to pass judgment on all my mistakes. One of the well-meaning stupid things that people said to me when my mother died was this: she'll always be with you, watching over you. Words of comfort, I'm sure, but not when you are 15 and driving without a license, not when you are 17 and sneaking out of the house at night to meet your boyfriend.

Maybe if I had been an athlete, I would have understood better what Paul was talking about. I would have known what it is to have a crowd behind you, to have their energy as a tangible force that impacts and enhances your performance. Maybe I would have known what it's like to have people in your corner, the home court advantage. Truth is, I'm not very good at recognizing support when it comes and I'm even worse at receiving it. Mine has been the ethics of survival, a "do it yourself" mentality complete with many of those individualistic self words that our society endorses -- self-reliant, self-sufficient, self-contained. I never was very good at group projects.

Despite my lack of athletic ability and teamwork intelligence, God kept on sending support, cheerleaders who came in different shapes and sizes, showed up in many different forms. Eventually even I couldn't miss it. There was a wealth of spiritual resource out there waiting for me to wake up and receive. People came with the gift of encouragement, people who recognized my need and were not put off by my inner curmudgeon. I am also surrounded by a great cloud of witnesses, a heavenly host which does not judge and does not stay behind the glass. These ones whisper in my ear, put people in my path, guide me in the way that I should go.

First time it happened, I was a sophomore in college, fresh off a year of defending my faith, a year of trying to justify myself and explain how someone as smart and sophisticated as me could believe in anything as ridiculous as Jesus the Christ. The last straw came late one night after another go-round with my boyfriend. Personally I was sick and tired of Jesus, tired of talking about him. I wasn't trying to evangelize anyone; I just wanted to be left alone, to co-exist in peace. I was sick and tired of prejudice and projection and how the fact of my faith kept me separate from others. I took it up with God. I let him have it, both barrels. I poured out my anger and my frustration, my anguish and my deep loneliness - the sense of betrayal. Along with Teresa of Avila, I shook my fist at God and railed: if this is the way you treat your friends, no wonder you have so few. I turned my back and fell asleep.

In the middle of the night, I come up from the depths slow and smiling. Someone has kissed me on the forehead. My eyes are closed, but I feel love and warmth radiating from just off to the left of my bed. There is such peace. Boyfriend, I think, has come, come at last to apologize and make up. I reach out my hand, but no one takes it. I open my eyes but no one is there. No one is there… and yet, something is there. I can feel it – warmth, radiating love, and a particular presence. Someone is there. I feel it, and then I feel it recede and disappear until I am, indeed, alone.

Freaked me out. I didn't know what to make of it. No one talked about anything like this in Sunday School. Well, actually, they did.   In the Old Testament, God appears to Moses in a burning bush, to Jacob in a dream, to Abraham and Sarah in the form of strangers passing by, to Samuel through a persistent voice and to Isaiah in a still, small voice.   Angels of the Lord appear to Zechariah, Mary, Joseph, Shepherds, three magi and many others as a clear discernable presence.   We did talk about angels, especially at Christmas -- angels, all the time showing up to say: Fear not.   Funny, how I doubted the existence of demons but I always believed in these messengers from God.   I always believed in them; I just didn't know they were still active.   The angels, I thought, had retired.

But from that night, my way of looking at the world changed.   Conventional wisdom says that we are each ultimately on our own, but after that, after the whole kiss-on-the-forehead thing, I have come to see it a little differently.   It's true that no one walks my exact same walk.   No one shares my exact same body or my experiences, but spiritually speaking, I am never alone.   Others are always there with me, even when I can't see them.   They are there, close at hand, giving me support.

At the time, I didn't know anyone who was on a first name basis with the angels, or the saints, or as some people call them, the guides.   In my own quiet way, I began to search.   In the hospitals and in the hospice, in the thin places between life and death, I stayed alert.   If heavenly spirit was going to be showing up anywhere, I had a hunch that it might be here, here among the dying, what with all those angels coming for to carry us home.

Sure enough, I came across people who had if not exactly a near-death experience, then a near-death awareness.   The Beloved Dead would come to offer comfort and to say: Not Yet, or Soon, or Be Not Afraid.   Whenever patients began to talk like this, I got very quiet.   Like a child up past bedtime, I got very still and listened for all I was worth.

I listened and people liked to talk.   It did them good.

Even when we're talking about angelic entities, talking about Spiritual Presence does not come easy. I met a young man with a brain tumor. One day he began to talk about these beings that would come and visit him. There were three, he said. They might be angels, but he didn't like to talk about them much. He didn't want people to think he was crazy. He did have a brain tumor after all. But truthfully, he didn't think it was just the cancer talking.

I was younger then and I didn't have the courage to talk about my own experience of Spiritual Presence. I didn't want anyone to think I was crazy either, and I didn't even have a brain tumor to account for it. But I listened and I believed and this alone seemed to help. These angels, he said, they brought him great peace. He called them: Friends of the Father, and because of them, he was no longer afraid to die.

Sometimes these spirits showed up as a distinct and particular presence. In Texas, for example, John died. John was Bob's brother but nobody wanted to give Bob the bad news because Bob was dying too. He didn't have very long to live and no one wanted to upset him. Next morning, Bob was alert and lucid for the first time in days. Hey, he called out, how come nobody told me that John was here? John, it seems, had dropped in to visit Bob sometime during the night.

For chaplains, death is part of the job, the meat and the potatoes of our ministry. We specialize in grief and I wanted to learn as much about grief as I could. From the death of my mother, I had already learned about the stupid things that people say, the words that don't work well. I wanted to learn how to do it right. I learned about the stages of grief and all the things that are supposed to bring us closure. There are many things that we can do to help people let their loved ones go -- rituals and prayers, the speaking of words left unspoken and the doing of things left undone. I got to be pretty good at it, and yet there was a piece of it that I got wrong, dead wrong.

What I know now is this. Good grief is not about letting

go. Good grief has more to do with holding on. We hold on to the good. We incorporate the love and bring that loving relationship inside, into our very being. We can keep our relationship alive through spiritual awareness and Self-to-Self connection. The Beloved Dead live on -- not only through memory or emulation, but in genuine spiritual presence. It's a kind of spiritual physics. Physical energy, they say, is never lost; it simply takes new form. So it is with spiritual energy, that very breath of God. Our souls are not lost; we simply take new form. Set free from the material world and released from the constraints of flesh, those we love may, in fact, be more available and accessible to us than ever. They are with us all the time. If we are open to it, they will walk alongside of us, informing us, guiding us. We have this spiritual connection, Soul to Soul, and wherever we go, they go along to cheer us on.

They often show up in distinct form, although many people experience them as something more amorphous; it's more intuitive, the sense that someone else is there, that some spiritual presence is there with them, guiding them along the way. People have the sense that someone else is there with them, watching over them. Sometimes that presence is much more active and intervenes in daily life. People will tell you, it's like someone was there, showing me what I was supposed to do or putting all the pieces into place. A friend of mine says it's a lot like when you go bowling and there's those bumpers in the gutter – just a gentle nudge to get you back on course. For others, the guides are even more forceful – a little appendectomy, a little car crash, a call so close that we wake up and start paying attention to the spiritual dimension of our life.

Whatever form they may take, these guys sometimes come with a message. They say things like: you will have a son, or, return to Egypt by another way, or, maybe you should pay that bill, or get on a different plane; do not go out with her. They may come with tidings, saying: Fear not, for I bring you good news of great joy for all people, for unto you is born this day in the city of David, a Savior. Some times they whisper words of encouragement to keep our hearts from fear. These ones work for God and they work for the good. If we are open, they will serve as signposts, guardian angels, Friends of the Father, guides along the way.

I've been thinking lately that I might have finally found what I want to be when I grow up. Maybe I could be a Guide. I don't know how it works, if you get to choose or not. Maybe you get drafted, or have to earn your place on the team, but thinking about it, I feel calm and confident -- not the least bit afraid, not even in the face of death. Maybe death is just another form of matriculation, just what it takes to get those angel wings, and when I do, you can bet that I'm not going to be sitting up there sidelined on any old bleachers. Nope, mine is a love that will never die and I'd like to be there for my friends and family, right there in their field, sending as much loving energy and support as I can, cheering them on as they run whatever race opens up before them. It's a new idea, but I like the sound of it.

There are Eight C's in Discernment

It's another dawn here in the southeast of Wisconsin. The household is slowly coming to life. The heat kicks on. Someone steps into the shower. Paws snick snick out in the hallway; my dog is ready for me to be up and about. I groan and sink myself deeper under the blanket. I am sick. At least, I think I am. Could be. It's not for sure. Last night was different, a lot better. I had this lovely little temperature, 101 degrees right there on the digital thermometer where everyone could see it for themselves: hard data, scientific fact, proof positive. But today, fever fails and I'm on my own. I have to figure this thing out for myself and even though it's not a decision of monumental proportion, I obsess.

It's true, I don't feel well. I'm tired and my head aches. Still, it isn't all that bad. Nothing that I can't handle, and I've been through a whole lot worse. Did I mention giving birth? Besides, there's another long list of things that need doing. Clients waiting. A shot of caffeine and I'll be good to go.

Or, maybe not. Maybe I should give myself a break. Maybe I shouldn't push so hard like this. After all, I know what it is to be driven. I've made this same mistake. I've walked around with a couple of pneumonias and gone too far down long, hard roads. So far, everything has worked out fine, but my daughter has grown wary. She has learned that she can't always depend me. She has to look out for herself, assert her needs. She won't go out with me anymore unless I promise right upfront that we will stop to eat.

Meanwhile, I still don't know if I'm sick enough to stay home. I go back and forth until in the end I give up trying to figure it out for myself and look to outside authority -- the health bulletin sent home from my kid's school. Turns out I meet five of the seven criteria for H1N1 flu. I make an Axis III diagnosis: I am sick. The bulletin is very clear, stern. I have no choice. It's a matter of public safety. I have to stay home.

I cancel my clients. Everyone is nice about it. Then again, it's not like they want to be around me either. I climb back into bed. I feel queasy but from whence does queasy come? Is it the flu, or the fact that it still feels like I'm playing hooky? Is it the being sick, or is it that being sick is weak and not anything I want any part of? Hypochondria steps in, just to spice things up a bit. Hypochondria is insidious. Maybe this is *It*, she whispers, the Big One… meningitis… lupus… hanta virus.

My stomach churns but the mind is worse, tumbling the same things over and over. Brain fever is back. Not once in this whole process do I settle me down. Not for a second do I take the time to get still and simply breathe. Whatever the heck it is that my body might be trying to tell me, I'm not about to listen. Whatever spiritual awakening that might lie in store can wait a little longer. I pop a couple of pills and sip a lovely little syrup laced with codeine. This knocks me out for awhile, which is a kind of being still, I think, and counts for something.

Learning to listen. Learning how to discern. It wasn't anything that I got in seminary. My own fault, no doubt, me too busy studying theology and searching out Official Answers to all my God Questions. I was enrolled at Duke Divinity School -- a Presbyterian fostering among the Methodists who, to their credit, did what they could to turn me on to John Wesley and to communicate that strange warming of the heart which comes in the presence of Holy Spirit, that or a great basketball team. They also taught me a tool for theological assessment known as the Wesleyan Quadrilateral. When testing for theological truth, we come at it, assess and evaluate through the four angles of scripture, tradition, reason, and experience.

Wesley would be proud, because this is what I've done with IFS. Evaluate and assess and bring each lens to bear. To my way of thinking, IFS is spiritually sound and it resonates with much of what Jesus said and what Jesus did. For one thing, it was through the model that I found personal healing, and for that reason alone, I know that God is in it, just as God is in the Salk polio vaccine, penicillin and chocolate. More than that, IFS has become a form of spiritual practice, a means of discernment, a way of listening at deep levels. IFS has taken me into the heart of Jesus' teaching and brought me into the very heart of God.

God is our alpha and our omega, Paul says, our beginning and our end, and if that's true, then it's taken me a long time to find my way back home. I spent a lot of time headed in the other direction. Let me just say, there are lots of ways to do this: run away... abandon your body, leave your life. You can remain in place without really being there. You can also pack your bags and head out of Dodge. You can be that rolling stone and just keep rolling on. You can bury yourself in your work or you can lose yourself in your relationships. You can drink or eat yourself into oblivion. You can deny the real in the pursuit of the ideal. You can deny so many parts of yourself in the name of what you think you could be or should be.

Leaving my life: it seemed to be the thing to do and almost everyone I knew encouraged it, in the most well-meaning and nicest kind of way. There are so many little catch phrases to reinforce it. If at first you don't succeed...try, try again. I think I can, I think I can. JOY means Jesus, Others, You. Forsake your past and repent. Leave it all behind and follow Jesus.

Those who lose their life will find it. Fix your mind on higher things. Why can't you just let it go… just do it. All right already.

Let it go. This is what I wanted for myself and God knows I tried. The parts of my life and the parts of me that caused pain, I tried to leave them behind. Cut them off, if I had to. Early on I learned to leave myself - to drift away and wander. I was always out of the house, and when that failed, I learned to disconnect and dissociate. Or I would take refuge in my mind. I tried to figure things out. At night, my mind worked overtime. When sleep refused to come, I didn't exactly count sheep, but I did recite scriptures about the Lost Sheep and Good Shepherds. I did sit-ups to the tune of the Apostle's Creed. As an adult, my mind was often still busy, anticipating and organizing, planning ahead, vigilant. In my centering prayer, I found it hard to stay centered. Thoughts would come and thoughts would go. Feelings would come and feelings would go. I tried to let it all flow through my mind like I'm supposed to, but some of these guys had come to stay. They wouldn't budge, so what could I do? I had no choice. I had to stop and face myself. In other words, Repent. Now there's a word you don't hear so much, except in church -- repent, which at its root means "turn around." Stop yourself and turn around, face up to things. It's the first step in the reconciliation of any relationship, if that's what you're about.

Stop yourself and turn around. Maybe that's what it takes, but in my Bible, first God's people run away. They run and run and run. For someone like me, it's encouraging. Moses ran. Jacob ran. Jonah ran. The whole tribe of Israel ran away. The disciples ran away. Jesus stands his ground, but the others, not so much. For God's people, growing in spiritual maturity means that it's time to stop running; stop and face the music, turn and repent. In the church calendar we have the whole season of Lent to help with this. Lent invites us into the process of repentance and reconciliation, but most of us do not go easily.

We go kicking and screaming, and we do it only when all the other options fail. Life...the universe... God... has a way of helping us with this. One day we find ourselves wandering in the wilderness, or stuck in the belly of a whale, walking through the valley of the shadow of death or sweating blood in some garden of Gethsemane. That's when we either turn away or turn ourselves around. We can walk away or we can walk straight into the dark. At times like this, we either lose our faith, or we find it.

As for me, I got tired of running... just plain ran out of steam. The 40's will do that for you. You just get tired. In the long run, running doesn't get you anywhere anyway. Wherever I went... there I was. Whatever I was running from, I carried with me.

Still, at the very edge of my turning, I hesitated. I contemplated. Jesus sat there on the fence with me, pulled out some gum. Fruit Stripe. I chewed. He chewed. We chewed together.

Remember how you're always wanting to follow me, he says. Walk my path? And that Apostle's Creed... how you used to say it over and over again until even the apostles got sick of hearing it, that part where it says that I descended into hell, and then I rose again from the dead? Jesus grins. Guess it's time to follow me.

It's going to be scary, isn't it? I whimper. It's going to hurt, isn't it?

Yeah, he says, but only for a little while. It's that whole dark night of the soul thing -- scary, but have faith. I'll be there and there will be plenty of help along the way. And remember, this is not a road that leads to death; it's the passageway into life.

Man, I had so been hoping to skip all of this, ascend straight into heaven somehow like Elijah. But no, I have to repent, own up to my life and to all the ways in which I let me

169

down. I have to wrap my arms around the whole of me, including the darkness in my heart.

In her book on spiritual direction Sue Monk Kidd writes:

> The Christ-life doesn't divorce us from our humanity; it causes us to embrace it. It makes us *more* human. It humbles us. Genuine transformation always connects us to our essential nature, both sacred and profane. When we go through its passages, we plumb the depths of our humanity. We become intimate with what lies inside – the wild and untamed, the orphaned and abused, the soiled and unredeemed...We stare into the sockets of our pain and glimpse the naked truth of who we are. All this we bring with us into the new life. It ushers us into a new humility. Oh, yes, no doubt about it. We birth Christ on a pile of ordinary straw. May Christ be born in you. That's the mystery at work.

Through IFS Dick opened a passageway for this kind of process. He showed me how to enter the depths of my humanity and how to do it safely, descend into hell without losing my way and without losing my Self along the way. IFS helped me embrace my humanity without being completely absorbed in it -- helped me be with my wild and untamed parts, my orphaned and abused, my soiled and unredeemed -- to be with them without being overtaken by them. IFS helped me open and embody more of the Spirit of Christ, so that in the end I could view myself through Christ's own eyes, and love myself from God's own heart. That's the mystery at work.

In other words: discernment. That's what this is all about -- seeing our earthly situation from a heavenly perspective, viewing our human Self from the vantage point of Larger Self. Through whose eyes do we look? With what awareness do we sift our options? Does the Holy Spirit dwell within? That's what we need to know. If we would seek Divine Will, then the first thing we have to do is detect Divine Presence. We need to know that God is truly with us.

How do we do that? Well, when it comes to detecting the presence of Holy Spirit, Dick has come up with a new formula, another tool for assessment. If you're Methodist maybe you can think of it as a double quadrilateral with eight points instead of four. Myself, I like to think of it as a kind of spiritual thermometer, a gauge for the Holy Ghost. It's those eight "C"s of Christ, those eight qualities that characterize Holy Spirit: calm, clarity, curiosity, compassion, confidence, courage, creativity, and connectedness. These qualities help us sense Sacred Presence. These qualities and something else. It's the way that my heart burns within me, and not from any fever. It's that strange warming Wesley talks about. When God is near, I tingle and glow on the inside. It's the radiant energy of the Self, the warmth of well-being. God is here and I am well.

A great gale arose, and the waves beat into the boat, so that the boat was already being swamped. But he was in the stern, asleep on the cushion; and they woke him up and said to him, "Teacher, do you not care that we are perishing?" He woke up and rebuked the wind, and said to the sea, "Peace! Be still!" Then the wind ceased, and there was a dead calm. He said to them, "Why are you afraid? Have you still no faith?" And they were filled with great awe and said to one another, "Who then is this, that even the wind and the sea obey him?"

(Mark 4:37-41)

Calm

When it comes to crisis, I am probably the one you want. Me, or someone like me. I am trauma-center trained. This means that I am calm, cool and collected – a safe port in any storm. At least, that's how I used to be… until I met panic. Panic took me back to where I never wanted to be in the first place – to Fear and Helpless and Out Of Control. Chaos and Crazy. Turns out, panic was in me all along, and not as distant memory, but as a living, breathing beast -- which really, I don't think is acceptable. Let the dead bury their dead; let the past stay in the past. Get thee behind me, Satan. That's what I say. But like it or not, I found panic there inside where it was apparently hiding all along. I've made a little progress, gotten to the point where I can acknowledge it, but even so, I'm not about to shake its hand. I don't care what Dick says about welcoming all parts; panic is not my friend.

Now, anxiety. That one I can do, and do well. Anxiety is related to panic. First cousins, once removed. But of the two, anxiety is much better behaved. Panic is running fast in no direction. Panic is your heart out of rhythm, beating wild without purpose. Panic will grab you by the throat and drag

172

you down.   Anxiety is a kinder, gentler way to go.   You simply chew yourself to death.

The disciples were going down.   They were out in a boat, caught in a fierce storm.   The boat was being overwhelmed with water and the boaters were overcome with fear.   Meanwhile, Jesus is below deck getting his beauty sleep.   He is sleeping like a baby.   It's so like him, just the kind of thing to make you mad, especially if you've got a little anxiety on board; anxiety is nothing if not collegial.   It likes to share.   It will reach out to others… reach and reach and reach.   It's a little needy in this way, not to mention manipulative and controlling.

The disciples are anxious and it feels to them like they are out there on their own.   Understandably, this makes them a wee bit resentful.   Don't you even care, they said.   We left everything to follow after you and this is what we get?   We are going down, and where are you?   Asleep, and not even at the wheel!

Jesus responds, but he is not a bit reactive.   With the waves and wind, he is firm.   He is calm, and he calms the stormy sea.   Everything gets still.   The disciples try to give Jesus a taste of their anxiety, but he just won't bite.   He won't take it on. He simply turns it back to them.   Why are you afraid?   He asks. What happened to your faith?

What happened to your faith?   Good question.   What did happen to their faith?   Sometimes I think to myself, if I had been with Jesus, if I had heard him speak or seen him perform all those miracles, then I would have a lot more faith.   I wouldn't be so afraid.   Well, the disciples had gone through an awful lot with Jesus, but they are still afraid.   They still don't trust.   The waves out there are definitely dangerous, a physical threat for sure, but the greater threat is psychological. Ultimately, it's the fear that drags them down. Panic shatters their inner calm.

Jesus soothes the wind and waves and the disciples are impressed.   Jesus calms a raging sea, and this is a nifty trick, but

173

to my mind, it would be far more impressive if he could calm the storm in me. In me, and in a lot of other people that I know. Many of us live with turmoil on the inside. Many people, Dick notes, "especially those who have experienced some form of trauma, feel a constant tension in their bodies, like a tightly wound spring, that makes them hyper-vigilant and agitated. If you're like them, this state of physical arousal makes you overreact to other people and prevents you from truly ever relaxing."

Life comes with all kinds of hardships. Challenge comes to everyone -- inevitable disappointment in relationships, setbacks at work, or something that goes wrong with our health. There are little traumas and then the ones that go above and beyond, accidents or acts of violence that scar us deeply. Some are worse than others and some just seem to land with greater impact. When it comes to determining degree of difficulty, there are a lot of factors and, if you're like me, you want to know where your trauma falls on the scale. How does it measure up? I consider my experience and my reaction and I wonder: was it really that bad, or am I just making a mountain out of a molehill? Are my reactions justified, or is it just me? Are my feelings legit? That's what I want to know. And if I'm crazy, could it be that my being crazy makes a lot of sense?

That's how it is for me. I examine the situation scrupulously, trying to figure it all out, trying to figure me out, trying to get the world to work right for a change. I do just the thing that Dick talks about; I am just the person Dick describes: wrapped a little tight. And I am so ready for release, a spring waiting to be sprung... longing for a little peace and quiet and for a calm that will hold no matter what storms around me or within me.

Jesus had this kind of calm. He wasn't all that anxious -- not in that boat, or when his enemies lie in wait, or when he stood on trial before Pilate. He's only twelve when his mother blasts him for hanging out too long in the temple but he doesn't even flinch. Jesus could stay still on the inside even though other people raged around him and at him. He embodied what systems theory calls a non-anxious presence, and what the IFS model identifies as the spiritual quality of calm; what Dick calls the "I" in the storm.

No matter how it looks on the outside, not every calm you see is spiritual. Some of us are sure and steady, impassive. Like Spock in Star Trek, we manifest a Vulcan kind of calm, and in order to do this, our parts keep us from being fully present. They cut us off from any strong emotion. They block out any sensations that might prove too intense. We may experience ourselves as calm, but that's only because we've turned into stone; we can't afford to feel.

My mother had a way of bringing calm to our family. She was the peacemaker, the one who soothed and smoothed and swept things under the carpet. My dad had a different way of calm. He imposed it. He was one to yell and swear until I learned to keep my mouth shut and stay out of the away.

There are so many ways to keep things quiet. One pastor I know isn't very comfortable with conflict. As soon as the conversation starts to heat up, she stops the action and calls for prayer. Now I am all for going inside and I am all for prayer, but in her case the move is more like a bid for control. It sounds like a good idea, but what it really creates is a partial calm, by which I mean that it's a peace imposed by parts. It's a façade and no one is fooled, not for long. Here's the irony: false peace creates the very thing it fears, which is conflict. Oppression ultimately causes more unrest, and in the long run, our attempts to control evoke chaos. Some people may go quietly crazy, but the others erupt in rebellion and revolt.

There are all kinds of calm, but genuine peace is a spiritual quality. It comes from the Holy Spirit. It comes when we're in Self. It's the peace that is of Christ. Calm like this stretches across the horizon, extends outward into eternity. Have you ever been with anyone like that? Have you ever been with someone who embodies this kind of calm? You sense quiet at their core, and this alone has a way of making you feel steady and secure. You can throw anything at a person like this -- not that you should -- but calm like this: you can dump everything on it, and you can empty yourself into it. There is room for everything that you bring, and more. It's like walking your crazy self into a room with padded walls. It's like having someone who can hold you together though your world is falling apart. You might be going down in flames, but still your soul finds rest.

Hard to imagine, especially when life is rocking my little boat. Hard to imagine, when panic shows up unannounced. The world is full of feelings, but why do they all find harbor in me. Do I have to feel all of them? Really? I would be OK with less, a smaller palette, less intense. Oh yeah, when feelings start to overwhelm me, then I am all for any kind of calm, just give me back my heart of stone. I am a rock. I am an island.

Fortunately, calm, like anxiety, is contagious, especially if your leader can embody the calm of Christ. Several years ago my congregation was in the midst of a building program. In church life, the only thing worse is when you try to change the hymnal. The steering committee had done its homework, assessed needs, crunched numbers and come up with a preliminary plan. Now it was time for the congregation to vote. Our church family, our lovely home away from home, was divided. People, being what they are, had differing opinions, but everyone agreed about one thing: we were afraid of conflict, afraid of a fight that might split our congregation. Now we were facing a vote and voting polarizes. Anxiety was running high. I had been studying IFS for a little while and was intrigued by its potential for use in larger systems. Here was a good chance to try it out. It seemed like it might be good for the congregation and I knew for sure that it would be good for me. I was going to need some help with a few of my own parts, especially the ones afraid of conflict.

My co-pastor, Melanie, and I agreed to trust in process, to trust in the leading of the Holy Spirit. We each faced serious challenge. I would moderate the meeting, and as moderator, I would affirm the vision behind the project, but I would not endorse any specific plan. I would affirm our desire to create a welcoming space for anyone who might walk through our doors, but I would not give advice. That was my challenge. Melanie would sit in the congregation during the meeting. She was there to pray, hold Self-energy as it were, and keep her mouth shut. That was her challenge.

I opened the meeting with prayer, as good Presbyterians do. Then I practiced the basic principles of IFS as good IFS therapists do. I welcomed all points of view. I affirmed positive intent and expressed appreciation for the passion of parts. I asked people to speak on behalf of their emotions and beliefs. I acknowledged that it might get a little rocky but that it would be OK, so long as they could address their comments directly to me. And I got permission to intervene if things got too extreme. Everyone liked the set-up and even I felt more secure.

One by one the members spoke, some more heatedly than others. Some came with financial concerns, remembering times when we couldn't meet our bills. Some spoke with affection for the windows and the walls and how they wanted the church to be as it has always been, as it was in treasured pictures of family weddings and baptisms. Some worried that we would lose the feel of our congregation by changing its form. Others worried that inaction would indicate a loss of vision. Several urged a faith leading into the future. Some came with legacy burdens: vestiges of earlier issues and generational conflicts that continue. Believe me; I did a lot of breathing. That and a little tongue biting, but I didn't offer an opinion. I tried to treat people and their parts as Dick taught me – with respect. I acknowledged the concerns, validated the perspectives, asked about the fears. Melanie, who had never met Dick, did what Christians have been doing for centuries, she prayed and trusted in the leading of the Holy Spirit.

I don't remember the vote, but I do remember what people said afterwards. That was the best congregational meeting we've ever had…Everyone was treated with respect… We didn't all agree, but we all felt heard… I didn't get what I wanted, that's OK because I felt like people listened to what I had to say…Hey, we actually made a decision… Hey, we took a step forward *and* we still like each other!

That's what they said. I said to myself, hey, this IFS stuff really works.

Melanie said: God is good and it's good to trust in the leading of the Holy Spirit.

Yes, God is good. Held in the palm of God's hand, my anxious mind can settle down. And when my anxiety runs wild, there are people who will wrap their arms around me and keep me close. I lean on others, that's true and it's good. I get by with a lot of help from my friends. Thank God for good friends. And it's good too when I can reach that place of inner peace, that deep and steady pool of Being. Through the spiritual quality of calm, I find that I can handle the intensity of my own inner world and I can hang with intense people in the outer world. I don't overreact. I don't take on other people's anxiety. I just stay calm.

I know, sounds impossible, doesn't it?! Especially for someone who is wrapped a little too tight like me. But the other day I had an episode of calm and I was all by myself. It lasted for, like, a minute. It sounds so short, but it was *so* amazing. It's not like anything in my world was any different. I still had my same life: my same family, my same work, my same me… but on the inside, everything felt different. I breathed in the spaciousness of Eternity. Tell you the truth, I don't even know what that means, but I know how it feels… Eternal Calm. I think it must be that peace that Paul talks about, the peace that surpasses all understanding, the peace that Jesus gives. Peace I leave with you, he said. My peace I give to you. I do not give to you as the world gives. Do not let your hearts be troubled, and do not let them be afraid.

The peace of Christ. A little Self can do this for you. A little Spirit goes a long way.

The other day, when I was calm, we had a little pow wow, me and my new friend, panic. We ended up in the same room together. Panic freaked, but that's nothing new. Panic is what panic does. The new was me, me being with my panic, but not in it; me, watching myself without worry, without a single twinge of anxiety. Me holding on to myself, wrapping my arms around my parts and holding me close; steady and calm, just like Jesus, until the waves of fear subside. Together we rock and rock, a little boat on the endless sea.

For now we see in a mirror, dimly, but then we will see face to face. Now I know only in part; then I will know fully, even as I have been fully known.

(I Cor. 13:12)

Clarity

It's a return trip to the eye doctor and now there's another voice in the chorus, just to say: you're getting old. Older, but not old, mind you -- not that I'm obsessed or anything, but geez Louise, every time I turn around -- another voice like the cuckoo on a clock: old-er...old-er...old-er. My time is running out. This life is brilliant and brief. Or maybe more like that Woody Allen joke in *Annie Hall*.

Two elderly women are at a resort in the Catskills. One says, Boy, the food at this place is terrible.

And the other says, Yeah, I know; and such small portions!

Time is running out, and these days, whatever my life serves up, I am glad for the portion.

Anyway, the eye doctor tells me that I have presbyopia; my corneal lens is losing its elasticity. It's getting harder for me to focus. That's what it means. I have a hard time seeing things, even when those things are right in front of my face. If that's the case, then presbyopia must be a common condition and not just for aging Presbyterians.

I am getting older, and aging impacts our perception in more ways than one. Perception is shaped by previous experience, and there is more behind me now than ahead. I look at life through the lens of lessons learned. In some respects, you could say that I was old by the age of two or three -- two or three years, two or three months, two or three days, two or three minutes. Attachment theory says that the kind of care we receive as little kids has a lasting impact, and the subsequent wounds we bear have a way of bleeding over into everything. They color the relationships that we have with other people, especially the ones who are right in front of our face, the ones that we love most.

From childhood, we are conditioned to see the world in a particular way. We learn to see ourselves in a particular light. We come to believe certain truths about ourselves and the world. Families indoctrinate. It's not like they do it on purpose -- well, some do, but it's also just the way it works. It's in the water. It's in the air. Stories are told. Labels are given. Roles are assigned, and it's not all bad. It's like being in your school play: if you have a role, then at least you have a part. You're part of the cast. You belong.

The problem with roles is that you get stuck in them, defined by them, and judged for them. There is always a "good" one and a "bad" one, a hero and a villain. In my family, I was the youngest and only female, forever "too little and a girl," as though this explained everything. Well, it does explain some things -- why I have worked so hard, accomplished so much, and still find it hard to resist any challenge thrown down by a man; why I have championed the rights of women while doubting my own self-worth.

In every human grouping there are preferred roles, though the favorite may be different in different families. Some families like the smart ones or the responsible ones. Some families prefer the athletic ones or compliant ones. Some encourage a lot of blackness in their sheep. Whichever role it is, one gets privileged over the others. Some jobs are held up as better, but if we're lucky, there is someone in our life who doesn't define us by our role, whatever it might be; who doesn't judge us in terms of our behavior, who doesn't mistake us for any of the parts we play. Someone who knows better. Someone who sees us as God sees us. The Lord, Samuel reminds us, does not see as mortals see. We look on the outward appearance, but the Lord looks on the heart.

If we are lucky, we have someone like this, who sees with a God's eye view. When they look at us they see beneath the surface, and what they see is Heart. What they find is Soul. It might be a grandparent, or a teacher, a youth group leader or a friend. For me, it was a dog, and let me just say, there's nothing wrong with that. My dog knew me, through and through. She knew me in all my axe-murderer multiplicity, knew all my moods: sometimes nice and sometimes not; sometimes good and sometimes mean; sometimes welcoming and sometimes just wanting to be left the hell alone. Dog knew all of me and loved me still in the tail-wagging way. Don't get me wrong. Dog wasn't stupid. She knew when to keep her distance. But for all of that, she loved me through and through. It was grace, and it's for good reason that dog is god spelled backwards.

When my mother died, roles in the family shifted. I went from "Lost Child" to "Identified Patient," from "Apple of my Mother's Eye" to "Filler of my Mother's Shoes." I have worn several different hats and there are many different aspects to me. I don't always know who I am. It's like, will the Real Me please stand up? I like to know who I'm dealing with. It's why I like those tests. You know: the ones that tell you who you are. You can find them anywhere. You can pay five bucks and get one out of the women's magazine, or you can pay five hundred bucks and get yourself some serious psychological testing. I love them all. It's like I'm still little and looking in the fractal mirror, still looking for my butt. I take all those tests – the ones that inventory my personality and identify my leadership qualities, assign my DSM diagnosis and my conflict management style, my love language, my emotional intelligence quotient and my enneagram type. I am taken with the fortune cookies, the Ouija boards, the palm readings, the tarot cards, the Magic 8 ball, and the man on the street. I just want someone who can tell me who I am, *really*.

Whamo!

From out of the blue, it's Jesus again, socking me with a pillow. It's soft and fluffy, and from the outside, this probably looks like fun. It's not. Underneath, I can feel the frustration. Jesus is fed up. Jesus is fed up with me. I don't think that's really allowed in a personal Messiah, but there it is.

Oh my god, he says. *When are you going to get it?! What more can I say? What more can I do?*

It's true. It's not his fault. Jesus has tried to help me see myself as I truly am -- a Spirit, a Soul, a Self, a cherished one of God. He tells me this, but nothing sticks for very long. I get plenty of help in this regard, far more than I deserve – visions and dreams, guides and God in the flesh and blood of good people, many good people that Holy Spirit sends my way as means of support. Jesus has tried to love me into my wholeness. I've even got it in writing. It's all over the Bible:

You are not a servant any more, you are my friend.
You are in me and I am in you.
I am with you always, to the end of the age.
See what love the Father has for you that you are called
    child of God.

Poor guy. He's practically tearing his hair out. I don't mean to be difficult, but really, forget Jesus, don't you think there's something wrong with me?

There *is* something wrong with me. I make mistakes. I mess up. My bad. My big bad. Just ask my kids. I'm pretty sure they're keeping score. Surely someone must be keeping score, even if it's only Santa.

I do make mistakes, and when clarity comes, what I get is an eyeful of myself. I see my scorecard, the whole enchilada and what I see hurts. It hurts to see the ways in which I have failed. It hurts to see how I hurt others and hurt myself. It's also a big relief. The secret is out so now I can stop pretending, stop deceiving myself and deluding myself. I can look into the blind spots and do it without being defensive. I can see the things that I've done wrong and this means that one day I might even apologize for them. Or pay for them.

Just the other day I got this ticket in the mail, a ticket from the state of Illinois where they have installed Big Brother video cameras at every intersection between the Wisconsin state line and Oak Park, where Dick lives and works... not that it's his fault or anything. It said: you ran a red light, pay up.

I read it and I saw red alright. I was incensed. I was outraged. I did not run a red light. I am an excellent driver and I do not run red lights. I ranted for awhile, then went to the State of Illinois version of You Tube and watched myself roll right through the intersection. There it was: proof positive, empirical fact, data for everyone in the world to see, including me.

I had to stop and reconsider, see myself in a new light. It reminded me of the time a few years back when a cop pulled me over for failure to yield at a stop sign. Boy, was I mad. I couldn't believe it. I am an excellent driver, I am a good person, and I do not run through stop signs. I am so convinced of this that I argue with the man. I actually argue with the nice police officer about the fact that I couldn't have run a stop sign because there isn't one there because if there had been, I would have stopped, because I'm the kind of person who stops at stop signs. This is really stupid because all you had to do was turn around and see the stop sign standing there, silent witness.

You'd think I was the kind of person who needs to be right all the time, and that could well be, but it isn't the need to be right so much as it is the need to be "not wrong," to not make a mistake. Mistakes are costly for me. I can't afford to make too many because I am a perfectionist and I have a way of holding on to my sin. Not so much the individual sins like running a red light... well, yes, that too, but more the sense I have of being sinful... not good, but bad, and somehow undeserving. I have the sense that there be something wrong with me, that I am fundamentally and permanently flawed. I just can't seem to shake this belief. On the other hand, there's no need to have it confirmed, and by Law Enforcement, no less.

One thing is perfectly clear. This sense of inevitable doom that I have, it is not of God. When I am seeing clearly, I know better. God loves me and God is a liberationist. God is a freedom fighter and the Holy Spirit wants nothing more than my freedom: freedom from sin, freedom from the need to justify, freedom from perfectionism, freedom from all oppression, including my own. When I look at me with the spiritual quality of clarity, I see me through God's own eyes. I see all of my mistakes, it's true, but what I see is so much more. Underneath it all – the different hats, the different roles – I see me as I am: my own true Self, heir of grace and child of God. I see how I belong.

Jesus had unusual clarity and with it came an unusual sense of belonging. As Son of God, Jesus had a leading role. He knew it in his heart and felt it in his soul. I don't know how he arrived at such clarity, but you can bet that his mother had something to do with it. Mary not only gave birth to this boy, she raised him, and she raised him to be the kind of man he was, a man supremely secure in his Self. OK, it wasn't all her doing, but she did a darn good job, and if mothers are going to get so much blame, then they should also get their due.

Jesus was securely attached, and this was not just because he had good enough mothering. He knew his connection with the Divine. He knew who he was and what he was about. The Spirit of the Lord is upon me, Jesus said, because he has anointed me to bring good news to the poor. He has sent me to proclaim release to the captives and recovery of sight to the blind, to let the oppressed go free.

It's a radical vision and it comes with the territory.

Clarity has a way of opening our eyes to the sacred will that waits to unfurl in each one of us. We see the spiritual possibility that waits to unfold in every earthly moment. We dare to dream those dreams. We imagine. We envision relationships which embody both justice and mercy. We picture everyone free from whatever burdens they carry. We move past fear and live into love. It's the Kingdom of God that we see and nothing less.

It works something like this. I stand next to God and together we look out over all the earth. For miles around, all I can see is chaos and confusion, just like when I watch the news. I despair, just like when I watch the news. Then God takes off his glasses and hands them over. I put them on. Lo and behold, the prescription miraculously fits; presbyopia disappears and I see with fresh eyes. The fuzzy comes into focus. Yeah, there are still a few floaters, but they don't get in the way. Everything looks different to me. Before I saw only the problems, but now what I see is promise. I get the bigger picture. Amid all the chaos and confusion, what I see is the Kingdom of God as it slowly comes; the Spirit of God as it works its way through the world, unannounced, and often unrecognized, but still it comes, slow and sure. This is at the heart of our matter.

Jesus was really good at seeing things clearly. It was like a party trick for him. Throw out a situation, any situation, and he can size it up before the timer runs out. Just try and stump him. Throw up a roadblock and he will work around it. Throw out a conundrum and he will unravel it. The Pharisees ask him a question about paying taxes to Caesar. It was a trick; Jesus knew. They brought a woman taken in adultery. It was a trap; Jesus knew. The devil offered him food and power. It was temptation; Jesus knew. On a daily basis, people came to Jesus with their trouble. They were in deep need. Jesus knew.

Jesus saw the need and he was glad to help, but he isn't one to wave a magic wand. He addresses the presenting problem, but he does it in a way that reframes the issue – makes it broader, makes it deeper, makes it clear. He asks a lot of questions:

Why are you searching for me?
What do you want from me?
Do you want to be healed?
Who do you say that I am?
Who is it that you're looking for?
Why do you look at that speck in your neighbor's eye,
    but do not notice the log in your own?
Why are you sleeping?
Isn't life more than food and the body more than clothing?
Who is greater, the one who is at the table
    or the one who serves?
What will it profit you if you gain the whole world,
    but forfeit your soul?

Now that I think about it, it's just like all those tests I take to tell me who I am. Only better. Jesus asks questions, and in the answers, we find ourselves revealed. Issues are clarified. Burdens stand in bold relief. We see what really calls for our attention.

In fact, this is how Dick defines clarity: as the ability to perceive situations without distortion from extreme beliefs and emotions. In other words, we understand things better when we're not all whacked out.

I'd like to see me more clearly, but mostly, what I want is to be more secure. Insecurity has a way of wearing people out. It wears me out, and if it gets to Jesus, just think what it does to my not-quite-Jesus friends. I'd like to fix my eyes on Jesus and let him sweet-talk me into wholeness, but that isn't how it works. I do not see me the way that Jesus sees me. There's something in my eye, some log in my lens. It obscures my vision and distorts my worldview.

Extreme emotions and beliefs get in the way of our clarity. They cause us to see dimly. They act like spiritual cataracts. Everyone knows about this, even if they don't use the word *burden*. The Random House Dictionary lists over 60 meanings for the word clarity, and almost all of them involve the release of what the IFS model would identify as burdens. Clarity is being free from obstruction; free from guilt; free from blame; free from confusion; free from entanglements; free from limitation; free from debt; free from impurities; free from suspicion; free from illusion; free from doubt; free from uncertainty; free from ambiguity, and so on. So many different ways to be free and clear.

I lay my burdens down and when I do, things look a lot different. When I am "in Self," I have the eyes of Christ, and I see old things in new ways. I see things that I never saw before. In a flash, I get the whole picture. Solutions suddenly show up. Things come to me, even in my sleep. I don't know how it happens. Some people call it intuition or insight, but it seems to me that someone seeds my brain. Tell no one. That's how it feels, but I try not to talk about it very much. Thought-insertion, they say, is a sign of psychosis. Call me crazy, but from what I can tell, this is just how the Spirit works. In times of great clarity, I know myself to be informed by an even greater Intelligence. I know things without knowing how I know them. Information downloads. I see right into the heart of a matter. I know just the right thing to say or do. I am an empty vessel and the Holy Spirit moves right on through.

In the end, maybe this is what it's all about: not that I see clearly, but that I myself am clear…open and unobscured, translucent. Holy Spirit: it shines in me and through me and so out into the world. I embody the ultimate meaning of clarity: I serve more perfectly in the passage of Light.

And they were bringing children to him, that he might touch them; and the disciples rebuked them. But when Jesus saw it he was indignant, and said to them, "Let the children come to me, do not hinder them; for to such belongs the kingdom of God. Truly, I say to you, whoever does not receive the kingdom of God like a child shall not enter it." And he took them in his arms and blessed them, laying his hands upon them.

(Mark 10:13-16)

Curiosity

The first time I introduced my congregation to the idea of curiosity as a spiritual quality, I thought they were going to stone me. My little lambs, they howled like wolves.

No way, they said. Not curiosity. Curiosity is not good. Curiosity is inquiring minds that want to know. Curiosity is getting the inside scoop, getting the goods on someone else, gossip and innuendo. Curiosity killed the cat, they said, and we want none of it.

Yikes! It took a little while to calm us down, especially me. We took another look, and I had to admit, they had a point.

Curiosity may be a spiritual quality, but like any spiritual quality, it can be hijacked. It might look spiritual, but it's not -- more like an evil twin. My best friends from high school are identical twins -- I mean like super identical -- so I should know. Not evil, though every now and then, they would swap identities, swap classes, swap dates. I got to know them well and I learned to pay close attention. I do the same with my parts. I get to know them well and pay close attention. They're less likely to pull a switcheroo, but if they do, I catch on pretty quick, and they actually like this. It feels surprisingly good to have someone who knows you that well, who knows when you're up to your same old tricks and will call you on it. It's feels good to have someone like that, even if that someone is

189

you.

Why would anyone want to co-opt a nice little quality like curiosity? For some, it's the parts in us are anxious and insecure, parts with that middle-school kind of social anxiety. They need to know who is wearing what when or going where when with whom and why?   Information gathering: it's strategic. Armed with information, we can make plans, make alliances and negotiate our way through the lunch room or the board room. Knowledge is power, the power to build ourselves up even if it means bringing someone else down. When it comes to social stuff, I'm pretty clueless -- the last person you want to go to for good gossip or advice on clothes, or who to sit with in the lunch room, for that matter. I'm just not that curious.

I suppose I could get curious about not being curious, but I'm not. I'm not a particularly curious person, though after that encounter with the congregation, I do find that I want to learn everything I can about curiosity. I want to read about it, analyze it and master the material, and while this might look like genuine intellectual curiosity… it's not. It's just my need to know -- fraternal twin to the part of me that likes things done decently and in order. They both get to feeling all warm and fuzzy inside when that last puzzle piece slips into place, when the last leaf is swept out of the garage, when the last Lego goes up on the shelf. Put them together and I can be a little compulsive, not to mention driven and demanding. I love these parts, but they aren't what you would call kid-friendly, and they're not so good with mess.

If we want to enter into the kingdom of God, Jesus says, we must be as little children.

Ah, God bless the little children. I love little children and I love them most when they belong to someone else and go home at the end of the day.   Unless, of course, they're mine, in which case I love them all the time. But here's a real world bulletin: children are noisy and needy, and not real good with bodily fluids.

That day with Jesus, no one wanted to care for the kids, and yet there they were – gumming their cheerios and dropping their crayons and whining their way through the sermon. You know how it goes. People begin to stare hard and make snarky comments in the general direction of the poor parents who are already feeling harried and inadequate, helpless to do anything but snap and snarl at their own young. The disciples do what they can to manage the situation. They try to get things back under control. They tell the children, go away. Shoo! Beat it! Scram!

It was one of those days and, God knows, there are so many. The grown-ups are feeling driven and so they drive the children away.

But Jesus stops, mid-sermon. Jesus says, let them come. Let them come, he says, and they do: a long-haired girl with a rainbow pony tucked up under her arm, a bright-eyed boy who wriggles with all the right answers, two sisters who hold hands and a boy who snuggles in real close; a shy little girl who stands off to the side and a really little guy with snot running down his nose. It's time for the Children's Sermon, and all are welcome. Jesus loves the little children, all the children of the world.

If you have ever led worship, you know that there is nothing quite like the Children's Sermon, the five minutes in which all your best-laid plans go to hell. There you are, prepped for a two minute lesson on love when Suzy starts talking about her soccer game and Johnny pipes up with news about the new puppy. Joey, sensing a break in the action, punches his sister.

Yes, it's the weekly installment of "Stump the Pastor," and congregations love it. They especially love it when the pastor's pride and joy are numbered among the children gathered. One fine Sunday during the Children's Sermon my daughter announces to the world at large: *my mother threatens me.* Yeah, and there I am muttering under my breath, *one more word out of you and you're going to get it when we get home.* They're still

191

laughing about that one.

Congregations love the Children's Sermon because it is spontaneous. The children are spontaneous and unrehearsed, fresh and full of life, open and uncensored. Some of them wander around the front of the church while others lie down on the floor and stare up at the ceiling fan. Kids are curious and they ask good questions, better than the ones that I have prepared. These days when the Children's Sermon rolls around, I try to stay curious about what these little ones will come up with. It works better that way.

Come, Jesus says, like a little child.

Not a chance. That's what I say. At least, not when it comes to me. You can get all nostalgic about childhood if you want to, but I'm not about to go there. Being little was the last thing I ever wanted. I wanted to be big and strong, like my older brothers, though the idea of being like a child did make a lot more sense to me once I had two of my own. I don't know about your babies, but mine were amazing, like great big sponges, soaking in the world. As an infant, Miranda would lie there and carry on a conversation with sunlight as it streamed in from the window. As a toddler, Matt would open the dresser drawer, then pull it closed to within a half inch of his little fingers. I'm freaking out, but over and over he does this, and looks at me as if to ask, how low can I go?

Yes, children are born curious, innately programmed to explore. They reach and touch and taste. Everything goes right into the mouth where it can be digested, or not. A little older and the curiosity comes in question form, darn good questions like the ones found in *Children's Letters to God*:

"Dear God, I read the bible. What does begat mean? Nobody will tell me."

Love, Alison.

"Did you mean for giraffe to look like that or was it an accident?"

Norma.

"Dear God, Instead of letting people die and having to make new ones why don't you just keep the ones you got now?"

Jane.

"Dear God, Who draws the lines around the countries?"

Nan

Children come with open minds. They're too new to have a normal. They learn quickly from their experiences, but they can also remain open for a long time. They don't have preconceived notions and they don't take anything for granted. They literally have what the Buddhists call "beginner's mind."

One of the sad things about growing up is that our curiosity gets trained right out of us – by education or experience. We are taught to color within the lines. We are encouraged to set side our natural love of learning and study toward the test. We give up our own interests and lean into the expectations others set.

Here's a factoid: on the average, visitors to the Louvre spend 37 seconds on any one piece of art. Children, on the other hand, can spend ten minutes staring at the crack in a sidewalk. Curiosity like this will drive you nuts, especially if you've got somewhere to go. Curiosity like this scares the bejeebers out of me. I look at the world and I see danger. I don't want my children out there exploring; I want them safe. I want them right where they belong -- home with me. It's a funny thing. We are so vigilant and we think that we are protecting the children, but mostly we are protecting ourselves. We think children are vulnerable, and it's true, they are, but there is no one more

193

vulnerable than a parent. Having a child means that you have extended the perimeter of your risk. You have given up your ability to control. You have shared your gene pool with another person, donated your flesh and blood, and even if you are not the biological parent, if you love a child, you have given your heart away. It is out there right now, walking around in the world without you. Now who thought that was a good idea?

No wonder parents get so protective. Have you ever noticed that the key feature of modern baby equipment is restraint? We have restraints everywhere -- in the baby seats and the car seats, the high chairs and the bouncy chairs, the strollers and the walkers. Yep, strap those kiddos in; let's tie those babies down. Keep 'em safe. They grow older and our means of restraint grow more subtle. It comes in the form of schedules so structured that no one has time to go out and play; there is no explore. The children grow older still and instill the constraints of fear. In my day it was instilled through scary videos about sex, drugs, smoking and *Red Asphalt*, that gory film from Driver's Ed. Our children grow up safe, but stunted.

Jesus suggests something altogether different. Come as a little child, he says. Come follow your curiosity. See the wonders of our world. Albert Einstein said, "Curiosity has its own reason for existing. One cannot help but be in awe when he contemplates the mysteries of eternity, of life, of the marvelous structure of reality. It is enough if one tries merely to comprehend a little of this mystery every day. Never lose a holy curiosity."

A holy curiosity. Wow! Wonder what would happen if I had the spiritual quality of curiosity? What if I relinquished my stranglehold on schedules, agendas and lists; released my inner constraints and my need to get everything in its proper place? What things might I see? Whom might I meet? What mysteries might be revealed along the way?

Dick sees spiritual curiosity as a way to connect.

Pure, guileless curiosity is disarming. People and
parts of us sense that they no longer have to protect
themselves because they can tell that we intend only
to try to understand them. Since, usually, all they
want is to be understood, there is no reason for them
to remain angry or defensive. Instead, they are often
glad to tell their story and feel heard by a person
who is not trying to change them. In this book, this
is what is meant by the term witnessing – asking
about and listening to a person or part with genuine
curiosity and with the intent...of compassion.

Jesus had a lot of childlike qualities and he had a way of
drawing people near. He was one of those kids that always
seem to come home messy. Even as an adult he dabbled in the
mud and wrote with any old stick. He poked around, asking
questions and inviting people into a holy curiosity. Jesus was
all the time trying to get the grown-ups to set aside their agendas
and move beyond their preconceived notions, to stop and
consider sparrows in the sky and lilies in the field. He was
pure and guileless and irresistible.

Jesus is still at it, throwing pebbles at my door even
though I am working hard to meet another ever present
deadline. He's out there right now, doing his best Winnie the
Pooh imitation.

Let's go on a bit of an Explore, he says. Wonder if
there's a pot of honey somewhere out there? Can you smell it?

Jesus Pooh Bear. Now, that's a curious thing for sure.

So I grab my coat and off we go, and as we do, he smiles
a little smile. He sings a little song beneath his breath.

Come on out and follow me; come on out, and play.

Then Jesus went about all the cities and villages, teaching in their synagogues, and proclaiming the good news of the kingdom, and curing every disease and every sickness. When he saw the crowds, he had compassion for them, because they were harassed and helpless, like sheep without a shepherd.

(Matthew 9:35-38)

Compassion

As a spiritual quality, curiosity might come as a surprise, but everyone gets compassion. Everyone knows that compassion is spiritual. Just the word makes us feel all warm inside. Other words can do the same, words like fireplace and friend, payday and Friday, margarita. But compassion, it just seems to go with God. Mother Teresa said, "To me, God and compassion are one and the same."

Jesus is compassionate. Jesus oozes compassion.

When Jesus saw the crowds, he had compassion for them, because they were harassed and helpless, like sheep without a shepherd.

In story of the feeding of the Five Thousand, Jesus came ashore, and seeing the great crowd, he had compassion for them and cured their sick.

A widow's only son died and when Jesus saw her, he had compassion for her and raised the man from death.

When I picture Jesus the Compassionate, I see him with a sheep slung across his shoulders, just like the guy in my nativity scene, the one that goes on top of our piano at Christmas. Jesus the Compassionate who risks it all for one lost sheep.

I have never carried a sheep, but I did wrangle once with a good-sized dog. We are out there, Dog and I, wandering the wastelands of Florida, empty lots filled with sandy soil, drainage ditches and stray palmettos. We are poking our way along. We are deep into an empty lot when Dog suddenly comes to a complete and sudden stop. Cockleburs. She has thorns stuck in her paws. I pull them out, but still, the dog won't move. I get mad; we have places to go. I get worried; we are out there all alone. She is a good-sized dog, and I am a small-sized girl. She's too big for me to carry. I try everything. I order and demand. I threaten and explain. I plead. Dog will have none of it. She just looks at me with those big brown eyes that say, "Mine Field." She looks at me with such utter calm and trust. Who does she think I am? I look at her, and when I do, my heart melts with compassion. I pick her up and haul her out. It isn't pretty, but we get the job done. We struggle through that field together. We share the pain.

As it turns out, compassion comes with pain. Compassion isn't just a warm and fuzzy feeling; it's a churning in my gut. The Greek verb for compassion is *splangchnizomai*, which builds on the word *splangchma*. *Splangchma* are the entrails of the body, the innards. I can't pronounce the Greek, but I know what it means: compassion isn't a mental construct. It's neither abstract nor removed. It doesn't live in my head. Compassion is much more visceral; I feel it in my gut. I resonate with pain.

I like to think of myself as a compassionate person. I'm pretty good at sitting with someone in pain, but sometimes my parts do get in the way.

Here's me at the Feeding of the Five Thousand, or serving up a meal at the shelter, or trying to get dinner on the table -- any hunger will do.

My critical parts begin to comment:
    What were they thinking, come this far without food?
    Why didn't they plan ahead? Pack a snack?
    Lazy, irresponsible Whiner Babies.

My helpful parts try to help:
    Let's organize them into small groups.

197

Let's sort them out by age and gender.
Let's get some kind of plan going here.

Other parts of me get scared:
    These people are really getting hungry. That's not good.
    Hungry people are ugly people.
    They will turn on me.

I get to feeling hopeless:
    I can't feed all these people.
    There's too many.
    It's impossible; it can't be done.

I get overwhelmed:
    Stupid sheep. Shoo! Beat it! Scram!

I get resentful:
    Why should I feed them, anyway? No one ever feeds me.

Some parts may resemble compassion, but they're a little
off. I can feel sorry for someone, but in a way that keeps me
from being fully present. I keep myself a little apart, buffered
from the pain. Others parts can do the opposite, zoom right in
and make assumptions, interpret, over-identify. It might look
like I have compassion for the other person, but the pain that I
am feeling in my gut, mostly it's my own.

To me, the spiritual quality of compassion works a lot
like a tuning fork. You sound your note and it registers on those
little hairs in my ear, but it also reverberates within my soul.
You transmit and I receive. We resonate. You speak and in
your words I hear lament. We are attuned and the song you
sing is so tender and true, that my heart is rent. In the very
bowels of my being, I am touched. Splangchnizomai.

When I have the compassion as of Christ, when I embody

Self, I am present to you in such a way that we are both one and apart, together and separate. I am present to your pain, but I don't have a need to take it from you, or take over for you. I honor your suffering and respect you with it. In her poem, *the Invitation*, Oriah Mountain Dreamer invites us into this way of being with one another:

> I want to know if you can sit with pain
> mine or your own
> without moving to hide it
> or fade it
> or fix it...
>
> I want to know if you will stand
> in the centre of the fire
> with me
> and not shrink back.

What?! It's the responsible Christian in me. All that sweet talk about compassion... it lulled her into sleep, but now she's wide awake.

What?! She demands. She can be a little shrill. What are you talking about? What about our responsibilities? Aren't we supposed to help others? Aren't we supposed to save them... save them from themselves, if that's what it takes?

I am just about to say something smart alecky to her when Jesus steps in. He looks at her and I see that he loves her. Can't imagine why. She's such a buttinski. I was going to say something smart like: we don't save people, *Jesus* saves people. I really wanted to get that one in there.

But Jesus looks at her with what I think might be compassion. It's hard, he says. He is so kind, and tender. It's hard, I know. You love someone and there they are, doing things that are destructive and damaging. Hurting themselves.

199

Hurting others. Hurting you.   All that hurt, it's hard to take.
Happens to me all the time.   You do what you can, but they
don't listen.   You offer help, but they turn you down. People go
their own way.   That's how it is. You can't save someone from
themselves. Not even I can do that. You can issue the invitation,
but not everyone will accept.

Well, then what am I supposed to do, she asks?

Try a little compassion, Jesus says. Set limits if you have
to. Walk away if you have to, but have compassion – for them
and for you.   This life is hard.   And remember, sometimes
suffering is what it takes.   Sometimes more suffering is the only
thing that gets our attention, the only thing that wakes us up.

Besides, Jesus says, how did you get stuck with the job of
saving others?   That's a pretty big job, not to mention… mine.
I'm wondering: if you didn't have to do that any more, what
would you rather be doing?

Eating ice cream, she says.

Eating ice cream?! Even I am surprised. Who knew?

After a little more negotiation, she agrees to let Jesus do
his job and she heads on down to the Sugar Shack. I decide to go
with her. I go because I am being compassionate. I want to
share her pain, that and her Betty Boop Sundae.

When it comes to compassion, Jesus is a whole lot better
at it than I am, and the saving of souls: it isn't up to me.   It helps
when I remember that; it helps me feel more free.   Practitioners
of IFS trust in the power of spiritual presence and so they
experience this same kind of freedom.   They know, as Dick says,
"that the other has a Self, that once released, can relieve their
own misery. If people relieve their own suffering, they learn to
trust their own Self and they learn whatever lessons the
suffering has to teach. Compassion, then, leads to doing
whatever possible to foster the release of the other's Self rather
than becoming the other's healer."

These days I am trying to be more compassionate with
myself and this is a lot harder than you might think.

I remember the first time that I met Compassion. It came in the form of my first supervisor, a Methodist minister. What I remember most about Compassion is me turning it down, keeping it at bay. This man was there for me. I knew it. Holy Spirit right there in the room. But for all that, I just couldn't take it in. It felt like it would be too much. I couldn't let myself be that vulnerable with this man, representative of God. This was exactly what I needed, of course -- to come into the presence of God, to bring myself into the Light - to be fully seen, fully witnessed, and fully loved. Even though I couldn't accept it at the time, I saw it for what it is; compassion is an invitation into grace.

I am not the only one who turns it down. I'm not the only one who doesn't like feeling vulnerable. How are you? I ask a friend whose husband died recently. Tears well up in her eyes. I was fine, she says, with her voice full of reproach. I *was* fine... until you asked.

Come to Christ, and there is pain involved. Come to Self, and you'll be fully seen. It's what we both fear and long for. Compassion helps to melt the walls that lock me even as they shut others out. Compassion disarms my arsenal, dissolves my armor, and beats my swords into ploughshares. And yes, I can refuse the invitation. I can keep myself from grace, but there's a price to pay: it's all that shrapnel in my heart.

Being compassionate toward myself; that's hard. It's hard to treat me on the inside as Jesus treated people on the outside. Being merciful to others is challenge enough, but to have mercy on myself, I think not. I don't have a lot of compassion for myself except when I'm in Self. When Holy Spirit dwells within, that's when I can look at me through Christ's own eyes, and this makes all the difference. I look at me and when I do, I see myself as I once saw Dog. I see my own brown eyes. I feel the thorns in my own side. I sense the minefields all around. My heart melts, but when it does, it melts this time for me.

Confidence

I'm in my early 20's, just bouncing through another day at work, when a colleague says, I envy you. You're so young and confident. The whole world is out there waiting for you.

What do you mean? I say in a sticky sweet voice. You're great. There are a lot of good things out there just waiting for you too. Of course there are.

This is what I say. I pretend that I don't know what she means, but I know exactly what she means. I am young and firm of flesh. My whole future lies ahead. She is in her mid-fifties, dealing with a divorce and failing health. I, on the other hand, am bold and brash. I walk as young folk do, the ones who are unself-conscious in a self-conscious kind of way, the ones who project self-sufficiency and cool.

Some of us learn early on that about 90% of what passes for being confident lies in convincing others that you are. We learn how to walk, we learn what to wear, we learn to speak in ways that make others sit up and take notice. And that's just middle school. Add on a pedigree, or a PhD, put on a veneer of confidence, and the world just opens right up; we breeze on through.

On TV, the Christians always look confident – pastors who preach from ornate pulpits and people with placards who stand outside family planning clinics. I don't get this. Maybe it's the company I keep, but most of the Christians I know are conflict avoidant and not all that confident, especially when it comes to issues of faith. The ones who talk the most or speak

202

the loudest often turn out to be the most insecure. Me, I'm a chicken, especially when it comes to Jesus. If I had to, I would sell him out in a heartbeat, just like Peter.

Those disciples, they were all chicken. In the gospel of John there's this story about how Jesus has been crucified and the disciples are left quaking in their sandals. Following Jesus is well and good, but no one ever thought it would turn out like this. No one at the recruiting office ever mentioned crucifixion. No one ever signed on to be the next in line to suffer. So there they are, those disciples, overwhelmed with fear. Makes sense to me. They hide behind locked doors, but Jesus, newly risen, comes looking. By the time he catches up with them, they are under the bed. To his credit, Jesus isn't mad or resentful or even the least bit disappointed. He just slips his Spirit in underneath the door and crawls right in there with them. Peace, he says. I've come to bring you peace, and then he breathes a little more Holy Spirit into them, which is a good thing, because they are in serious need of a little inspiration. Then he sends them right back out into the world. There's work to be done.

Jesus was no chicken. He was a confident guy, though you wouldn't know it to look at the pictures of him in our Sunday School curriculum. The white Jesus is a little anemic and lacking in bone structure, but in the Bible, the confidence of Christ is clear. It's one thing people noticed right off. They were astonished at his teaching, for he taught them as one who had authority, and not as the scribes. Even when he is on trial for his life, Jesus is not intimidated. Instead, he puts Pilate in his place: "You would have no power over me if it were not given you from above."

I could be cynical about this. Why wouldn't Jesus be confident? He was the son of God, for God's sake! It's kind of the ultimate in being the boss' son. It seems like a pretty privileged position to me, but then again, maybe that only goes to show how I think about confidence -- as though it's something that comes from the outside, as though confidence is what comes from holding a certain position, or from knowing all the answers, or from being connected with the right people. That's mostly how it works for me: confidence from the outside in.

You want to know what makes me feel confident? A steady paycheck. A big bank account. Private health insurance. Friends in high places. Health, wealth and a great big brownie. You want to know what makes me lose confidence? No surprise: it's when I lose those exact same things. Yes, I put my trust in things that can be taken away. I put my faith in things that are fleeting. I know that, and I am totally fine with that just so long as I can hold on to what I've got. The way I see it, you can respect the poor without having to become one of them. No need to romanticize poverty. Here's my take: it's totally fine to have these things just so long as I don't get too attached to them. Possessions aren't the issue; attachment is the issue.

Right.

So I try letting go. Right away, I find an attachment. I let something else go; damn, another attachment. You want to find an attachment or two, just try giving up what you've got. It's what Janis Joplin knew all along: freedom's just another word for nothing left to lose. Lucky for me, I'm looking for freedom, so things are going according to plan. I give up a few more things, a few little things like a steady job and a steady paycheck and the really good health insurance that comes with it.

I start freaking out. What was I thinking?! I can see everything slipping away, everything that I worked so hard to get, everything that I *earned*, and everything that I am owed. The sky is falling! I'm melting... *melting*!

This is how I feel, and it's so ridiculous. Embarrassing. I mean, it's not even true. I have more than enough and I work with people who are jobless and uninsured, some have no place to lay their heads. I know better than to be like this, but I can't help it. Parts of me absolutely believe in the power of power. They remember Powerless and they didn't like it much the first time around. This time, they're not going down without a fight. I do not trust me to be OK, and I don't think that you can count on God to pay the bills, so let's not even start with that. Forget being a therapist. I should get a real job, recoup my losses. This is the real world solution to my real world problems. I can rebuild me. I have the technology. I can make me better than before. I will rebuild, and this rebuilding will restore my confidence, at least on the outside. At least, for as long as it lasts.

For all of this, I am not fooled by me. I can rebuild, but I'm old enough to know that this earthly foundation is pretty shaky. Sooner or later, my ability to work will end. Sooner or later, my health will fail. My income will peter out. In what then, shall I trust, and in whom? I need a different kind of confidence, a different way to take care of myself. Not that I have a choice. I'm not going to be rich enough to pay someone else to take care of me. Not that I would, I'm just saying… it's not an option. I've got to find another source.

I lift up my eyes to the hills. From whence will my help come, asks the psalmist. It will come from the Lord. The Lord will keep me from all evil. The Lord will keep my life. The Lord will keep my going out and my coming in, from this time on and forevermore.

This is exactly what I'm looking for. Spiritual confidence. It's knowing that with God, I will be OK… no, that I *am* OK. My soul is safe, no matter what may happen in my flesh. With confidence like this, I can stay the course. I can go through all those ups and downs of life and remain calm. Spiritual confidence helps to get me out from under the bed.

Sometimes I have this kind of confidence. I experience myself as being held in the holiness of Spirit. This is the truth about my innermost being. At some level, I know this; I just find it hard to live on a daily basis. I still have parts that fear. They have learned their lessons well and they are holding on to anything that represents security. They think I need it and they've been taking care of me for a long time. They don't see another way. The problem is they're young… like 13, and 11, and 3. Little kids with grown-up jobs. Child labor. Parentified parts -- that's what I've got, and they do pretty well, considering. They don't trust in me, don't trust in my Self, and why should they? So many times I wasn't there for me when I needed me, so many times when even God seemed absent. But I'm here now and here to stay, full with Self and fully embodied. This is what I tell them, but it takes time to win their trust, and that's OK.

Confidence is something that grows on you. It's a form of trust, and we only come to trust through experience. I trust in my chair because I sit on it every day, and every day it holds me up. It is there for me. After awhile, I don't even think about it. I just sit. But let's say one day the chair gives and I go crashing to the floor. Believe me, that's a crisis of confidence. Now, every time before I sit in that chair, I stop and think about it. Check. It takes awhile before I'm going to put my trust in that chair again. That's just how it is, how the process works.

Through IFS I am learning how to trust – to trust in me, and God with me. I am learning how to be with myself, with the whole of me. These days I am taking myself more seriously. I used to try and talk me out of me, but I don't do that any more. Whatever it is, I don't try to talk me out of it, or tell me to just get over myself. I stop and listen to what my parts have to say. I am learning what I need to know. I am learning what needs to happen in order for me to be made well. In the end, I discover that even ancient wrongs can be redressed and my most painful wounds can be healed. Best of all, I am becoming more confident in my sense of Self, and in the Spirit as it works through me.

It's like a client said: I used to pray for God to heal me, but this is much better. It's like it says in the movie, *Evan Almighty*: If we ask for patience… does God give us patience, or the chance to be patient? If we ask for courage, does God just make us brave, or does he give us the opportunity to be courageous? Instead of just healing me, God has given me the opportunity to heal.

IFS facilitates healing through Self and it builds confidence in the Self. It's one of the lasting benefits of IFS. Through IFS, Dick says, people come to feel "Self-confident in the sense that their Self has healed those parts and has shown its ability to protect them, or to comfort them if they are hurt again."

Make no mistake; we will get hurt again. Jesus never once said, follow me and life will be a piece of cake, although I do think that a lot more people would have shown up for that. We all get hurt, and everyone I know is in the process of healing and recovery. We call it Life. It's just that some people engage it, embrace it, and move through it with the kind of grace and elegance that comes only through spiritual confidence, the confidence that comes when we trust in divine presence and allow ourselves to participate in the flow of divine process.

Confidence like this is a spiritual quality. It isn't a gift; it's innate capacity, and it grows each time we establish a genuine connection with God, each time that we find that God is trustworthy and reliable. Holy Spirit unburdens us, heals us, comforts us, liberates us, transforms us, reconnects us, reorients us… gives us whatever we need and takes us wherever it is that we need to go. When you have this kind of experience, when this happens over and over again, some of it eventually begins to seep in, some of it starts to take hold. The seeds of confidence sprout, take root, sink deep. Confidence grows -- confidence, not in the power of your parts, but confidence in the steadfast love and presence of God, confidence in power of Self-energy, and this confidence empowers us to live a more full-bodied kind of faith. It allows us to move more freely through the world. We come out of the shadows. We become vibrant and fully alive and no matter where the road may lead, we can walk it, steady and sure, secure in the love of God, who keeps our going out and our coming in, forever more.

And going a little farther, he threw himself on the ground and prayed, "My Father, if it is possible, let this cup pass from me; yet not what I want but what you want." Then he came to the disciples and found them sleeping; and he said to Peter, "So, could you not stay awake with me one hour? Stay awake and pray that you may not come into the time of trial; the spirit indeed is willing, but the flesh is weak."

(Matthew 26:39-41)

Courage

Every now and then Jesus comes up with a bright idea, some new gimmick that he seems to think will get the Good News out. Maybe I shouldn't hold him responsible for this kind of thing, but who else would be in charge of marketing?

In recent years, meaning within my lifetime, there were the "I Found It!" bumper stickers, followed by the "I never lost it!" bumper stickers.

Another year, strange hieroglyphics began showing up at sporting events, large posters inscribed: Jn 3:16. You can still find these signs at most sporting events, along with the body paint, beer and anything else that can be sold to make sure we have a really good time at the game.

But nothing has topped the whole *What Would Jesus Do?* campaign, a movement which has spawned WWJD bracelets, necklaces, T-shirts, notepads, hats, rings, and yes, even tattoos.

Whoever came up with this, I'm sure, has only my own good in mind. The question is meant to wake me up, get me to pay a little more attention to God, at least as God is found in the person of Jesus Christ, and I am all for that.

What *would* Jesus do? It's a tricky question. Maybe even a trick question, so I go straight to the horse's mouth looking for an answer. I turn to Jesus. So... what is it that you would do?

Jesus is busy in the kitchen, whipping up a batch of huevos rancheros.   He is wearing a ridiculous striped apron and makes a point of not looking in my direction. If I give you all the answers, he says, how are you ever going to learn? Besides, it's not my homework.

I can hardly believe my ears, even though this is exactly the kind of thing I would say to my own children. A smoldering starts in my chest. Just do it, the commercial says, but what am I to do? Jesus is the Way, the Truth and the Life; he has all the answers. That's what they say, so why can't he just tell me what I'm supposed to do, so I can do it?   Everyone makes it sound so easy: all you have to do is go to God, but when I go to God, this is what I get. Really, am I the only one with a Jesus like this?

Besides, I whimper, my homework is very hard.

Jesus hands me a plate. I know, he says. Here, honey, have some eggs. And a little guacamole. Guacamole always makes it better.

What *would* Jesus do?

Since I can't get it straight from his mouth, I consult the official instruction manual, Cliff's Notes for Christians, otherwise known as The Bible.   What I find there confounds me.   There is no step by step. Jesus is there, but he is magnificent and wild and unpredictable.   He dismisses the law and then he fulfills it. He turns the other cheek, but then he turns over tables in the temple. He forgives but won't let us off the hook, or let us forget what we're about. Follow me, he says to some, but to others, he says, stay home.   From what I can tell, the scriptures do not give us a single formula for the life of faith. You have to make it up as you go along.

Jesus is an enigma. I try to get inside his head, but I can't. I don't even know why I would try.   I spent enough years trying to figure out the normal people.   I've put in enough time as a mind-reader, trying to figure where someone else is so

209

I can figure out where I should be – the things I should do, the things I should say, in order to fit myself into somebody else's picture. I want to make Jesus happy, but it turns out that he doesn't want me for a copy cat Christian, or a cookie-cutter Christ; no mini-me messiah for him, and this is hard because it flies in the face of so much that I have been taught, which is this: mimic Jesus; do what he would do.

Actually, Jesus wants something very different. Like any good parent, Jesus wants me to grow and mature into my own person. Jesus, like every good teacher, wants me to gain mastery over the material. In order to grow spiritually, I have to work out my own faith; no one else can do it for me. Well, Jesus can, but mostly he won't, although from time to time, he does offer food and words of encouragement. He stays close by while I sweat it out.

What would Jesus do? It's a good question. The question is meant to make me stop and think before I act, and I am all for that, except for one thing: the acting is automatic. You know how when you're really mad, you're supposed to stop and count to ten before you open your mouth. Well, it's a great idea, but if I had what it takes to stop and count to ten, then I probably wouldn't need to.

I am at a national youth conference in Fort Collins, Colorado. We are some forty strong, youth and adults who represent the Presbytery of Milwaukee. My role is Adult-in-Charge. It's a dubious honor. Back at the dorm, something is up. I feel it in my bones. I smell it in the air. I stroll down the hall where the young people are spread along the floor. They are happy to see me -- too happy. The conference is great, they say. We are great. Everything is great. They are eager, and they are eager for me to be on my way. Something is up, but there's nothing I can do but wait.

The next morning, right after worship, it happens. Hundreds of people stream out of the worship center. I see young people holding up signs and holding out baskets. My young people. They have come up with a mission project. These are my girls, and I think, this is not so bad, but then I see the signs say something strange like: "Bikini Run – Racing Money for the Hungry." Sure enough, other young people are racing through the crowds. They wear bikinis. They are mine; they are the boys.

One of the conference leaders forgets to count to ten. She reacts. She is loud and blaming and abusive. In this case, there is no doubt what Jesus would do, but I am not doing it. I vacate my body. I lose some portion of my life. When I come to, when I come back to myself, I find that my legs are walking me away from this confrontation, and this is not a choice; it's automatic.

Sometimes, even when we know what Jesus would do, something else gets in the way. What gets in the way for me is fear. When I am under attack, there's no time for my lovely neo-cortex, no time to work my way through the menu options. Let's say that my mind registers the fact that a dinosaur is coming right at me. Now is not the time to consider the categories of herbivore, carnivore, omnivore. Nope, it's time to run. That's why I have an amygdala, that place in the brain that knows how to short-cut my neo-cortex and cut right to the chase. Later, over dessert or a drink, I can work my way through the decision tree, rehash all the things that I wished that I had done, instead of all the things I did.

Truth is, I have a lot of fear. Many things frighten me. Mostly I'm afraid I'll make a mistake and get punished for it. I want Jesus to tell me what I should do, so I can get it right the first time. I'm afraid of getting hurt, so in the face of threat, I fight, or flight, or flee, and none of this has anything to do with my faith.

For the most part, I'd like to get rid of my fear, but I've come to see that it has a place. It keeps me safe. If you're a parent, you know that there's nothing scarier than a child without fear; they don't know danger when they see it. They will pet that loose dog. They will talk to that stranger. They will jump off the roof in Superman's cape.   A little fear is worth having. As the Wizard of Oz says to the Cowardly Lion, "You, my friend, are a victim of disorganized thinking. You are under the unfortunate impression that just because you run away you have no courage; you're confusing courage with wisdom."   You can have courage and still have parts that fear, it's just that your fear doesn't lead the way.

Jesus felt fear. His life curriculum was difficult -- post-graduate level. And though he may have been the son of God, he was not a super-human; he was a man and he felt pain, just like the rest of us. He got tired, just like the rest of us. In the Garden of Gethsemane, he worried, just like the rest of us. The final exam is coming up, and Jesus wants out. His Spirit is willing, but even *his* flesh is a little weak. Still, no one else can do it for him, and in his case, as it turns out, there are no words of encouragement. No one else can stand the heat; they all get out of the kitchen.

In life, as in death, Jesus was courageous, that or stupid. The two look alike; I sometimes get confused. It's not enough to heal people; Jesus has to break the law and do it on the Sabbath, even though his enemies are sitting on the sidelines, shucking peanuts and just waiting for him to mess up. It's not enough to break the purification laws and eat with sinners, Jesus has to go and accuse the Pharisees of being self-righteous. He not only saves the woman taken in adultery, he confronts the crowd with their own sin. This is not the way to win friends and influence people, although it is a darn good way to get yourself killed.

That's the thing about courage. Danger, by definition, is involved. Courage helps us stand in the face of cost.

So what makes courage worth it? Why would we take a risk?

Well, sometimes you do it because you just get tired of living in the fear and sometimes you just get tired.

Rosa Parks had courage, but as she tells it, our country changed mostly because one woman got tired. She had finished another long, hard day at work and she was worn out -- tired physically and tired of the prejudice and injustice. She couldn't take it any more. Rosa Parks knew that she had to sit down, even if sitting down meant standing up for herself, for herself and all the rest of us.

Jesus was a man of compassion, but he also had courage. He stood up for those who could not stand up for themselves. This kind of courage is a key characteristic of Self.

As Dick points out,

> One might think that the Self's "it's all okay" sense of grace would lead to a detached passivity and acceptance of the injustices of life, but that's not the nature of the Self. The clarity of the Self makes it hard for people to deny injustice and ignore suffering. The compassion of the Self leads people to resist tyranny and fight for the oppressed. The words of the Self bring hope to the hopeless. The energy of the Self seeps into the cracks in the tyrant's walls and gradually erodes them.

Courage comes with a cost, it's true. It might even cost you your life, but then again, what is it that we believe? Isn't death and resurrection the great paradigm of the Christian faith? Those who want to save their life will lose it, Jesus says, and those who lose their life for my sake will find it. We die in order that we might be born again. We do it again and again, die to old ways of being so that we may be reborn, renewed. This is what it takes, so why do we resist this fundamental principle of spiritual growth?

Courage is part of the process, and it comes when we learn how to calm our fear. I'm not real good at this. You want to know what I do when I'm scared? I yell at myself. STOP IT! I say. Just stop it, RIGHT NOW! It's what I do, but it's no help at all. And it makes no sense. I'm already scared, so how does the yelling help?   Sometimes I try to talk myself out of being afraid; I scold myself and tell me that I'm being *irrational, ridiculous*. I call me names: like *baby*, or *wimp*. Now I'm not only afraid; I've hurt my own feelings.

I wish that Jesus would just tell me what to do. It would make it so much easier. It would help me feel more brave. But I have come to see: there is no one-size-fits all approach to faith and there are no short-cuts. I may follow in the footsteps of Christ but I still have to find my own path. I have to stand on my own two feet. Turns out that the spiritual quality of courage doesn't come from me trying to get in Jesus' skin; it comes when I let Jesus into mine.

You know what does help? It's the heuvos rancheros and all the little things that Jesus dishes up to help me know I'm not alone. It's the way that he is firm with me and stands his ground; it makes me stand on mine. It's this little thing that Jesus does: he places his faith in me, until eventually I have to find it in myself.

Jesus trusting me: it used to be a scary thought. I didn't trust my Self. But now it's kind of nice. I don't need quite as much help as I used to and Jesus is a lot more relaxed. He's moved on from the huevos rancheros and working now on soufflé. Soufflé must be more difficult. He's muttering under his breath; he's banging pots and pans. Once that would have been enough to scare me out of the kitchen, but now I'm not afraid. I think I'll stick around. I'll offer a few words of encouragement, and when the time is right, I've got the guacamole.

In the beginning when God created the heavens and the earth, the earth was a formless void and darkness covered the face of the deep, while a wind from God swept over the face of the waters. Then God said, 'Let there be light'; and there was light... God saw everything that he had made, and indeed, it was very good.

(Genesis 1:1-3, 31)

Creativity

Every family has its secrets. At six, I find one. We are housed temporarily with my uncle in a large complex that supports the Yale Observatory. It is winter in the woods of Connecticut. My whole life I have lived in the tropics, and now for the first time -- snow. It's white. White and cold and wonderful as it drops through the snow-globe world around me. Inside the big house, flames dance in the fireplace. The room is warm and cozy and the adults speak Dutch. Here it's magical. I can tell because even the grown-ups are laughing.

After awhile I get bored and wander off to explore. In the upstairs kitchen, I find my cousin who is home from college. She is hunched over the table, stirring something. Little pots and vials and tubes surround her, scraps of paper and brushes and nasty smelling goo. She looks like a witch, only without the hat. I don't think she even sees me. She is lost in her work. Someone takes me aside. I am given somber news. My cousin is an *artist*.

I am stunned, but secretly thrilled. My mother was a high school math teacher and my father a civil engineer. I am the daughter of equations: facts and formulas, hard science and a hard-nosed approach to life. Apply the principles. Do your math. Follow the rules. Paint within the lines. But now, the shadow side. This creature in the kitchen... she's cousin, she's kin, she's me.   There are others out there like me.   Come to find that my family sports a creative streak that hopscotches its way across the generations, popping up unpredictably in artists, church musicians and addicts.

One thing I always knew for sure: creativity is divine, heavenly... a spiritual quality, one of the distinctive characteristics of Holy Spirit.   In the beginning, the scriptures tell us, when God created the heavens and the earth, the earth was a formless void and darkness covered the face of the deep, while a wind from God swept over the face of the waters.   Then God said, 'Let there be light;" and there was light.

Dick interjects.   I have a problem with this, he announces -- this reference to Creation.   He's a little edgy about it.

O-kay, I say, what's that about?

It's not scientific, he says.

Dick, I explain, you're talking about Creationism, not Creation.   Creationism is when people take the stories of creation literally as scientific fact.   But the theology of Creation isn't about science; it's about the spiritual quality of creativity – creativity and intentionality.   Biblical accounts of creation affirm that God has a positive intent toward us and that the Holy Spirit is creatively at work in the world.

He is not sold.

I think people are going to get to that, Dick says, and they are going to be turned off.   They're going to think that we're coming from a fundamentalist perspective.   I don't want to be associated with it.

Dick, I say, no one would ever mistake you for a fundamentalist and the theology of Creation is really important in the Christian tradition.   We can't just leave it out.   I don't want to leave it out.   It's about *cre-a-tiv-i-ty*.   I say it slowly, just like that so he can't miss the point.

But let me make it clear: Dick is not a fundamentalist of any flavor.   He's not even a Christian, though he's kind of taken with Jesus, and a little with me.   Dick does not believe the

216

scriptural accounts of creation to be scientifically accurate. Me either, for that matter. But you can use the model, regardless of what you believe about our origin.

What Genesis describes is your basic blank slate experience. It's the black computer screen. It's the empty blue book. It's the churning void of meetings not yet begun. It's the murky feel of combat or family dinners. It's what happens when I'm confronted with absence: me...my mind... blank. I have a big blanking part.

Like last week. I'm working with a couple and -- tell no one -- but frankly, it's not going all that well. Attack, counterattack, withdraw... attack, counterattack, withdraw. I look out over this very raw material of human relationship, this formless void of marital potential and I sense that something else is needed in the mix. There's a missing ingredient, but what? A therapist. That's what it is. These people need a therapist, I think, and then I remember... that would be me. I am the therapist and something is required, but what? Nothing comes to mind. No words to say. No explanations to give. No interventions to make. Nothing.

Nothing is not a problem. Jesus speaks up. He's standing a little off to the left and behind.

I jump. Geez, I say, you startled me! I didn't know you were there.

I know, he says. I got tired of waiting. Nothing is not a problem, he repeats. We can work with that.

I have no idea what he's talking about, but I sure like the *"we"* part of it. A gentle wave of relief washes over me, like a soft breeze on my fevered body. That's when I realize that this is part of the problem; I am part of the problem. Pressure and responsibility and feeling like it's all up to me. I've got the whole world in my hands again. All of this gets in the way of creativity. I can see that it isn't all up to me, and I'm really glad for the Jesus help, but I'm still a little confused. What is my responsibility exactly?

So help me out here, I say to Jesus. What about my homework? What about me learning to stand on my own two feet? What about me not looking to you for help all the time, waiting for you to bail me out?

He laughs, but in a friendly sort of way. Yes, he says, well, here's the thing. You gotta know what homework is yours. Not everybody gets the same assignment. Your homework is not to do other people's homework. In fact, your homework is to do less homework.

I can feel my eyes cross. Oh yeah, there he is again: Coyote Christ. Confuse a Cat. Jesus of the Parables, speaking now in koan. *Your homework is to do less homework.* My brain turns like a kaleidoscope, the little tiles scrambling to reconfigure. This is disorienting, and I am nothing if not nausea averse. I think we've already established that. I try to put a stop to the action. I'm not sure where he's going with this. I'm not sure I like where he's taking me. Less is more? Nothing is not a problem? I have to stop and think about this. I go back to safer ground, to thinking and to what I learned in seminary. I go back to the Latin.

Creation ex nihilo: this is the ability of God to create something out of nothing. This is what happens in Genesis. Holy Spirit moves over the formless void and comes up with a proliferation of life. God takes fragmented bits of dirt and breathes us into life. You can fight all you want about whether such accounts are fact or fiction, but you'd be wasting your time and you'd be making a big mistake if you missed the whole point. What looks like "nothing" to us turns out to be fertile ground for God. What looks like "chaos" to us turns out to be the breeding ground of sacred potential. In other words, from a spiritual perspective, there's no such thing as *nothing*. *Nothing* is a figment of our limited imagination. We're the ones who come up blank. We're the ones without vision. We're the ones who give up hope. But through creative capacity of Spirit, all kinds of things become possible.

With God, all kinds of things are possible because God's creative energy is still at work: *creation continua*. Holy Spirit works with what is. The Holy Spirit works with us. We are raw material continually being fashioned in the crucible of life, and our spirits are resilient. We can be reworked, reshaped, refashioned, and renewed. We are people in process. We are souls in a continuing project of sanctification, and the creativity which moves all of this is much bigger and far more vast than anything we could come up with on our own. Alfred North Whitehead said, "God is in the world, or nowhere, creating continually in us and around us. This creative principle is everywhere, in animate and so-called inanimate matter, in the ether, water, earth, human hearts."

God says, I am doing a new thing; now it springs forth, do you not perceive it? I will make a way in the wilderness and rivers in the desert.

Jesus says, A new heart I will give you, and a new spirit I will put within you.

If any one is in Christ, Paul says, he is a new creation; the old has passed away, behold, the new has come.

For some people I know, this is not good news. *New* is not good news. *New* means something different, and not everybody goes in for that kind of thing. Some people like it best when things stay the same. Me, I like change, but I have to admit, I like change so long as I get to choose when and where and how it happens. I like to be in charge of change; otherwise it can begin to feel like loss of control.

Not every change is for the good and sometimes chaos is just that: chaos. We call it creativity, but it's really a cover for inner personal and interpersonal chaos, an excuse for the non-payment of bills, the neglect of relationships, bizarre behavior and the reckless use of drugs. Creativity can be used to justify many things, and this is one of the reasons that parents of college age young people dread the words "fine arts." Let me just say, in my extremely limited experience, drugs can make you *feel* creative, but that's about as far as it goes. Get a good chemical on board and you may think that you are brilliant, that you have all the answers, but then you sober up and see that you have actually come up with nothing and your life is even more chaotic than ever.

You want to know when new is good? New is good when your old ways don't work any more, when the defense mechanisms fail and you are just too tired to try again. In times like this, different is a word that brings delight and hope. When I look at my life and draw a blank, when I look at me and come up with nothing, the fresh breath of creativity is just what I need.

Nothing is not a problem, Jesus said. We can work with that.

We, Jesus says. *We* can work with that. It's a team approach. We don't have to do it all on our own. We can't do it on our own. Trust me, I tried. But what we can do is participate in the process. We can be colleagues, partners in Christ's service. We can be spiritual conduits. Open to guidance and inspiration, we can be part of God's divine flow. As a spiritual quality, creativity is always right there within reach, hovering in the midst of nothingness and emerging through the chaos. It is available to us all.

No way! That's what people often say when I introduce creativity as something that is universal and accessible. No way, they say. I don't have a creative bone in my body!

So I ask them:

Do you quilt?
Do you garden?
Do you sew?
Can you tell a story, make a joke?
Can you jerry-rig the plumbing?
Do you come up with interesting lesson plans?
Can you open up a lane to the hoop?
Have you ever come up with a business plan,
    or a mission statement?
Do you find ways to work with all kinds of people?
Can you reach that difficult child?
Have you redesigned an office or streamlined a system?
Can you stretch a dollar, or a meal?
Have you dreamed up ways to feed the hungry
    or house the homeless?
Do you find ways to skooch over and make room for more,
    as many as Jesus calls?
Have you ever had a moment of inspiration or intuition?
Do ideas come to you in your dreams,
Do visions come in the waking hours?

I pause to take a breath. Good thing.

Oh, they say. We never thought of it like that. We never thought of that as being creative. We thought creativity was more like a kind of a special gift, spectacular, unique – you know, a few people have it, but most of us don't. We thought it had to be something really big, something really splashy, extraordinary… like Picasso or Michael Jackson or Michael Jordan. We never thought of ourselves as being creative before.

They kind of like the knowing. It makes them happy inside.

Working with clients, Dick also came to see creativity as an important part of healing. It's a key characteristic of Self. Creativity is an innate spiritual quality that arises spontaneously when constraints are removed.

Clients, he says, begin to tap into a kind of creative wisdom as their inner noise diminishes and their Selves arise. Solutions to long-standing problems emerge, often involving lateral, "out of the box" thinking that was not possible when they were dominated by the parts of them that had so many rules about their lives and relationships. It seems that peoples' Selves have an innate wisdom about how to create harmony in relationship, whether those relationships are with people around them or with parts inside them.

I guess Jesus must have had a lot of Self, because he was always going "outside of the box." He was always coming up with new and unexpected solutions. Good solutions.

Four thousand people come to his day-long workshop. They get hungry. They get grumpy, edgy, dangerously hungry. Four thousand of them. I don't know about you, but in my family, four people hungry is a problem. It begins to look chaotic out there, and the disciples make a move for control. Get rid of them, they urge. Send them away. Instead, Jesus gets creative in a way that makes for miracles. He takes up a collection of resources. Now some people think that the miracle lies in the creation of more food. Other people think the miracle lies in the fact that people shared their food. Either way, everyone gets fed.

Another time, the disciples are out on the sea, caught in a storm. Most of us would have been stuck on the shore, drawing a blank, out of options, but Jesus walks on the water. That was creative.

Jesus had a dream of what could be. He called it the Kingdom of God. It was a vision of justice and mercy, but to those in control, it looked to be chaos. They killed him; but then he rose from the dead, escaped the tomb, literally out of his box.

222

That was creative.

  Myself, I like creativity and I like change, but I'm not looking to perform any miracles. Just want to get that out there in case any of you get your hopes up. My mind is very small. Tiny. A wee bit of brain, hardly worth mentioning. On the other hand, it's not about me. It's definitely not about me, or about you either, for that matter. It's about serving God, allowing the Holy Spirit to flow through us and out into the world. Participants of divine process. Dreamers of the divine dream. In the book of Joel, God says:

> I will pour out my spirit on all flesh;
> your sons and your daughters shall prophesy,
> your old men shall dream dreams,
> and your young men shall see visions.

  Holy Spirit flows. Spirit-filled people embody creativity. We can't always control the circumstances of our lives, but we can respond to those circumstances in a creative fashion. We can let the Spirit lead within and as we do, we become artists in our own right: co-creators, co-authors in our own life's tale. More than that, we ourselves become works of art. We become masterpieces shaped through the moving of Divine Mystery.

  When we are full with Self-energy, we look out over the raw material of our life with eager anticipation. At one time, it looked to be chaos. At one time, we appeared to ourselves as Nothing. But now we look at our very being and what we see is a field for divine potential and miraculous possibility. We look out across the shapeless void, and there, ready to emerge, is Life.

There is one body and one Spirit, just as you were called to the one hope of your calling, one Lord, one faith, one baptism, one God and Father of all, who is above all and through all and in all.

(Ephesians :1-6)

Abide in me as I abide in you. Just as the branch cannot bear fruit by itself unless it abides in the vine, neither can you unless you abide in me.

(John 14:4)

Connectedness

A misfit, that's what she said.

I'm out riding horses and I have just fallen in love with the girl who is my guide.   She is all of fifteen, but the horse she rides is alive and rocking.   The stables here are alive and rocking.   The whole place is a riot of life.   There are cats, dogs, horses and children, all of every size and shape and color.   I'm wondering how you get to be in a place like this.

I just didn't fit at home, she says.   So I came here to live.

Misfit.   If that's all it takes, I think, then I'm in.   Already I can see the genius of it.   In a house full of misfits, everyone fits.   In a land where no one belongs, everyone is at home.   Sweet.

OK, so I have a few issues with attachment.   I never feel like I belong.

Don't be silly, Jesus says.   You're one of the lucky ones.   You know where you belong.   You've always known.   You belong with me.

Yeah, I know, I say, but I want a *real* family, one like I was supposed to have in the first place.   You know, the ones like they show on TV.   Beaver Cleaver.   The Brady Bunch.   The Waltons.

What Waltons? What real family? Jesus asks. Who
are my mother and my brother? Those who hear the
word of God and do it. Remember, I said that.
Check it out: Luke 8:21. Less TV, more Bible.
Think about it.

It's not that I believe everything that I see on TV, but I
totally believe that some kids got lucky and grew up in real
families, the ones where people play board games all the time
and eat chocolate chip cookies fresh from the oven. They laugh
from their bellies, and you feel all safe and warm on the inside.
Where is *that* family? Where did it go?

Like Sally in a Charlie Brown Christmas, all I want is
what I've got coming to me. All I want is my fair share.

I wonder sometimes, does everyone feel like this --
disconnected? Like we don't fit very well with other people and
that we don't mesh, even on the inside?   I feel like this and I
know a lot of people who feel like this.   Then again, I'm a
therapist; so it could be the company I keep. I'm also a spiritual
seeker and I travel with those inclined to search. In other
words, my sample might be skewed.

Which begs the question: Is there help for the misfit?   For
those who have no home? For the neglected, the abused, the
abandoned?

There are a lot of people out there who say "No."
Developmental theorists will tell you that if you didn't get good
enough parenting, then you're out of luck. If you didn't get a
secure attachment to your primary caregiver, a sense of
connection at the beginning, then you are doomed, permanently
damaged. That's what they say. That's what they say, but I
don't like it when they talk about me like this. In defense of my
parents, let me just say that it wasn't all bad, and they don't
deserve all the blame. For another thing, "doom" is not in the
vocabulary of faith.

The way I see it, we're all misfits. We all have experiences of rejection and embarrassment. We all know the sting of exclusion, the not being invited to the party or the being passed over for promotion, the proverbial being picked last for the team. Feelings of shame and humiliation; no one gets out of them. No one escapes these painful experiences, though we may try hard to forget. We try to leave them in the past. We blow off the injury and bury the pain. We cut off from key experiences in our lives because they hurt too much and they don't fit with the story that we are trying to tell about ourselves. In this way we deceive ourselves and fool others. We can be quite brutal about it, angrily defensive on the outside – rejecting feedback and blaming others. We can be quite critical and cruel on the inside. We blame and punish ourselves for having tender parts that got hurt in the first place. These vulnerable childlike parts could be counted among the despised and rejected whom Isaiah talks about, that very ones whom Jesus came to save.

Do you ever wonder what happens to them? What happens to the parts of us that we don't like, the ones that we no longer welcome? Where do they go when there's no place for them at home? They go looking for love. They will lead us in search of that idealized family, the one we never had, or the idealized person, the one who must be waiting for us out there somewhere. The knight in shining armor. The woman who will make you feel like a man. The one who will make you complete. The Church of Perpetual Embrace.

Sounds a little sickening, but we do it all the time. It looks like love and it talks like love, but it's really a parts-led connection, and connections like these are fueled by our exiled, unmet need. We enter adult relationships with the little ones in charge. These guys want what we never had. And who can blame them? They want to make up for lost time and make up for all the mistakes that our parents made. They want to forge a new family, better than what they had before. They want someone who will love them and do it right this time.

Underneath, there's deep longing, smoldering desperation and the fear of misfit all over again.

Now we really are doomed because we tend to create the very thing that we fear. We bring too much expectation to the relationship and put too much pressure on the other person. Who could live up to all of that? Not to mention how hard it is to be in an adult relationship with a two year old or a twelve year old. Now there's a mismatch and it happens all the time. Just think, how many times have you wished that your partner would just grow up? How many of you actually said it? *Why don't you just grow up?!* If you've ever said it, then you probably know by now… it doesn't help. The other person won't like hearing it, and in that moment, they probably can't do anything different anyway. Caught in the grip of our parts, we might as well be two or twelve years old. In a way, we are. And would you tell a child to just grow up?! Ok, so don't answer that. If you've ever done it, then you know it doesn't really make any sense and it doesn't help. It just makes you both feel bad.

It's hard for me to hold on to my Self when my husband is coming at me like a needy child and it's even worse when *I* am the child, when some little kid is running my relationship. I don't like it at all. I feel small and vulnerable, needy and dependent and that gets my protective system going. All kinds of interesting things happen. I get resentful and rageful. I get aloof and act all grown-up. I might pull out a surly adolescent or a super super-ego. I act badly and then I blame him for it. I know for a fact, it's all his fault. But underneath, I know that something isn't quite right. Something doesn't fit. I think it's me.

It doesn't have to be like this. *I* don't have to be like this. I am not doomed to repeating these relationship patterns, not doomed to a life-time of disconnect. It's not how I want to live and it's not how I'm meant to live. I am meant to work toward common understanding and peace – peace of mind and peace in my world: harmony in relationship at every level of my being.

Through the IFS model I have learned how to welcome those wounded parts in me, the ones that have been abused and abandoned, the ones that I myself have despised and rejected. I go seeking after those little lost lambs. Jesus comes along. Good Shepherd is one of his best gigs. We go to these challenging parts and I find it easier to be with them now. I couldn't before. I couldn't be there for me, but now I can. In Self, I help them get what they needed the first time around. It's a "do over." Blows my mind, but it totally works. Spiritual presence: it heals and transforms the past; it sets me free to live in the present.

As with other spiritual paths, the IFS model points us toward a life-giving relationship with the Divine, with God. Despite what the developmental theorists say, our ultimate connection, our primary attachment is not to our parents or to our partner or to any other person; it is to Self. A healthy spiritual relationship is the only thing that can make us secure in the very core of our being. Divine connection is the only authentic, enduring cure for our existential angst. Spirit alone heals. God is the only one who holds us with eternal embrace. Any other love is less.

When I am securely attached to God, I find that I can care for myself. I can take care of myself and because of this I can trust myself to be in relationship with another person. I can be with all my parts, yet lead from a place of spiritual grounding. I am available to other people in a way that invites a stronger kind of connection: Self to Self. Love like this is liberating. Freed from my burdens, I no longer need you to help me carry my load. I no longer love you from the place of my need so I have no personal agenda; I love you just for being you. Doesn't that sound nice?

What do you mean, *take care of myself?!* I don't want to take care of myself?!

It's me again, reacting to myself.

I've been doing that my whole life! I'm tired of taking care of myself, depending on myself. Been there, tired of doing that.

Jesus looks up from his latte.

What Self do you think we're talking about here, he asks?

Myself, of course. Me, Myself and I.

Well, he says, that's a little narrow, isn't it? A limited way to look at things. There's life outside your cranium, you know, and there's a whole lot more to you than you.

My head starts to throb. What is he talking about?

My *Self*. Your *Self*, he says. We're not talking about lil' ole you. We're not talking about your little "s" self and all your self-reliant parts. We're talking about your big "S" Self, he says. The indwelling of the Holy Spirit. God's own Self. Divine Self. Transcendent Self. Spiritual Self. Being held in the Everlasting Arms. I'm pretty sure we covered this material already. Doesn't any of this sound familiar? I think you wrote it.

It does sound familiar, now that he mentions it. It was a temporary lapse; it happens. I still forget. It's basic information and yet I forget, a lot. But then, thank God, something comes along to help me remember about Spiritual Presence. Some angel comes to wake me up. I come to my Self, and when I do, it is such a relief to remember who I am, whose I am, what I am: heavenly treasure in a jar of clay; Holy Spirit infused throughout flesh. Holy Spirit is my life-blood, and the life-blood of authentic relationship, the nexus of my connections, heart to heart. We are one in the Spirit. We are one in the Lord. Apart from me, you cannot bear fruit, Jesus says. Abide in me, as I abide in you.

I guess the Spirit is a lot like sap, sap that flows within the branches, sustaining life, nurturing growth, bearing fruit. Sometimes I can even see it for myself. In sudden mystical moments, everything is transformed. Everyone becomes translucent. People walking, people talking. Whatever it is that they are doing, I see in them the shimmering pixie-dust of Soul. They shine. They shine, those little lights, so lovely; all of us shining on our way through life. All around, Spirit sparkles -- off waves in the water and stars in the sky, the twinkle in your eye. We are so beautiful. My heart is full, so full that I think it might explode, flash out across the sky in sparkling bits of glittering Soul, fireworks for the world.

I like to think that someday everyone will see it like this, that everyone will see us like this. Everyone will see the Holy Spirit shining within us and that we will all experience the spiritual quality of connection -- the quality of spiritual connection. We're not the same, but we are one and we can live together in peace.

They will not hurt or destroy on all my holy mountain; for the earth will be full of the knowledge of the Lord as the waters cover the sea.

Isaiah calls this: the Reign of God.
Jesus calls it: the Kingdom of God.
I call it: Family for the Misfit.
Finally... home.

We know that all things work together for good for those who love God,
Who are called according to his purpose.

(Romans 8:28)

Come to me, all of you who are weary and carry heavy burdens,
and I will give you rest.

(Matthew 11:28)

The Meaning of Life, or Burdens as Lessons

People are stupid.

I know. You're not supposed to talk like that. I'm a Mom and most of the time I'm maternally correct. We don't call people *stupid*. At least, that's what I used to tell my kids. But honestly, sometimes it's the only good explanation.

As a mother, I was trying to teach my kids something important, an important lesson about respect. After all, Jesus warned me about calling other people "fools." And calling someone stupid, well, that might not be all that Self-led. My friend, Jon, says that if you're trashing people, you can be pretty sure that you're not in Self.

Self aside, I was trying to teach and so I wasn't really listening. I had a point to get across and I was so focused that I didn't really hear what my kids were trying to say. They were trying to make sense of something, and I said, we don't call people *stupid*.

One day my son, who was born to prove me wrong, changed all that. He came home from school with yet another tale of playground cruelty. Man's inhumanity to man, or in his case, third grade inhumanity to third graders. I don't remember the details, but it was so extreme that even I forgot to set him straight. People are stupid, Mom, he said. On the inside, I could feel my parental structures teeter and collapse like a tower of building blocks. You're right, I said, people *are* stupid.

It was a milestone moment in our relationship. I decided to teach less and listen more. Instead of training them up in the way that they should go, I decided to meet my children first, right where they were. I began to deal with their experience in a whole new way, which was relief for us all, since the old way wasn't working very well. After that, I let them speak their truth: call a spade a spade, and a stupid spade, a stupid spade. I acknowledged their reality. Still, being their mother and all, I tried to shape that reality just a wee little bit. Maybe we could be a little more precise in our use of language, a little more careful with our words. People are not stupid. People do stupid things, and people say things that are stupid, but no one's stupid through and through. We are dumb in different ways, and few of us know what to do or say in the face of suffering.

When things don't make sense, we don't know what to say. And yet we try. Instead of staying with people right where they are, we feel the need to move them forward. We feel the need to share some words of wisdom and it's amazing how often we manage to say just the wrong thing:

> God needed him more than you do.
> She's in a better place.
> God is trying to teach you a lesson.
> It's all part of God's plan.
> Everything happens for a reason.
> God won't give you more than you can handle.

I may have said something like this myself once or twice. It seems likely. I'm not really sure. That's how it works, at least for me. I don't set out to be stupid on purpose. I don't offend people intentionally; I'm too well-managed for that. If you see me being stepping on someone's toes, it's usually because I've missed something. I'm not being mean; I just don't know any better. And maybe it doesn't make much difference in the long run. Inhumanity is inhumanity, and hurt is hurt, however it comes.

When it comes to death and suffering, I generally know how to act. I know because I've been around the block a few times and I took darn good notes. I've been privy to a lot of mistakes. I've heard the things that people say. You want to walk on the edge, you just try and tell somebody what the death of a loved one means, just try and make sense out of it for them. Reduce their suffering to a sound byte and get ready to duck.

Poet-undertaker Thomas Lynch has seen it too -- people who rush in, quick to reassure.

> Right between the inhale and exhale of the bone-wracking sob ... some frightened and well-meaning ignoramus is bound to give out with "It's OK, that's not her, it's just a shell." I once saw an Episcopalian deacon nearly decked by the swift slap of the mother of a teenager, dead of leukemia, to whom he'd tendered this counsel. "I'll tell you when it's 'just a shell,'" the woman said. "For now and until I tell you otherwise, she's my daughter."

Yes, if beauty is in the eye of the beholder, then meaning is in the hands of those who must make it. It falls to the suffering to make sense of the insensible. No one can do it for them, and we who love can only watch and wait close by. We yield to the power of presence. Spoken word makes way for Living Word.

In the face of suffering, I find it best to keep my mouth shut. It's a simple all-purpose rule, and I like rules, especially the ones that keep me from making stupid mistakes. There is another side to this coin, however. If there is a time to be silent, then there is also a time to speak. If there is a time to hold back, then there is also a time to offer hope. Timing is everything.

We are people of faith, and this means that we have faith in *something*. We trust in some higher power. Christians trust in the powerful presence of the Holy Spirit as it comes in the person of Jesus Christ. Practitioners of IFS trust in the powerful presence of Self as it comes to us from within. We have this spiritual understanding, and this understanding strengthens us even in times of terrible suffering. We share a light that shines in the deepest dark.

When you're in trouble, it helps to know the tenets of your faith. What has been taught and what of it do you believe?

Jesus says that not one hair falls from my head without the Father's knowledge. Personally, I find this hard to believe; my people have a lot of hair. Still, it is a great teaching and I get the point. I matter. Every part of me matters. I matter, and you matter, and we mean something to God. Our lives count and our suffering is significant. Though small, we are relevant, even in the grand scheme of things. And when things go from bad to worse, God is right there with us.

I know people without any kind of faith. They don't believe in the existence of God or in a spiritual Self. Atheist, they say, and when they do, they often say it with some defiance and pride. I get it, but then again, I don't really get it. Spirit lies too deep within my grain. Self lies in every single cell and every part of me. It's true that I get mad at Jesus. He makes a lot of mistakes and he, of all people, should know better, but I guess that this just makes him real. Holy Spirit is the Source of all Being, and this knowledge keeps me grounded in *my* being, no matter what. I trust in the goodness of God, and this keeps me from being blown about in every wind, or tossed about by every storm. Faith holds me up when life comes crashing down.

I know the Holy Spirit and this helps me in times of trouble. And those same times of trouble in turn help me to know more of Holy Spirit. My experiences of Self help me in the hard times, and those same hard times provide new opportunities for me to experience Self. It's a recursive relationship. It's a loop. It's an education in love first-hand.

Life comes crashing down, and when it does, I like to get

a handle on it. I try to make sense out of it. I ask the Big Questions. What is the meaning of life, and why do we have to suffer? Why me? Why now? I don't know for sure, but I do know that the hard times have a way of waking me up, and when it comes to my life, I think there's material that I'm meant to master. I think I'm meant to grow.

For spiritual seekers, life is one big lesson plan: a pilgrim's progress. We are born, and everything which comes after serves as our curriculum. Everything that comes our way, both the good and the bad, has the potential to teach us important spiritual lessons and develop in us a greater spiritual capacity. Life events can expand our awareness, build our character and grow in us our faith. In Romans 5:3, Paul says, we "boast in our sufferings, knowing that suffering produces endurance, and endurance produces character, and character produces hope, and hope does not disappoint us, because God's love has been poured into our hearts through the Holy Spirit that has been given to us."

I'm not so sure about the boasting part, and it's not like I'm going to go out there deliberately looking for more trouble, just so I can grow and all. Trouble seems to find me well enough on its own. Every life comes with a full measure of suffering and opportunities for growth and all of it can work for our good. Even our worst enemies can become great teachers. Even our worst tormentors, Dick says, can become our mentors.

I know, I know. All of this comes dangerously close to the category of less smart things that people will say in the face of suffering. I've heard it myself, the quoting of Paul in hospital hallways and in the parlors of the funeral home. All things work for the good, they say. This is just a test, they say -- which makes God out to be a sadist, as though God would send evil on purpose. If suffering is just a test of my emergency spiritual preparedness, then let me tell you, I'm going to get up and turn the channel. There's got to be a better way to learn. Me, I like those smiley face stamps and the glittery gold stars.

235

I just can't get excited about suffering, especially when it's my own. I'm kind of a chicken that way. I'm opposed to pain in principle and I avoid it in practice. I do what I can to prevent it, but it seems to find me anyway, and when it does, I try to deny it, minimize it, disown it, fix my mind on other things, bury myself in work, and keep on keeping on.

I hate my suffering and do what I can to get rid of it, but you know, at the same time, I have these other parts that seem to accommodate it. Parts of me have this terrible, unhealthy tolerance for suffering and they are willing to settle in for a long-term relationship. They say, and with such utter conviction: that's just the way it is. That's just the way the world works. This is how it's meant to be, at least for me.

Even worse are the parts that would blame me, see my pain as some kind of fitting punishment. You only get what you deserve. You brought this on yourself. You made your bed, now you have to lie in it. That's what they say, and when I listen to them, when I listen to stuff like this, I no longer see my burdens as an invitation into new learning; they now become God's way of teaching me a lesson. Suffering no longer serves as a knock on the door of my consciousness; it's more like God knocking me upside the head. There is no hope, only hurt. Punishing parts are not my favorite. They don't like me and I don't like them.

So here's the thing: suffering can serve a purpose and pain may have a positive intention. They might wake me up. They might point me to parts in need of healing. But suffering without the experience of spiritual presence is a problem. Suffering without the presence Self-energy is pointless, even destructive, and prolonged suffering is insidious. It wears me down and wears me out. It separates me all the more from my Self. It cuts me off from God. I get overwhelmed and I lose perspective. That's how it works. Some of life's lessons are just too hard for us to master on our own. It helps to have a framework of faith. It gives you something to hold on to. And

236

it's important to have a community of faith, people who will hold on to you when you have lost all hope for yourself, people who can embody the Spirit of Christ when you are feeling completely lost and abandoned.

When I am suffering, I need people who can hold onto hope. Hope is what I need, but even that is hard, maybe the hardest thing of all. It's too risky. I'm afraid to get my hopes up. What if things don't work out? What if this is my last hope and then those hopes get dashed? Better to stay safely with the suffering I know than risk losing it all.

I whine this way to Jesus. I expect a little empathy but what I get is irritation.

What, he says, and are you such a tough case?
What, out of all the people in the world, you think
that you're the only one beyond all hope, beyond my
help? Suit yourself. You can suffer if you want to,
but when you're ready, there's a way. I'm the Way.
Look me up.

When do I get the real deal? That's what I want to
know. When do I get the nice Jesus?

I'm going to see Dick, that's what I tell him. He's a
lot nicer than you are.

Jesus laughs out loud. Go ahead, he says. See how
far you get. Better yet, see where you end up. Self,
Spirit; it's all the same and it all leads back to the
same Source. We share one hope – the love of God
poured in our hearts through the Holy Spirit. All
your roads lead back to me, baby, so rock on.

Here we go again. It all comes back to the hope we have, poured into our hearts through the presence of Holy Spirit. It's

237

a big deal in the Christian faith and a big deal in the IFS worldview. It's hope, based on the presence of Self in all people. It's healing that is available to us all for all our parts. It's the possibility of goodness. Positive change is always possible. We have Spirit at our core and our inner relationships are far more fluid and flexible than we think. Our inner systems are not fixed, not stuck on one setting, and because of this, far more is possible than we previously imagined.

It's true that we can't change the past, but we can change the way it affects us. We can't change the facts of our life, but we can reorganize our relationship with those facts, make new meanings and discover new narratives. Within the mind itself we can create new neural pathways of connection and new ways of being in relationship, even with our Self. We can come to our parts with spiritual presence, heal them and help them find new roles. We don't have to settle in for a lesser way of life, we can live into abundant life. This is, I believe, the work to which we are called. This is what we're meant to do, and for most of us, it's a whole life's learning. Maybe more.

It's a big job but one worth doing, not only for ourselves, but for the sake of the whole world. Every piece of healing makes our the world a healthier place. Every act of reconciliation moves us all toward world peace. Every change that we make on the inside has a ripple effect on the outside. As Ghandi said, we are to be the change that we would like to see in the world. If we let Self lead in our internal relationships, we will manifest Self-energy in our external relationships. Spirit leads in our lives and as it does, it leads us back out into the world. We go to love and serve the Lord with gladness.

As Christians, we know our need of change. We know of sin and suffering. We know the value of conversion. We know where we want to go and IFS gives us a way to get there. IFS gives us a framework. It gives us a means of discernment. It gives us a practical way to deal with damage. It's a clear and enduring path toward healing. It's what my friend, Bill Wilder, calls "grace with legs." With IFS, we now have the means to delve deep within our very being. We can get right down to the heart of the matter and to the things that weigh heavy on our heart. In the IFS model, these things are known as burdens, and all of us have them.

In his book *Traveling Light*, Max Lucado describes the effect of burdens:

> Don't remember seeing a baggage terminal? That's because the carousel is not the one in the airport; it's the one in the mind. And the bags we grab are not made of leather; they're made of burdens. The suitcase of guilt. A sack of discontent. You drape a duffel bag of weariness on one shoulder and a hanging bag of grief on the other. Add on a backpack of doubt, an overnight bag of loneliness, and a trunk of fear. Pretty soon you're pulling more stuff than a skycap. No wonder you're so tired at the end of the day. Lugging baggage is exhausting.

What are these burdens? In the IFS model they are extreme ideas, behaviors or feelings which can exercise great influence and power in our lives. They are the residual effects of painful experiences and destructive relationships, places of wounding that can drive everything else in the inner system. Burdens are often messages that we have internalized, the lies that we've been told and come now to believe. They come to us through many means, but the message is clear: we are worthless, useless, ugly, stupid, no good, we get what we deserve, and what we deserve is to be punished; we are damned to hell. Tell the truth, many of us are there already, tortured by feelings of abandonment or depression, isolation and emptiness.

Like all lies, burdens are insidious. They worm their way in and once inside, they have a way of taking hold. They get entwined with parts. Sometimes the burdens have been there so long that we can't remember ever being without them. Sometimes these burdens can be so close and so familiar that we can't see them for what they are. We believe the lies, take them for gospel truth:

I *am* useless.
I *am* worthless.
I *am* ugly.
I *am* dumb.
I *am* to blame.

We believe the lies because burdens blind us to the truth about ourselves, the deeper truth that we are beloved and precious in the sight of God.

In the Christian tradition, we may not use the word *burden* very much, but we do speak of sin, and we understand this sin as anything which separates us from God. In the IFS model, burdens look a lot like sin; they emulate that sinful state of separation and to the same effect. They fill us with shame and guilt. They cause us to hide. They distort our perceptions and separate us from the truth. Burdened parts disconnect us from our Self. In other words, they take us away from the very thing that we need in order to heal; they take from us our hope.

Given all of this, you'd think that having burdens would be a bad thing and it's true: the IFS model works toward the release of these burdens. Jesus worked for that same release. Come to me, he says, all of you who are weary and carry heavy burdens, and I will give you rest. At the same time, just as the experience of sin can lead us into an even greater experience of God's grace, burdens can open us to a powerful experience of the Self. Burdens are important features in the development of our faith. They serve as essential elements in the process of our spiritual education. They are, in short, the lesson plans in life.

Tina had breast cancer and the diagnosis took her right to a burden that she carried for a very long time, the belief that she was unattractive and therefore doomed to a lifetime of loneliness. Married to Bob for thirty-five years, she still had parts that believed in her essential ugliness. They knew for a fact that one day Bob would leave her, and he would leave for a more beautiful woman. In the beginning, the diagnosis of breast cancer plunged her into an agony of anxiety and depression, but not even that could drive Bob away. Eventually, Tina came to believe in Bob, and then she had to look inside herself. She found this burdened part and approached it from a place of compassion. She helped it heal and let that burden go. What she found in its place was a sense of great inner beauty. It's a mixed bag. It's not that Tina is glad about her cancer, but she's grateful for the lessons learned. She is freer now to live her life, however long or short it may be, and she's a lot happier now with her Self and in her life with Bob.

Keith fell in love with the woman of his dreams. Lauren was funny and smart, the life of the party. When Keith was with her, he felt special. He also found himself filled with a jealous anger. He began to criticize and control. Things got worse until one day he crossed the line and hit her. Lauren insisted that it was over between them unless Keith got some counseling and got himself turned around. Keith faced up to himself and found the part in him that held memories of ridicule and humiliation, a childhood burden that grew into a deep-seated insecurity and showed itself in acts of rage. He treated Lauren badly, there's no doubt about that, but this extreme behavior confronted him with his issues and it forced Lauren to achieve new levels of self-care; it led them both to a place of healing and away from life-long patterns of harm.

When Carol came to see me, she was carrying a heavy load, burdens of guilt and the long-standing belief that she was a bad mother. Carol had an adult daughter who was addicted to drugs, a daughter who had been lost to her for ten years. Things began to go wrong for Carol, one thing after another. She needed major surgery and she needed someone to help. Carol reached out to her daughter. The daughter moved back home and nursed her mother. Things were better; things were worse. The daughter still took drugs, and this caused a lot of problems between them. One night, while her mother dozed in a chair nearby, the daughter died of an overdose.

Carol was filled with resentment and remorse. She was angry at her daughter. She was angry at herself. She was angry with God. But Carol was a woman of faith and she committed to the process of healing. She got to know her parts and own her parts and acknowledge the part that she had played in this sad affair. In time, she found compassion for herself and compassion for her daughter. She released her burdens and then she released her daughter, gave them both into God's care. Carol was able to forgive -- her daughter and herself.

She began to make sense of all the suffering, to see a sense within the suffering. Despite it all, Carol saw the Spirit at work in her life for good. If I hadn't needed this surgery, she said, I wouldn't have found my daughter. If I hadn't found my daughter, she might have died on the streets and I would never have known. I would have always wondered what happened to her. As it was, on the day she died, she picked flowers for me. She combed my hair and told me that she loved me. That was a miracle and I will always treasure that memory. As it is, she died at home, and I was there. She was clean and safe, and I was there. That was the grace of God. She is dead, and it's not what I wanted, but I am at peace. I am grateful to God and ready now to live my life.

Every life comes with burdens, and for many people, the process of unburdening is a profound spiritual experience. It opens us to life-changing experiences of Divine Presence. Specific burdens are released, which is great, but even more important, we learn the love of God. We learn to trust in the Holy Spirit. We develop a whole new relationship with Self. Burdens come and burdens go, but we find that the steadfast love of God endures forever. Is there any better life learning than this? I don't think so.

The steadfast love of God. It is a matter of faith, and it's the kind of faith which comes through personal experience. It comes from the experience of being lost then found. It comes from our experience of burden and release, of sin and salvation. Go through the pattern enough times, encounter Divine Presence enough times, and you too will begin to believe, even where you can not see. Do your own work, and you will come to know God for yourself. Bring enough Self-energy to your parts and you will find a blessing buried within their burdens.

This is totally true, but you gotta be careful with talk like this. It's best if you let people say it for themselves. It's best if you let people discover it for themselves, come to their own spiritual understanding. That or you can always buy them a copy of this book. But mostly, we have to learn it for ourselves. You can't learn someone else's lessons for them, and you shouldn't try to bear another's burden -- not that I haven't tried.

I grew up with Donny Osmond and his rendition of the Hollies hit: "He ain't Heavy, He's my Brother." *No burden is he to bear?! I'm strong enough to carry him?!* Oh, it just fit so nicely with that whole misunderstood passage in Matthew about giving a man your cloak as well as your coat, about going the extra mile with someone who has forced you into the first. It plays into the whole Christian culture of self-sacrifice.

If you are truly in Self, if you are genuinely filled with the Spirit of Christ, you can give away both your coat and your cloak and you can get away with it. You can go that extra mile and it might effect transformation for the both of you. But when we make those same sacrifices out of a sense of "should" and "ought," when we are coerced or we give out of guilt, there's usually some kind of backlash, some hell to pay for it later. We end up feeling resentful or taken advantage of. Oh yeah, there will be more lessons to be learned and more burdens to uncover.

There are ways to lay down your life and do it authentically, out of Holy Love, but much of the time, self-sacrifice comes more from our burdened parts. We put the

243

needs of others first because that's what we've been taught to do. That's what Jesus would do, that's what Jesus wants us to do. At least, that's what we've been told and come to believe. If we don't sacrifice, we feel selfish, guilty, ashamed and bad. We have disappointed or angered someone else, but it feels like we have disappointed or angered God himself. We put the needs of others first, but we don't do this from a spiritual core. We do it from our Christ-like parts, the ones that mistake themselves for Christ.

These Christ-like parts do a lot of good work in the world, but they often bear a great burden of responsibility. We feel responsible for the well-being of others. Heck, we feel responsible for the well-being of the entire world. We have our own need of healing, our own life lessons waiting to be learned, but we ignore our issues and concentrate our energies on someone else. Before we have mastered the basic principles of self-care, we go for the advanced placement level of self-sacrifice. Somehow we have gotten the idea that we are strong enough, smart enough, enlightened enough, faithful enough to bear another's burdens. Not content with the crosses we already bear, we go out looking for others. And believe me, people are more than willing to share. You will always find someone willing to hand off a cross or two, someone more than willing to let you help them with their load. The Christ-like parts don't know how to say "no," not to a brother or sister in need. We take on more and more, and over time, and in time, we walk around with the weight of the world on our shoulders. We turn into martyrs, and not in the best sense of the word.

This is a problem for nice people the world over, the good people of the world, but women have it bad, and religious women, worst of all. Our natural inclination toward relationship and our socialization toward caring for others combine with the religious ethic of sacrificial love, and this makes us particularly susceptible. Our sense of boundaries stink.

How to love others well, and without sacrificing ourselves at the same time: for people of faith, this is a real dilemma. We don't know how to do it and we're not sure it's even allowed.

I go to Jesus about this. I quote him at himself:

No one has greater love than this, to lay down one's life for one's friends. Isn't that what you told us to do?

You know who you sound like? Jesus asks. You sound just like Caiaphas trying to trap me with my own words. *Better to have one man die for the good of all.* That's what the man said, and it sounded like wisdom, but he was just justifying himself.

Turn the other cheek. Forgive and forget. It's what everyone says when they're trying to bend you to their will, when they're trying to get you to do what they want. They will take your faith and use it against you. They will tell you to sacrifice yourself and they will do it in the name of God. They take my name in vain. So do you.

But what about Donny Osmond? I wheedle. What about that whole *"I am my brother's keeper"* thing? That whole *"doing it unto the least of these"* thing? What happened to *"laying down my life?"*

Look, says Jesus, talking straight at me. He is as serious as I have ever seen. This is important, he says, so be sure you get this one right. I already did that. *I* am the good shepherd who lays down his life for the sheep. Love your brothers and your sisters, yes. Encourage them and support them, yes, but let them walk their walk and leave the saving up to me.

245

That's *my* job.

People need to do their own work and you are
stepping in where you don't belong. Do their
homework for them and they'll never learn. Take
on their burdens and you will deprive them of their
healing. It's a form of stealing, really, and in the
long run, you only prolong their suffering. Who are
you to mess with God's curriculum?

Why don't you take up your own cross, which, by
the way, in case you haven't noticed, is plenty big
enough? Do your own work and let your own life
serve as witness. Let my light shine in you and that
will be sufficient.

I hear these words and I get the truth of them. I have
lived the truth of them. But still, shouldn't we be doing
something? Shouldn't we be fixing things? I look at the world
and it looks to me like we are one big bunch of burdened parts
colliding and bouncing off one another, like atoms on the loose,
like a wild ride in bumper cars. It's a parts-led life. Burdens
101. It's a wonder anyone gets out alive.

Oh yeah, we don't. I forgot. We aren't in this world to
get out of it alive. That's not the point. We're here to learn, as
long as we're alive.

I am trying to follow Jesus and I am not the only one.
There are many others out there who dance to his tune, sing to
his song, smile at the sound of his voice. There are many others
on the spiritual path. From my perspective, we're all on the
spiritual path, it's just that some people know it and the others
haven't seen it yet. We are all here, walking our walk. We are
all in the process of waking up. We are all, in our own ways,
coming to God, and even though we each have our own work to
do, we do not walk alone. In the Spirit-led Life, everyone serves

as a teacher and at the same time, everyone is a fellow student. The course load comes with a mighty fine cohort. We are joined in a common journey, and where we walk: it's Holy Ground. When you look at life through a spiritual lens, it's all Holy Ground.

I am following Jesus and I've got a few more lessons yet to learn, though if you're going strictly by that standard, I'll be here forever, and some of the lessons I have to learn can only be learned in the leave-taking. I look at the whole of my life and I say: so far, so good. I am glad for the work that I have done and for what the Holy Spirit has accomplished in me.

I've learned some big lessons and I've been fortunate enough to meet some darn good teachers. It's been a pretty good ride... a wild ride, but those bumper cars, they're not all bad. And my burdens, many of them have, in fact, become a blessing. They led me to where I am and to the person I am, and as they say in the old gospel song: I wouldn't take nothin' for my journey now.

*And the Word became flesh and lived among us, and we have seen
his glory, the glory as of a father's only son, full of grace and
truth…From his fullness we have all received, grace upon grace.*
(John 1:14, 16)

Grace: to be continued…

On the street where I live, there aren't many lights. It's a lovely neighborhood, but dark, and when the winter comes, you have to watch out… watch out for kids walking home from the bus and for people out rushing their dogs around the block. In the dark, danger lurks around every corner. All the time, you have to be alert. Closer to home, I see the lights, porch lights and the little twinkle lights that hang on our stairs year round, just to keep things bright, at least on the inside.

When I was a little girl, I traveled through the dark on foot or on my brother's Stingray bike, and as I went, walking or wheeling, I would look in at the houses as I passed by. I would look into the lit windows and wonder: Who lives here, and what's it like? Even now, driving across the wide expanse of Wyoming at dusk, a lone house sits on the empty plains and I wonder: who lives out there and why? An apartment above a bar in downtown Racine; a trailer in the hollows of Tennessee; or a house in the hills above San Francisco: I wonder, who lives in there, and what it is like on the inside?

Years ago, when we first moved to Wisconsin, my husband and I bought an old house, a lovely Queen Anne along the lake. It was grand and it looked to me like home. I took some pictures and showed it to my friends. I pointed to the gables and the trim and the lovely little balcony off the upstairs bedroom. I tell them that I'm feeling hopeful, that this will be a place of peace. It's lovely, Jeanette says, but peace, I think, is an inside job.

Peace is an inside job. The peace of Christ; it comes from within, and even though I am longing for peace, I am no longer willing to wait for it to simply show up. I am willing to work for well-being in the world, but I am not waiting on the world to make me well. I am old for my years and running out of runway. I'm tired of waiting, waiting for the world to change, for other people to change; tired of waiting for someone else to set me free - to approve or certify or endorse, to sign off and give me permission to start my life. No more waiting for the children to go to bed, or get home at night, or graduate from college. No more waiting until I retire, or for wars to cease; no more waiting for death in order to become more fully alive.

Thanks be to God! It's Jesus again. He dances a little jig.

Maybe you're finally getting it, he says. Maybe I'm finally getting through to you. I came so that you can have a full, rich, abundant life, and you don't have to die in order to get it. In fact, that would be counter-productive. The Kingdom of God has already begun and you don't have to go through the Pearly Gates to get in. You don't even have to move into a better house or a nicer neighborhood. All you have to do is open the door and welcome me in.

Internal Family Systems does just that. It helps me welcome God. It gives me a way to work for peace in the world, and that peace begins with me. I must be the light that I would bring. That's the way to overcome darkness. I bear the light. The light of God, it shines in me.

Sometimes the darkness can still overtake me. My lens is distorted and at times my vision limited. My jar of clay, it's wrinkled for sure, if not completely cracked. But, it seems to be enough. I seem to be enough. I look out at the world through

Christ's own eyes, and we are not deceived. The world is still a mess. The difference – it's in me. I've got a C or two on board; a little Self. I am a Self within the sea of Self.

There must be something to this model, because the world looks different to me now. I look different to me now. I look at me through eyes of love. More than what I used to anyway. I see it all: my good, my bad, but what I feel the most is grace, the grace of God; and every now and then, some peace.

Grace: it's so amazing. It makes you wonder, why does anyone turn away? It's our human nature, our parts and the burdens that they bear.

Some of them do not trust.

Some of them are afraid of change.

Some of them don't want to give up their roles.

Some of them are afraid, and others hold on to hurt.

Some of them feel guilt and shame; they hide.

Some of them hate what they've been taught about God.

Some of them have no relationship with Self.

Parts like this can take the lead. They dominate, and they can be so strong that I forget that there's more to me than my parts. I lose my way. In the worst of times, I can lose all sense of Self. I forget all about God. I hate it when that happens.

Many people picture hell as a particular place, a land of torment, but if you're asking me, hell is not so much a place as it is a state of being, and you don't have to die in order to get there. Hell is what happens when you lose all sense of Self, when you disconnect from God. There are many ways to disconnect from your Soul. You can get caught up in an explosive rage that turns outward in violence and hate. You can get lost in a chronic sense of responsibility that makes you resentful and self-righteous. You can lose your Self in the haze of addiction. You might simply dissolve into puddles of need.

We get separated from God, and when we do, we suffer. If you've ever been there, you know: you'd rather be dead. You usually wish you were dead.

Some of us are as good as dead, though yet we live.

I feel empty, Claire says, dead on the inside. I don't know what happened to me. I used to be so full of life. I used to be the life of the party, but not anymore. Something's missing. Something in me died. It's gone forever and I'll never get it back.

I listen and it seems likely to me that she is right. Some part of her has died. It might have been a slow death over time, failure to thrive. Or it might have come in a flash, parts severed from the Self in times of traumatic experience.

Usually it's the young who get sacrificed in this way; the young, vulnerable and lively parts of us get buried alive or blasted into outer space. We have survived difficult life circumstances, but we are not yet fully alive. We are not fully alive because these deadened parts still belong to our inner system and they hold elements of our life force. Apart from them, we may survive, but we will not thrive.

Parts of us may have the experience of death, but it is not true that they are gone forever. They are held in a state of suspended animation, in the hell of separation from the Self, and there they wait. They wait for us. Embodying the Spirit of Christ, we are now the seekers of lost sheep, the searchers for lost treasure, the lights that shine in the dark. Our parts wait for Self. They wait for God to gather them up in the arms of love, to bring them back into the light and breathe them back into life. Christians call this resurrection, and it happens with the inside just as it does with the outside.

Jesus said, "I am the resurrection and the life. Those who believe in me, even though they die, will live, and everyone who lives and believes in me will never die." It's the same energy for life that we find unleashed in the IFS model through the presence of Self and in the power of Self-energy. This is the same process of divine love which always seeks our healing and always looks to reconnect us with our soul. Behold, Jesus says, I stand at the door and knock... and knock... and knock.

It's never too late.   The invitation stands, whether we know it or not.   Self is always there, whether we believe it or not.   As Bono says, it's not that I believe in love, it's Love that believes in me.   Divine Love: it does not let us go and will not let us go.

All it takes is a little Self; a little Jesus in the room.   It's good to check, just to be sure.   I run through those eight "C"s of discernment, just to be sure that I'm in Self and not leading from a part, not even a Self-like part.

Yeah, Jesus says, it's like that old joke. What's the difference between you and God?   …God doesn't think he's you.

Jesus laughs, but I am not amused.

I'm doing my best, I say. I'm back to whining. Following you is a lot harder than you would think. It might be simple, but it sure isn't easy.

Never mind, Jesus says. Come on down. Grace is waiting behind doors #1, 2, *and* 3.   Let's make a deal. I'll live in you, if you live in me.

Do we get to live happily ever after?   This is what I want to know.

Absolutely, he says. I am the life that will never, never die. I'll live in you, if you live in me.

And with that, we're on the road again. God knows where, but it looks to be another Explore.   This time I'm hoping to be there for all of it.   It's the only way to go: fully present and fully alive, in tune with parts, yet filled with Self, and a song in my heart -- the Spirit-led Life.

Spirituality and the Internal Family Systems Model; Conversation with Richard C. Schwartz

How did you get to be a marriage and family therapist?

Well, there are several answers to that. The simplest one is that I got interested a little bit in psychology in college, but it was rat psychology. It didn't fit for me that much but my father got me a job at the psych unit at the hospital where he worked, at Rush, here in Chicago, and so I did that for about four summers in a row.

I was an occupational therapy aide and I would get to know these kids really well. I could see that, when they were in the hospital, they would do a little better. They would tell me about their sessions with their analysts. It was a very analytic place. But I could also see -- because I would come back on holidays and work there, and in the summer -- the kids would go home and get all screwed up again, and then come back.

I got really close to one girl in particular. I was working on weekends and I would be in the day room when her family came to visit. I would hear them berate her and scapegoat her horribly, that she was embarrassing them because she was in the hospital and so on. Then she would tell me about these stupid sessions with her therapist where if she wouldn't start a conversation, he wouldn't say a word the whole session. I just thought: there's got to be a better way. And then she wound up killing herself.

But this was before I ever heard of anything like family therapy. This was in the early 70's. I had a friend who talked about community psychology, and I thought: well, at least they're working with a bigger system. So I looked around for a program that might be good for that. There was something called a master's degree in community mental health at Northern Illinois. I went there and quickly learned that I wasn't any good in organizing communities and developing programs. I also wasn't really good at not having really clear outcomes and not getting reinforcement of your work.

While I was there, I heard about family therapy. There was a guy who had just come there named Earl Goodman, who was a family therapist and was in the counseling department. I hooked up with him and lowered my sights from changing big communities to changing families. I was introduced, through him, to systems thinking and got really excited about that. I began to see a few families not knowing what the hell I was doing. Then I graduated and decided to call myself a family therapist.

I got hired by that same psychiatry department where I had worked and got paid to be sort of a token family therapist. I was there about a year in Chicago and it became clear that I didn't really know that much about what I was doing, that I was faking it pretty well. I decided to go back and get a doctorate at Purdue. They have a marital and family program.

In sum, I got the idea when I was on that unit, that there's got to be a better way to do this. It was out of that impetus that I ran into systems thinking, and then that took me into family therapy. What I try to do with the model is expand systems thinking to intra-psychic worlds so it is a more complete systemic way of doing therapy.

You referred to your interest in outcomes. In other places you've talked about the importance of being scientific in your approach. How did you come to embrace a component of

spirituality in your model and in your work?

I was brought into it kicking and screaming.

I wasn't very spiritual when I was a young man. I came from a fairly non-spiritual family, a scientific family, and also was in this department of psychiatry when I was working on the model. So there were a lot of forces trying to keep me from becoming very spiritual. Also, as a young man, to try to help myself with tension and anxiety, I learned Transcendental Meditation and meditated for about six or seven years straight, fairly routinely. Through that I could tell that there was a state that was different and the mantra would get me there. That gave me an inkling into there being something different inside of us.

I didn't get into any of the spirituality that went with meditating; it was mainly just a tool to calm myself down. I began to explore this internal world and then discovered that there was a way to access that state that I had tasted in meditation by getting parts to separate. I was amazed to find that when they did that, people would automatically know how to heal themselves.

Initially I thought: okay, it makes sense from an evolutionary point of view -- that just like the body knows how to heal itself, people who could do that for themselves emotionally would be selected for natural selection. I concluded that, while it is contrary to most psychotherapies, it made sense evolutionarily, so that it didn't have to jar my world as far as spirituality at that point.

But then my clients would start to have more spiritual experiences as I was doing this work with them, and in some cases getting information that seemed to be coming from outside of them that was very useful to them. In some cases the information could be coming out of an image that they would see or a presence they would sense or through some kind of light that would be shining on them, and it would be happening spontaneously. So that seemed a little weird to me.

What was that like for you, Dick?

It piqued my interest. I think it made me more sensitized for when the phenomenon would show up again. And it did in several other clients, similar kinds of experiences. Sometimes it would be an archetypal image, some person or a bird or a dolphin. Sometimes it would be Jesus, or it might be the Lord -- just kind of depended a lot on the person's belief system. These presences would be similar across clients, in what they would say and what they would encourage the person to do. Some of them were pretty active, too, and would actually help us with the work. I was very distrustful of it at first and very -- my whole thing was that the Self should be doing all this; the Self shouldn't be dependent on some external force. So I again resisted in the beginning. As they kept coming and I could see that they weren't taking over, I became pretty curious about it. My position is that if there is a phenomenon, then we should study it. We don't have to conclude anything about it, but I think William James called it radical empiricism. You don't not study something because it doesn't fit the paradigm that you come out of.

People refer to the IFS model as a psycho-spiritual model. What does that mean and how does that apply to IFS?

I think there are a lot of different meanings for that term. The obvious one is that it's a model of the psyche that includes spiritual elements. That's certainly true. In another way it's also a kind of a cosmology of the soul and the inner world of people

256

that doesn't preclude spiritual things.

Traditionally there have been religious or spiritual models of the mind and psychological ones, and they hadn't overlapped that much. It's starting to happen more with mindfulness seeping into psychotherapy. And then there has always been a Christian counselor field that turned out to be quite a large field, where therapists are bringing aspects of Christian theology into therapy. And there are other people who are more or less into Buddhism and applied Buddhism.

For most people, I think, when they go to do that, they are trying to put together two things that are fairly disparate. I've read some of Ken Wilbur's writings. They try to take an established psychological model like object relations or something like that and juxtapose it with spirituality. It's almost like, at least in Ken Wilbur's case, you have object relations mapped to the lower territories and his own ideas about spirituality in the upper territories. They don't really inter-permeate that much. I think there are a number of them like that.

Like I said earlier, I didn't begin with a real spiritual outlook at all about this. It wasn't until that moment when I became convinced that people have this Self, and I didn't have any explanations for its existence short of spirituality, that I think IFS shifted in that direction. I couldn't pinpoint the exact year that happened.

In a way, it is integration, because what I'm calling Self and what other people called other names is more and more a spiritual concept. It's the centerpiece of the model, so you could say it's really a spiritual model except that it applies to psychological healing. As I said before, the parts are clearly psychological, but they contain Self. The distinction between the spiritual and the psychological really gets blurred when you start to listen carefully to these inner systems.

It's psycho-spiritual in the sense that -- not in the sense that some of it is psychological and some of it is spiritual -- but more like it's totally both and it's the same thing; it's not separate components. It's kind of hard to describe, I think, as I try to describe it.

From what you're saying, there's a way in which to separate them out is a false dichotomy to begin with.

Right.

What's it been like to introduce a psycho-spiritual model into the marriage and family arena?

My field, my own? I didn't get very far in the beginning. It was bad enough that I betrayed the true believers by focusing on intra-psychic process, but then as I got more spiritual, I think I was written off more by even more… easy to write off by a lot of people. But I think in the last decade there has been more interest in spirituality within the family therapy field too. I think within all psychotherapy, this whole movement toward mindfulness is a good example of that.

I just did a big keynote address to the annual MFT conference and I didn't throw a lot of the spirituality into it but enough, and it seemed to be a big hit. It just feels like some of the field is starting to catch up with some of these ideas, and at least take them somewhat more seriously. Along the way, I've got a lot of scars from people ridiculing me or seeing me as betraying the cause.

In my writing, I suggest that Self is the same as Soul or Spirit.

When you started studying religion and spirituality, you saw similar parallels. Why did you call it "Self" as opposed to Soul or Spirit?

Well, because that's what people would call it. I try to stay close to the language of my clients in the whole model, so when they get into that state, people would say "that's more of who I really am," or that's "my true self." That was the reason initially, and at that time, I wasn't very spiritual, so it wouldn't have made sense to call it something else.

It seems to me that your understanding of Self has evolved over time, from something that was inherently human but not necessarily spiritual, into something more transcendent.

I don't have all the answers as to what it is, and as many traditions say, those who know do not speak, and those who speak do not know. You can see it either as God in us -- like spark of the divine flame, or the place in us where God can have some access -- something like that. It depends on your religion. I know most Christians can't go to "it's God in us," and there has to be a separation between people and God, but they can go to "it's the image of God within us."

Or the relationship connection.

Where we can connect with God somehow. I don't really care about that distinction that much, it's not really that important to me.

I'm really fascinated by the parallels at all these levels, and so, when people enter this state I call "Self," they certainly act in ways that parallel the way people see God, so I've become more comfortable using the word God. I didn't used to be comfortable with that at all, but I have no trouble using "the

259

ground of being" or "spirit" or whatever else people tend to call whatever that is.

It's not about the language, it's what it describes.

Right, that's my big thing is -- language is just a tool.

One could have the idea of Self as being more an abstract life force, or an energy field, and not particularly personal at all.

There is that, and there are traditions that see it that way: many Christians, and also some psychotherapies and more spiritual psychotherapies.

Growth theories have the idea of self-actualization.

Yeah, the humanistic and the transpersonal schools. They often make a distinction between what they would call a transpersonal self, or a higher self, and then a more executive self. That higher self is more of a passive witness state -- it's more of a state of oneness and clarity and a lot of nice things, but it doesn't meddle at this level. Maybe the goal is to help this lesser self connect with that so that we have some of that wisdom.

For me that has never felt right. I've always taken the position that the Self that's doing the healing in my inner system and my client's inner system isn't really different from that more transpersonal state. It's just the same Self in different states. So when you're meditating you get very, very high -- that's you getting into that oceanic state, and then when you come back to this world, it's like photons are both particle and wave. There's a wave state and then there's also this boundaried particle state that's in this world.

The transcendent Self, or transpersonal Self, is also personal. It has a generic, universal initiating quality, but it is also unique to each person in some way. It's not impersonal. In a somewhat literal sense, it's down to earth.

There are spiritual traditions that try to spend as much time up there as possible, out of this world. That's also never felt right to me. I think it's important to spend some time there, and I try to do that, meditate occasionally, but a lot of my work has been designed to bring that more into this body, and into this world, rather than trying to get out of here as much as possible, or to leave this world as quickly as possible. So the goal of going up there is, in part, to embody more of that, and bring it here.

As that happens, people just naturally begin to expand in their ways of thinking and their ability to connect with others. They naturally begin to act the way God or Jesus or Buddha might act in this world as they become more Self-led. Again, that's what I see as the goal of the work, is to bring more of that here.

As I said, for that to happen, most of us have to learn a lot of lessons and often have to be led to those lessons kicking and screaming, in much the way you write about the Coyote Christ. The lesson plan is in the burdens we carry, and as we are forced to work with those burdens, then the burdens fall away or are transformed, and there's more room to embody.

Multiplicity is a key concept in the IFS model, but many of us think of multiplicity as a bad thing. We make moral judgments about it because we don't like the experience of it. What would you say about that – the goodness or badness of multiplicity?

Culturally, we've been taught that people with multiple

personalities are very strange, and so there's a bias against multiplicity. There's a bias towards saying you've got one brain, and you've got one body, so you should only have one mind, and the people who talk to themselves are crazy. That's been part of my crusade, to counter that whole belief system, to say that, not only is having parts and being plural inside not crazy, it's also a huge source of richness.

Now how is it a source of richness, because when all those voices are talking, it doesn't really feel that good?

When there's a huge conflict in a community of people, and there's no leadership, it doesn't feel good to be in that community either. But if you improve leadership and you help work out a lot of the conflicts and everybody gets together and works together and works in the same direction, then it's great to be in that community, and it's much better than not having a community.

So your point would be: it's not the multiplicity that's bad, it's the lack of leadership.

Lack of leadership, and all the polarizations and all the pain that drives polarizations and so on.

The solution is not to have one unified voice; it's to do the other work that we need to do around those issues.

It's not to eliminate members in the system, or to homogenize them even; it's to heal them and then celebrate the diversity of their talents and qualities.

Honoring the gifts that each one brings: that's one of the benefits of "multiplicity," both as a word and a concept. In Christianity there's been this struggle to affirm our diversity

and at the same time be one in the Spirit.

That's the paradox. I think everything surrounds that tension between the one and the many.

That's also where I love the parallels because, while it's true that inside of us there is a Self that has a lot of unity, and when all the parts are connected to it, people feel very unified -- the parts still exist. As you get to know each part more individually, you'll find that each of them is a microcosm of the person so that they have... each part has a Self, and each part has parts. I've once gotten to that next level down and found the same thing among sub-parts that have Self and parts.

At one level, especially when people meditate, it's possible to feel the unity. It's really just the Self that, in some states, is split up into lots of different entities, but when all that harmonizes, you feel the unity of it at the same time. And so, it could be the same cosmic way where there's the one God but there's these... Jesus, the Holy Spirit, whoever else, Mary, the angels... at different levels these are manifestations of God, connected to God, and at some point unified; one, and at other times, many.

That's always the struggle of trying to get your mind around the concept of Trinity, because there is that paradox of wanting to affirm the One, but also to make room for multiplicity and relationship. The important thing about divine multiplicity is that it allows for relationship, and affirms that there is a relational aspect to the Divine, or to God. It's not all hierarchical with God on a throne overlooking servants. It's the idea that we can have what Martin Buber calls that "I/Thou" relationship, and that God is interested in that same kind of relationship with us. One great thing about the model is that it acknowledges spiritual relationship all the way

through.

There are spiritual traditions that say that God decided to
subdivide for various reasons. So it was a deliberate act to
become multiple and then to help all the pieces reconnect. In a
sense you could say that's sort of what we're doing when we're
working with the individual. We're seeing how all these parts
have become disconnected from each other, and from Self, and
then we're just connecting the dots, and bringing them all back
together, which spontaneously creates this kind of inner
harmony. That may be the purpose of all this, really just learning
to reconnect both internally as parts to each other and to Self, but
also as people in order to connect at that Self-to-Self level.

**And that's such an important part, I think, of what IFS helps
illuminate for Christianity, because there's the same idea that
God creates us for relationship and the path is about that
reconnection with God, finding ways to reconnect. It's just
that in certain strains of the Christian tradition, there's the idea
that you reconnect with God by abandoning yourself instead
of reconnecting all the way through, with all the different parts
of you. With IFS, you get connected to God's spirit within so
that all of you gets reconnected with God, every part of you.**

Yeah, those parallels apply there too. So if you can come
to accept the parts of you that seem unacceptable, or seem totally
shameful, you can connect with those parts, and see they aren't
what they are seem, and bring them back into your inner family.
You can do the same with people who seem unacceptable, or are
outcasts as well. That's really the most profound thing that
came out of the Mississippi experience, when a guy named Bill
Richardson said that what we're trying to do internally is what
Jesus tried to do externally. And I think that's right. That was
when I started to wake up and say, whoa, I should look more
into this.

When people get to that part in this book, a light bulb seems to go off. They begin to understand. It's like a paradigm shift that helps them get not only the model, but the Christian faith.

Well… good.

In the IFS model, we value multiplicity and respect the multiple perspectives of our parts. It begs the question, does multiplicity lead to relativity? It would be easy to put IFS in the postmodernist camp in which everything is relative and there is no ultimate truth.

No, this is definitely not postmodern in that sense. It's also not a modernist theory; at least, I hope not, where there is an absolute truth. My position is very… I don't know if it's possible to know the absolute truth. All we can do is construct maps, but the more we stay close to the phenomena, the more accurate the map.

I think there are various positions. There are some positions that say there is no absolute truth, and there are other positions that say there is an absolute truth, but you can't know it because of the lack of quality of our instruments, which is more of my position, I think. But there are closer and further away approximations, and there are more distortions of that truth -- more or less distorted versions of that truth.

To whatever degree IFS is a less distorted version, is related to whatever degree I was able, at some point, to put aside most of my preconceptions and really just try to listen carefully to what I was being taught. I don't believe that it's an absolute truth. I don't believe that I've got the corner on what the whole cosmic game is about. It's not thinking that I know everything, that I've put it all together. It's trusting that there are wiser beings than me that I can rely on, and that what I've put together has come from them, and that it's one of these less distorted maps, even though it's not the actual territory.

What makes it less distorted?

I think because I got out of my own way at some point.

You said something in your answer about staying close to the phenomenon... in terms of your own experience of staying close to the spiritual phenomenon...

But also staying close to what my clients were saying. Instead of, when they were telling me about their parts, instead of saying, oh, this is one of my client's interjects and all the connotations that that would carry to it, and how that would guide me to relate to it, or have them relate to it... I didn't do that. Instead I just helped my clients get curious, and I got curious, and then we tried to ...

So you're talking about being open and listening...

Yeah, and not having my preconceptions and my own burdens influence what was created, and allowing my clients to tell me when I was going off, which happened many times. So if I'm proud of anything, it's that I really did let them teach me, rather than me imposing things.

And, in turn, one of the goals of the model is to help clients do that with their own experience so that they too can be open. One of the spiritual benefits of IFS is that it helps people to be more open to spiritual presence and open to their own experience of God.

Yeah, it's what keeps the whole thing organic, because as

we all in the IFS community stay curious, we're still learning lots of stuff, and the model continues to evolve, and there are still beliefs about it that are shifting. That's the delightful aspect of it.

That's where it parallels with the Christian idea of discernment and spiritual journey, that if you use that as a motif. You're always on the path, you're always walking and it helps to discern the presence of God as you're walking. We talk about a kind of praying without ceasing, so that kind of awareness, that God-awareness, is something that is, ideally, more continuous.

Dick, there are a lot of people out there who have some extreme parts, people who abuse children, or have committed great violence, or caused just a lot of pain and destruction, so given that, how have you come to believe that everyone has a Self, even people who do such terrible things?

You know, of course, I didn't believe that in the beginning because I had traditional training like you have and learned in psychology that only people that have a certain kind of parenting could have that kind of ego strength inside of them. As children, it's a critical period. If you didn't get that, you were out of luck.

As I was starting to play around with this and was finding this little technique I stumbled onto -- asking parts to separate -- the people would start to manifest these qualities that I couldn't believe was in them. It rocked my world and just took me a long time of seeing it happen over and over to believe it. And then as I began to work with the various populations of people that had very extreme parts, like a consultant to a place for juvenile sex offenders for about seven years, and to another place for really severely acting-out kids, and then did some work on inpatient units at the University of Illinois, Chicago, and so worked some with psychotic people, and as I tried to see if even those people had this, and as we'd get parts to separate, they would also manifest it. People with dissociative identity disorder, all those people -- we could actually get them in this state where Self was there.

Over the years it just became harder to buy the idea that that was pumped into them through parenting or some other external experience. It had to be something inherent to them. If people with these backgrounds, people who had been tortured, and a number of clients who'd had ritual abuse experiences -- people who had the worst kind of torture you could ever imagine, and they still had this place that was not harmed by that, and was the same, really, as the Self in people, in other kind of garden variety clients that I'd been working with… I started to cross over to the belief that it's in everybody. And then, as I said earlier, I first believed that that was an evolutionary reality, and now believe that it's more of a spiritual reality.

It seems like that would be a message of great hope, or if there's a good news of IFS, that would be it.

Yeah, the gospel of IFS.

The gospel according to Dick Schwartz.

It's that everybody's got that in them, and that there aren't any bad parts, which is equally hopeful. Even parts of the sex offenders that I worked with… all the suicidal parts, once you get to know them, will confess that they aren't what they seem, but they're stuck with the burdens that drive them in ways that they don't like, and would love to get rid of them. That seems to fit in some ways with what Christ taught, and in some ways contradicts what the church has done with it. It fits in the sense that everyone is redeemable.

So this is a struggle within the Christian tradition where, on the one hand, we really like the good news that everybody can be redeemed, or there are not bad parts, and, on the other hand, we find it extremely offensive. It's offensive to think that there are no bad parts.

Why is it offensive?

Because they're obviously doing bad things, and causing a lot of destruction.

I think that's the place where lots of traditions have gotten stuck. Wanting to believe that there's some inherent goodness, but how do you reconcile that with the destruction and the deliberate hurtfulness that's manifest in human nature?

I think that one of the things that IFS brings is an answer that in some ways does reconcile with Christianity. As I began to work with these parts, and they would talk about this thing that was in them, or on them, that was driving them to be extreme -- the more we got to know what that was, finding that it didn't really belong in their systems, their bodies, and it had come from the outside world, and that they could actually take it out of them, once they felt safe to do that -- once they got permission to do that, and once my client's Self understood where they got that, what I call a burden, in the past -- once that came out of them, they immediately transformed into their naturally valuable state.

The mistake that most psychotherapies and religions and our culture has made has been is to assume that the parts are what they seem, and so how could that be good? How could a part of a person that drove them to molest a little girl, how could that be redeemable, how could that be good?

269

But if you understand the concept of burdens, and the way burdens are ingested from the outside, and how once unburdened the part will transform immediately like a spell has been broken or a virus is out of their body that has been driving them, then it could make sense that there is a level of what might be called evil or sin, but it isn't inherent in us or in these parts of us; it comes into us. I think that reconciles this whole are people good or bad question.

As I understand it the Christian definition of sin is anything that separates a person from God, and that's exactly what these burdens do, they separate the parts from their Self, and they separate the person from accessing their guides or God. As people unburden, those connections just naturally start to develop and people feel much more spacious; they feel these open channels to the divine that were being blocked by burdens.

You're not minimizing the fact that parts can do bad things.

I think that's been a problem with some psychotherapies that in trying to say that everybody has good intentions, and everybody's basically good, they tried to paper over the bad things that families do to each other, for example. And I am saying that, no, these parts can be totally bad, and destructive and damaging, deliberately hurtful, but it's not the part doing that, it's the burden it carries that's doing that, and if we unburden that …

Or the part is doing that because of the burden it carries.

The part is doing that because of the burden it carries. Also, because it's trying to protect the more vulnerable parts. It's part of the system. Just like family therapy's big contribution was saying that you can't take the kid out of the family and expect the changes in that kid to last; you can't see a part in isolation from the set of relationships it's imbedded into and the burdens that it carries. But in terms of this question, are people good or bad: people are good, but we all acquire burdens through personal experience. Also through what we inherit from what we call legacy burdens that come into us through a family transmission, that can go throughout decades, or through ethnic group transmission, or through just the culture we're raised in. Those are what cut us off from Self and from God and what drive parts to be extreme.

So one message would be not to take bad behavior or a bad person at face value.

Right. If you see it as a part -- that's one level of not blaming the person totally, and then when you, say, take it another level, which is hard for a lot of people -- that even the part that did that behavior isn't bad, and at the same time you're not excusing what happened, you're actually trying to help the person achieve more accountability and responsibility in the sense of the ability to respond. While the part is carrying the burden, the person really has no choice but to really try to suppress it and hope for the best, and finds that in trying to suppress it, that makes the part fight back even harder.

So it's kind of an inner conflict that Christians talk about, where the harder they try to suppress what they think of as their base instincts, the more overcome they become with moments of weakness, which becomes a self-fulfilling, self-replicating prophecy. The more the part takes over, then the more frightened they become, the more dangerous they see it, the more they try to lock it up, so the stronger it becomes, and the more it tries to take over.

IFS and Christianity have similar goals. The end point would

271

to free the person and their system, or this part in the inner system, to free them, or liberate them, or heal them, or whatever it is, so they don't have to keep doing what they do. It's more that the approach is different. This doesn't come through judgment, blaming, shaming, scapegoating or cutting off; those things don't work.

Right, the goal is very similar in the sense that both traditions are trying to release the sins that people carry, if you allow for burden to be the same as sin.

The extent to which we are able to live harmoniously and connected spiritually on the inside has the capacity to greatly enhance our relationships in the outside world.

Yeah, as I say, it's all parallel. So to the degree to which we can do what Jesus would advocate, which would be to go to the exiles, to the lepers in our inner system, or the prostitutes, or whoever else he hung around with, and embrace them, and save them, in the sense of unburden them, which brings them into line with God in the inner world, with the Self, is to the same degree to which we can do that with people who otherwise would trigger us, because they're similar to these parts that we don't like in some ways. So how we relate internally to these different inner manifestations of God will dictate how we relate to the external manifestations.

I'm not sure I got that last part. How we relate to our internal manifestations of God?

Well, how we relate to our parts.

How we relate to our parts is likely to be how we relate to people.

272

Will translate into how we relate to people.

Right, so if we can learn to relate to our parts as Jesus did, we will more than likely be able to relate to other people as Jesus did.

Yeah. And if we can't do that, then the effort of trying to be Jesus-like with other people will involve locking up the parts of us that aren't that way, and will involve major effort and artificiality. We all know these pious people who are trying to be Christ-like when you know that it's totally hypocritical, or you know that it's a big strain for them to try and be nice to you, and they're dominated by parts that are very rigid, rigidly trying to make them nice.

They're trying to be Christ-like but it doesn't come from an authentic place within.

Right, it comes from these managerial parts of them that have learned that this is how you are Christ-like, and we're going to beat you until you are like that.

The beatings will continue until you are like Jesus.

Yeah, until morale improves.

IFS is another way to make the Christian experience more real?

Yeah, to make it more natural, to make it more spontaneous and embodied. You know how to make it who you are, not who you have to force yourself to be.

Okay, so Christianity has this strong tradition of self-sacrifice, this idea that you should lay down your life for your friends -- that you should not only bear your burdens, but take on the

burdens of another, so what do we make of that? Aren't we supposed to be helping others, Dick?

Yeah, but again, you can't force it. We should forgive people that hurt us...we should do all these things. Those are all things that, once people become Self-led, they do naturally and spontaneously, but until they become Self-led, the only way to get there, the only way to do those kind of things is to become dominated by the "should" parts, these very pious holy parts that are slave-driving us into being like that. My approach is to not tell people how they should live in any way, but instead help them unburden and find that they start to spontaneously become more Christ-like.

So take forgiveness for example, there's this big movement stemming from the Christian tradition, I think, for what I call "premature forgiveness," where you're supposed to know that the person was flawed and that's why they hurt you and show them compassion and let it go. While at the same time, there are parts of you that are still in total pain because of what that person did, and parts that are also enraged at that person. To pull that off you have to lock up those parts and just stifle and shut them down. If instead you are able to go to the rage and get permission and go to the pain, heal the pain, come back, unload the rage, then you have the choice about forgiving. Most people at that point see through the eyes of the Self, which in this sense has x-ray vision. When people look through the eyes of their Self, they usually can see the pain in the person that drove their extreme hurtful behavior. And they will have spontaneous compassion for that person. But it's not forced, it's not something that they have to try and achieve.

Maybe it's not unlike Desmond Tutu's Truth and Reconciliation Commission in South Africa, where the whole point was forgiveness, but it meant going through their

process of listening to the pain and really getting what it meant for the one who is suffering.

Yeah, although that experiment wasn't ideal - there were a lot of lessons learned on how to do that better. Because they would go into communities and spend two days having people testify as to what happened to them and stir everybody up and...

Okay, so maybe the converse is true... that you can stir all that stuff up, but if you're not coming at it from a place of Self...

If you don't unburden it, if you don't actually heal it, you just bring all the extreme parts out.

Right, which has also turned out to be true for trauma, just getting people to relive those experiences without unburdening it can be destructive.

Or without the Self witnessing.

Right.

Stirring it up and then leaving after two days can just stir it all up without any good end.

This is also one of the questions my clients often have about doing this kind of work when they start. What's the point? Why drag all this stuff out of the past, why stir it up?

So my constant answer is: we're not going there to stir it up, we're going there to unburden it. We're going there to unload it, but to really unload it you first have to see it, and know what happened, and help the part get that you got it. You don't relive it but you have to return to it.

When we talk about healing, what kind of healing are we talking about with IFS?

Well, healing... the idea is that we enter the world with some unburdened parts, probably some burdened parts because of what we call legacy burdens and in the beginning, there probably is some trust in Self leading. Parts trust Self from infancy, and then life happens. Through both the kind of injuries that happen in attachments as children and traumas that happen, parts become more burdened, so they take on more and more of these extreme beliefs and emotions, and become more governed by those.

And they also, because they weren't protected by who they thought was the leader inside, they become less trusting in the system. From that point, because there isn't adequate leadership, and because a lot of the parts are already to the extreme, they start to polarize internally and they also lock up the ones that are the most hurt. The system transforms from what you might think of as a healthy system, to one that has these managers, firefighters and exiles, and very little Self leadership. Healing reverses that.

What we call healing involves several different steps. The most obvious one is the release of the burdens. It's obvious because when they are released, parts immediately transform into their naturally valued states, so they seem healed, and then we invite qualities in to seal the deal. After that, that particular part is in much better shape.

What's still maybe not evident is that there are still polarizations, and there still are other parts that are locked up and burdened, and there's still a lack of trust in Self leadership. That's why when we go to do the work of unburdening or interacting in general, we prefer, when it's possible, to have the Self be the one doing it: the Self interfaces with the parts. We're connected to the Self as therapists, because, for me, healing involves both the release of these burdens but then also the restoration of Self-trust and Self leadership; re-harmonizing the whole system to the point that parts get along with each other and can work together. The person can, internally, feel more and more in unison because there aren't these huge schisms inside. The exiles aren't locked up anymore, and none of the former exiles, firefighters, or managers fit those designations anymore, because they are flexible and doing things that they much prefer and they really trust the Self to lead and keep them safe. So that's the picture of the healed system internally.

So there's the healing of individual parts -- the exiles, the burdens; there's the healing of the relationship between parts themselves; there's the healing of the inner system ...

Healing of the relationship among parts and the restoration of the trust in leadership.

It makes sense when you come from the inside of the model. When we talk about the model to the outside, to people who don't know it... how to explain it... healing in IFS is one of those things that the usual categories don't quite fit.

Yeah. People can identify with the idea that they carry very, very powerful, and maybe ancient emotions, and beliefs about Self, so the idea that that's what we're getting to and that's what we're releasing... people understand that as healing.

Right, yeah, because to understand the healing, you have to understand what the problem is, or what the issue is. And if you define the problem in a different way -- healing is so often now a part of the province of medicine and biology...

Right.

When I think of being healed, a lot of times I think in terms of being cured. So I'm thinking of how that fits with the model. For example, if I have issues with depression, and I have healing through IFS, does that mean that I won't ever experience depression or have issues with that again?

No. What we can offer people—well, yes and no, really. Because what we can offer people is: life is a rocky road and you can't do a lot about that, but you can improve your shock absorbers. What we can do is, by unloading some of this stuff that people carry from past shocks, from past rocks in the road, then the things they encounter in the present are just that. Their reactions are based on what's coming to them in the now, instead of whatever comes to them in the now bringing up all the stuff that is any way related to it or similar to it, from the past.

It's not like you're going to be impervious to the slings and arrows, but it's a lot easier to handle the slings and arrows. Each one doesn't go in and set off a big depth charge inside that's sitting there because of similar things that happened to you earlier.

People may still get depressed. Let's say you get rejected by a girlfriend, you'll feel sad about that, but it won't bring up the fact that your mother wasn't there for you and abandoned you in some way when you were young and totally powerless and your life was at stake, which is what a lot of people feel when they feel rejected. It's like, I'm never going to be the same; I'm going to die.

That's coming from that part that's stuck back in time

when that was true. So now, you get rejected and feel really bad about it, but you don't feel like you're going to die. There is Self in there who can say, but I'm still here with you, I still love you, to that part. A lot of times that's really the main thing these parts need ultimately. They can't get everything from Self but they need the sense that even if this person leaves, there is somebody still there -- they're not totally bereft and alone. Self leadership can provide that.

In the western world we kind of think that healing is something that's biological and belongs to the practice of medicine. How do you see the relationship between the IFS model and medicine? How does the model factor into physical well-being?

Just like I was saying about spirituality and psychology, to me, this form of psychological healing is hard to separate from physiological healing. And the reason for that is, that parts and their burdens will powerfully affect your physiology. Some parts will use aspects of your physiology to either make a statement, or try to break through and get you to notice them, or punish you for breaking rules they have. There's a whole variety of ways parts will use people's bodies for their purposes. As things harmonize and there is less need to do that, as these parts can be heard and as they give up the beliefs that you should be punished for certain things, then they start letting the body alone too. They stop trying to use it and people start to heal physically too.

So, I'm not saying that it can replace medicine, and I'm also not saying there aren't such things as viruses and genetic predispositions and germs, bacteria, but what I *am* saying is there are a lot of chronic problems that don't respond to traditional medical treatment and part of the reason for that is because parts are using them.

279

And then also, whenever there's a medical symptom, it's sort of the same as in physical systems where you have a bacteria enter the system and there's all these cells that mobilize to combat it; a lot of autoimmune problems are an over-reaction to a perceived invasion. The same things happen with parts. When a part begins to affect an organ in the body, then there's another set of parts that will combat that somehow.

Also, there are physical problems that result just from the battleground. It's sort of like the body becomes an innocent bystander in this conflict between parts sometimes. Sometimes you have to start by just getting the parts that are reacting to the physical changes to back off, and then you can go to the parts that might be involved in creating it.

The other thing about physical things, it turns out that… I don't know if this is true with all people, but with a lot of people I've worked with, there are parts that know how to do physical healing but sometimes get exiled too. So you can find parts involved in the symptoms but then you can also find parts that know how to heal the body and haven't been able to be accessed, and bring those forward too, and that's very powerful.

Are there certain physical conditions that respond more naturally to IFS than others?

Well, the physical conditions I focus on the most are co-morbid with survivors of sex abuse, because that's been my population. There are a lot of what have often been considered psychosomatic conditions that I've worked with very effectively. We've also been doing research on arthritis. We hope to do research on other kinds of medical conditions that aren't traditionally thought of as psychosomatic necessarily, but which have responded very well. There's a variety of neurological conditions that French neurologist Francois Le Doze has been working with. I hope to be able to bring this to diabetes and just a whole range of things that I think this could have a big impact on. And also to the parts that drive people to do extreme things that then result in disease.

Such as?

Diabetes is very clearly related... secondary diabetes is very clearly related to being over-weight and eating lots of sugar, and those almost always are firefighters. I think there's a lot that we can do with prevention, too, for conditions that are related to behavior... so, behavioral medicine.

Historically, the art of healing has been part of religious traditions and spiritual practices. Some of these healing practices can be helpful, but others can be destructive or dangerous for people. So what makes for a good or a bad healing?

The litmus test for me has to do with how much the healer is involved and how much the healer is trusting in the Self of the client, the person being healed. So those practices that involve a kind of blind faith, that there's this person that can do this to you, I think they are not always harmful but they can be, because the ego of the person can get involved and become exploitative.

But they aren't nearly as helpful as practices that actually encourage the healee to do it themselves, because that's just much cleaner and leaves the person feeling like they did it themselves and they can continue to do it themselves. There's a lot less danger of the kind of dependence that leads to exploitation when you're working through the client's Self.

I do think that placebo has a lot to do with some practices. I think you can build up somebody's trust to the point where they totally believe in a kind of hypnotic way that what you're going to do is going to work for them. And it will work for them for a period of time. I think these parts that know how to heal are kind of sucked in for a period of time, but because the actual problem hasn't really been addressed -- the issues that the parts have for using that organ in the first place -- then it will regress after a while, which to me is what placebo is.

So some of the healings then maybe work for awhile in addressing the symptoms or how it's being manifested, but you're saying... unless you get to the function of what that serves or what the part is...

Yeah, if it doesn't touch the part, that is, I mean... if you're simultaneously unburdening that part, then it may well last. If not, then the part will either make it come back, or it'll find some other organ to attack, or find some other way to get the client's attention or punish them. There are forms of energy work that I do think unburden parts without all the rigmarole that we go through, without witnessing, without unburdening in a formal way.

The issue I have with that... there are two issues. One is, again, there's a need for the healer to do it, and then the second is: I just feel... we're here to learn lessons, and the lesson plan is in our burdens. A lot of the learning comes in the witnessing we do when we ask parts to show what happened originally, and as we watch that, and we have such compassion for ourselves, then we both learn what took place when this happened, but we also now have a new compassion for people who've suffered in a similar way. And that's a lot of what we're here to do. You miss all that with these sort of quick ways of releasing burdens.

282

For generations, Christians have tried to articulate the relationship between our spirit and our flesh. How do you describe the relationship between Self and parts?

Self and parts of the body?

To me, the body is the container for Self and parts and our parts will use our body for their purposes. The burdens our parts carry are denser energies so they clog up our body, make it harder for our Self to embody. So when parts want to punish us, they will use our body to do that often. If they are exiled and they want to script our lives, because they've been exiled, or they want to get some message through in some way, they'll use our bodies that way.

So the body can be a battleground. It can be a message system, in which we try to kill the messenger more often than not, by surgeries, or pharmaceuticals, or drown the messenger. And our bodies can be a temple when our parts have unburdened, are in harmony and open space for us to really be in our bodies. When that's possible, we can live in the present, because Self basically does a lot of the work that people have to do so laboriously to meditate so that they can be in their bodies or can live in the present—it can just happen spontaneously.

So parts are not specifically identified with the body, but the body is the medium of communication.

Yeah, people will be able to locate most parts in their body someplace. Different parts tend to be located in some areas, but that can shift. And it doesn't mean that that body part is where the part lives in any way; it's just that may be what organs it tends to use, so that's what you notice.

Okay, and what about Self and the body?

283

Well, yeah, Self often becomes disembodied when we've suffered various kinds of traumas. Burdens come in and fill up the body, and there are protectors who think that Self can be hurt, so they try to move it out of the body so it isn't hurt in the face of trauma, which is why there are these reports of watching yourself being hurt or being amnesiac, because you were in some other world while the body was being hurt.

Where does Self go when it's not in the body?

I don't really know. I mean, it's around. It doesn't disappear, but it's not in the body. When we work with people, we can ask somebody, how much are you in your body? They'll usually tell you a percentage. And you can ask parts to open more space so Self can be more in the body.... there is a kind of vibrating energy that I feel a lot when I'm fully embodied and that a lot of people feel that indicates that you are much more in your body. Self can't operate as well if it's not in the body, and parts don't trust the leadership of the Self as much if it's not in the body.

Say more about that, because that seems like that's a very important concept, both in terms of Self and parts, and also for our human understanding of spiritual limitations of God, at least in this realm.

I think that's another fascinating parallel to Christianity where there's this question of: "Why hast thou forsaken me?" How could this God, who's so powerful and so caring, allow this to happen to me? This is, as far as I can tell, a big question in Christianity.

And in everybody's life. Where are you when I need you? The answer generally is: God works in mysterious ways and we

can't know these things.

I don't know what the answers are in Christianity. There is a direct parallel to internal systems because, first of all, you come to some parts that say: where were you when I needed you? Why should I trust you? You let this happen to me. You let this person molest me. You didn't stop them. If you're so great, why didn't you stop them?

And there are other times where that same question goes for why, if Self is so powerful, does it allow these parts to totally take over and run things, and dominate in that way?

Parts of our lessons come with these tragedies. Trust is the big lesson, one of the big lessons, so we have to distrust to find it... have things happen that will create distrust, before we can come to trust the leadership of Self, or Jesus or God or whoever. If God or Self... if Self was always protecting the parts and didn't let anything bad happen to them, there wouldn't be anything learned. If God always did that with us, there wouldn't be anything learned.

It's a parallel with a dilemma in Christian theology. We want to affirm that there's some kind of a purpose and meaning in the things that happen but how do you balance that without getting into the idea that God is intentionally sending tragedies to people? It's a place of tension and we generally leave it to the individual to come to their own understanding of the lesson. It's really challenging when we try to tell somebody else what their lesson is. They have to find it, but we still affirm that there's value and meaning to the things that happen for those who have the eyes to see it.

You said that one of our big life lessons has to do with trust. There are strains in the Christian tradition which talk about

faith in terms of belief: an intellectual ascent to doctrine. But Paul, in another whole tradition of the Christian faith, understands faith in terms of trust... that what we're about is learning to trust God, or develop a trusting relationship with God, and that seems to fit very closely with what you're talking about in terms of Self and parts.

Yeah, parts learning to trust Self leadership, even though there have been tragedies, even though Self couldn't fully protect them. The biggest problem isn't fear, which I had thought it was, in part, but it's doubt. Doubt is the big obstacle for most people, parts that doubt the Self's leadership.

That's interesting, because I think a lot of more recent theology has gone with the idea that the opposite of faith is fear... that fear is the big issue, as opposed to doubt. So now we're going back to doubt?

I think a lot of doubt is based in fear.

Is that doubt or lack of trust, or do they mean the same?

For me it's pretty much the same. Well, lack of trust is complete doubt, right?

Well, yeah, except I think sometimes doubt might get applied to intellectual theological precepts and you're talking more relationally.

Totally relationally and nothing about anything else. So it's more lack of trust, doubt in existence of Self, or ability of Self to lead, or the connection of Self to larger Self, and so on.

Either way, I guess whether it's fear or doubt, the solution or the remedy is trust -- that if you can trust, and ultimately for

286

Christians that would be having that peace that passes all understanding -- you trust that no matter what, you're okay, and you trust that God's got you, whatever that means to you, no matter what's happening to you in the outside world.

That can be misused, too, as an opiate of the masses: just stay in your place and accept whatever government does or whatever the church does, and that's, again, coming from a part. The other quality of Self that I love so much is the courage and clarity. So when you really trust, when your parts really trust Self, and you really trust your guides or God or whatever, then you have the courage to stand up to injustice and to take care of your parts as if they were, literally, your children, so that you don't allow people to exploit you. It's the opposite of a pacifying kind of trust. Or a trust that if you just wait until you die then you'll be in a better world. When you bring Self to this world there's a natural drive for justice, and desire to create harmony, and to stand up to exploitation and abuse. Again, I think that the trust in the Lord has been also misunderstood or distorted in various ways.

Spiritual presence brings comfort, but it also brings courage. In fact, the more you embody it, the more you carry the liberation aspect of Jesus into the world, and you can do it because you know that you are safe, no matter what. It's kind of like what Martin Luther King said the night before he died... he didn't necessarily want to go to that speech that night, or whatever, but to be able to say, it's not about what happens with me now because I have a vision, a vision that is worth the risk of what might happen to me now.

Exactly.

Sometimes there's a dualism that can happen in the Christian understanding of where we think of Self, or our spirit, and

flesh as separate. Sometimes that's a language thing, but it seems like that can happen in IFS, too, that we can begin to act as if Self is a separate entity from parts. Earlier you were saying that parts have Self too.

Parts have Self and at that level it's all one, it's all connected.

So that becoming spirit doesn't mean leaving our flesh, in the same way that being more Self-led is not about abandoning our parts.

Yeah, it's really again, it's the opposite. The more you enter your body and embody Self, the more Self-led you become, because then you can more easily help your parts.

Christianity often emphasizes the transcendent aspect of Holy Spirit, the idea of God as the Other, the Divine Other. Why, from your perspective, is it important for people to develop an inner relationship with Self, or to trust the Holy Spirit as it works from within?

I think the belief that God is external has led to more of a dependence on that and the dependence on the spokespeople for God in the Christian world. That would be something I would try to counter by this suggestion that you can hear from God, whether it's God in us, or it's where God can get through to you in you -- that you can hear more directly that way. You can act from a God-like place without the mediators and also knowing that it's your action, even though it's being influenced by some other force.

What are the dangers when we get dependent on the people who speak for God?

Because then we're subject to their burdens; it's filtered through the burdens of those people. Just like with therapists who are very interpretive and are trying to tell us what's good for us. I mean, that's when I stopped being interpretive at all, is when I realized that if you listen to the parts and what they are trying to say... like I would do dream interpretation, for example, and I would be way off when I finally got to the parts. And every time I gave a misinterpretation, it decreased their trust in me. It's all being filtered through my own parts and my own stuff, and so the nice thing about this perspective is, and really is along the lines of what Jesus taught, because he was really against rabbis and priests and institutions, as far as I can tell, and really was saying: trust me, but also, and especially -- this is some of the more esoteric texts around Jesus -- he was also saying listen inside.

You can have a direct relationship with God without going through anyone else.

It seems like that was what he was all about.

It can be risky if we place too much trust in people who are designated as spokespersons for God but haven't done their own work of healing. They have burdened parts that can act out in extreme ways and hurt other people. They add to the burdens that people are already carrying and push them even farther from the direct, transforming experience of God.

Right. In Catholicism, for example, the actual process of becoming a priest, during which you renounce sexuality, not renounce it, but what would the word be, maybe you rise above it. In its own way, that can be distorting and create burdens because of the way sexuality is being portrayed and why you need to rise above it. So you're winding up exiling lots of parts. That then distorts what you teach and how God filters through

289

you.

Yeah, you create exiles that come back in extreme forms and act out within congregations.

There's a lot to be said for trusting the Self and then working to open up more connections to the Self, the big Self.

Okay, so that phrase right there is a problem: trust yourself. How can you trust yourself when you know that you've already led yourself into some bad places, you've made some bad choices? What people know from their experiences is that they can't trust themselves.

Yeah, well, the word "self" most commonly has come to be construed as the personality, and just like in a lot of other spiritual traditions, like in some areas of Buddhism and Hinduism, the ego has been the equivalent of the Self, and you can't trust it: it's a trickster; it's got all these bad impulses. You can't trust it and it pulls you down. The goal is to transcend that.

The problem, with not only Christianity, but these other spiritual traditions, is that in doing that you wind up exiling all these parts that aren't what they seem, They are -- I mean, what they say about the ego and the self is true in the way they use "the self." It is very materialistic. It is very comfort-focused and selfish in that way. Those parts, depending on how many burdens they carry, how much hurt we've had in our lives, are the way they are described, and they get in the way of us being spiritual beings.

So again, from that perspective, it makes sense to try and ignore them, at best, and maybe even fight with them or lock them up, but it doesn't work and it isn't necessary if you understand that all those cravings are simply from the burdens these parts carry -- the degree to which they feel disconnected from us, the degree to which they are protecting us, or the extent to which they have been hurt. If you work with these parts from that perspective, you unburden them. You bring them into the community of parts. You help relieve them of the responsibility of protecting and then a lot of those cravings go away. You don't have to fight them to be spiritual.

What we commonly refer to as our "self" would, in the IFS model, actually be our parts.

Yeah, self, or ego, are the parts and their burdens, the burdened parts.

What Merton calls "true Self" corresponds more closely to the model's idea of Self.

Yeah, or a soul, I guess. I don't know all the definitions of soul in Christianity. Or Christ-consciousness.

The idea of soul works. Everybody has a soul, and that spiritual dimension is what we're talking about. For Christians, we understand that after Jesus' resurrection, there's more capacity for the soul, more avenue for Holy Spirit.

Right, Jesus will save your soul, meaning maybe Jesus will access it.

Or help heal the parts.

Yeah, it's the leadership. Help unburden enough so there's some space for it.

How did you come up with the 8 C's of Self?

This is really the truth: I just needed a way to convey this concept of Self, and was very inarticulate in trying to do that, and people just weren't getting it. In my reading about it, of course, people would say you can't speak about it; it's ineffable it's unknowable, it's unspeakable.

Not very helpful, was it?

No, not very helpful. But it was clear that as I was doing the work that when people entered that state they would manifest certain qualities, so I set about to try to categorize them. At first there were six of them and it was odd that they all began with the letter C, and then a couple more that seemed really foreign. Again, I really shouldn't take credit for it. I think a lot of this was just guided too. Those eight C's are so robust that I don't think I could have dreamed them up on my own. I think that it was taught to me.

In IFS there's a key question: how do you feel toward that part? What is so important about that question?

Well, that question is important at several levels. First, it begins a clear demarcation between you and that part, so it begins a process of separating from something that you might be quite identified with. And then that there's a "you" who has feelings about this other thing. Then in answering that question, people are telling you how much Self is present or how much they're blended with other parts. So it becomes this parts detector or Self detector question.

We often talk about it as a "parts detector" but it also serves as a "Self detector" or "Spirit detector." We're trying to help people understand what it's like when we're in touch with the

Spirit. Those are the qualities.

Exactly.

We talked generally about the 8 C's but not each one. So maybe you could do that. You had come to an awareness of Self energy and the different qualities of it, so maybe just talk about each one.

As I caught on to the fact that this was there when people's parts stepped back, I got more curious about how I describe this, and most of the religious and spiritual texts said you can't really describe when it's ineffable. Clearly people were changing, they were manifesting differently, when they got in that place, so I could describe how they manifest, so I just started to think what are the qualities that show up and these 8 C's just came out of that.

The first would be compassion.

The first one to show up is usually curiosity.

Okay, and how does it show up?

People shift from "I'm really afraid of this part" or "I really hate it," to, as those parts step back, "I'm just kind of curious about why it does this, what it's doing here." Or some form of that. I'll say, okay, just follow your curiosity. And they'll talk to it. But also, they're curious and confident. Whereas they were really scared earlier, now they're not afraid of it, they're just curious about it and calm, whereas they might've been really agitated. The parts step back and they're just really calm and peaceful about it. So those three were obvious right away – curious, confident, calm.

293

And then, sometimes in addition to curious they would also have a kind of immediate intuitive hit on why the part was the way it was and have this kind of compassion for it or this sense that it doesn't like having to do what it does. They have compassion for it. Right away, when the parts step back. So those four would be kind of immediate in some cases.

And then if I were to ask the client to get closer to it or do something different, whereas seconds earlier they would be terrified to do it, now they have courage to actually go and get to know it and find out what it wants to do and so on. Whereas when they were looking at it earlier, it looked very menacing and evil, as the part separates, suddenly they see it in a totally different way and now it looks fragile, or sort of like they see past its protectors and see its exiles. So suddenly it looks younger or more fragile. So clarity comes with that and then connectedness, they'll feel some caring. They'll want to connect with it; they'll want to help it.

When their parts were around, they wouldn't have many options for how to deal with it, but they'll have this sudden kind of sense of: oh, it needs this, and they can be creative with how they relate to it.

It's interesting as you describe it because it sounds very fluid and organic. It's not like there's this self-conscious: "Oh, look, now I've got courage." It's just there.

Yeah, just suddenly they are like that. They manifest all that in their actions.

And as therapists and practitioners, we track the qualities of Self as they appear in our clients, but for the most part clients are not striving toward those qualities. They are just there.

It just comes. It's sort of the critical mass as parts separate. It's right there; it's not something they have to try to pull in. I think that's part of what is radical about this position in IFS -- it's that you don't have to work to get there; it's just there. Whereas most other systems you have to do something to get into that state.

As you put together the 8 C's, did you then cross-reference them with other spiritual traditions to see where they match?

Not too much. People told me that they matched some systems. But it was much more just the comparing notes with other IFS people and just trying to put it together.

People, when they experience the 8 C's, seem to they know when they're in Self.

Clients, you mean?

Yeah.

It's amazing how often they will use some of those words to describe how they feel. Most clients, when you get their parts to separate and you ask how they feel, will use one or more of those words.

It's been interesting for me, as I've taught them to people in the church, that a lot of them make sense to them immediately. They struggle with the idea of curiosity, just because they haven't really been encouraged to be curious, for one thing, and then the other is all the negative messages about how, in fact, you aren't supposed to be curious. You're not supposed to ask and explore. You're supposed to be obedient. Curiosity is what leads you astray.

Killed the cat.

Exactly, or gets you into trouble. What they understand is when I talk about the innocent curiosity of a child as opposed to a voyeuristic or prurient interest in other people. Creativity is another one that people sometimes struggle with because they have parts that have so taken on the idea that they're not creative. Some of it for people is expanding their understanding of what each of these qualities really are. We have narrow definitions. But there's something else. There are parts that have these same qualities but it's coming from a part, not Self. What's the difference and how can you tell?

Well, it turns out that parts have Self. So parts are little replicas of a larger system. Parts have parts that have Self. When they're healing parts in Self, it'll resemble a lot of those qualities. Sub-parts also have Self in parts, it turns out -- these nested systems. I don't know how far it goes down. At each level, when Self manifests it's the same. It's just one piece of it when nested within its larger system. One way to think about it is that our Self is nested in some other system that contains Self, too, which we call God. Who knows if that's nested in something else.

What's the difference between a part that has a quality of Self and being "in Self," and how might that be a problem?

There are parts that can sort of be… get you in a pseudo-Self state where… like there's some parts that pretend to be very spiritual and make you feel very lofty and good about your spirituality, but they're also protectors who are trying to keep you away from other parts that they don't think are so spiritual. There are parts that can seem very compassionate, but as you get to know them, their compassion is really defensive in the sense that, if they get you to take care of everybody else, then you

296

won't look at certain things, or take care of yourself. There are parts that are kind of curious about everything, but again, it's a way to not have to look at things inside yourself. You could take each of those C words and describe a part that uses that quality but uses it as parts use things, for some kind of protective role.

The way you tell is, if you stay with it long enough, the part will kind of tip its hat. It'll show that it isn't pure Self, that there's some agenda behind that piece of good quality, and then you say, okay, let's get this part to separate too.

I imagine they're not happy about that.

That can be very disconcerting for people who are identified with all these Self-like parts. When one separates, some people have an "Oh my God, I'm nobody now" until they really get to know who there is.

Especially if they're serving the protective function of keeping you away from the "not spiritual" parts.

Yeah, then they get really scared that you might be swarmed by those parts to do something bad.

Related to that is the quality of an oceanic state that people sometimes describe, which can be Self but it can also be just a part.

Yea, it can be a part doing that, a dissociating part, and it can also be Self, but then there are parts that will make you addicted to that, to keep you out of this world.

Say more about that. So, even if it's a genuine experience of Self, then you have parts that get attached to it.

297

Right, and will be attached to the framework.

I love those parts.

Right, they'll be attached to frameworks that encourage that and then you become addicted to the practice. There are ways that parts will use the Self experience for their own purposes.

And how do you recognize that?

You know some of these people that seem so spiritual, but you can tell it's kind of brittle. They're addicted to the practice and they've got to do it all the time.

As a therapist, you just have the courage to keep inquiring about the part, even though they're insisting that it's not a part, that it's Self.

Right.

You said there are no bad parts, only parts in bad roles. Can you say a little bit more about that?

There are only burdened parts that are stuck in bad roles. I like the metaphor of a family of an alcoholic whose kids are in these different stereotypic roles like the lost child and the savior. I forget all the names... the mascot... and those roles aren't the essence of those kids. They don't define those kids; they're just what they got forced into by what happened to their families. The same is true with this internal system. Some of these parts needed to protect and some of them were too hurt, and by virtue of being hurt, they became a liability, so they had to be locked up.

It's communicating that basic idea that people are not their parts and parts are not their roles.

Jesus says: Love your enemies and pray for those who persecute you, and you talk about tormentors as being mentors. Do you want to say something to us about that, because I think in the Christian tradition and in human nature in general, it's easy to want God to have vengeance on our enemies and for us to see our enemies as enemies. You're suggesting something different.

I think that too many Christians have taken that to mean that you should let your enemies do whatever they want, but it's possible to love someone while you're still stopping them from hurting somebody. By that I mean you can see their pain is driving them and you can see that they have a Self, and you can also say that I am not going to allow you to keep doing this. You can act from the courage, clarity, confidence that Self contains as well. So I think the "turn the other cheek" and all that got construed, as when someone's mugging us, we should be forgiving them, and I think that's a distortion of what Jesus was saying. There seems to be a number of places in the Bible where Jesus was very forceful but, at the same time, I would guess he was maintaining a perspective of love for them at some level.

You can love someone and still set limits on what they're doing.

Right. When you're Self-led, again, you don't want to have forced love, forced forgiveness, that's premature, but when you're really in Self... I know when I'm really in Self and someone is out of line, what used to make me really judgmental of them and cut off from them, now I can see the pain that's driving them. I can be very clear and firm with them, but because I'm still in Self, they don't feel the huge disconnect when

I try to adjust their behavior.

You have coined the phrase tor-mentor.   What is a tor-mentor?

It coincides with the idea that we're here to learn lessons. A lot of people around us are here to teach us and they teach us by provoking us. So a person who upsets me the most, if I go inside with that and find the part that's being triggered and work with that, it becomes what I call a trailhead to find a key thing that I have to heal. This provocation actually mentored me in the sense of teaching me where I need to go, to try and unburden, and so that the person now becomes a tor-mentor. By tormenting me, they're mentoring me in my lesson plan.

That's a tough one for a lot of people.

And the fact that someone is a good tormentor doesn't mean you should stay with them. There comes a time when you matriculate. You learn your lessons and you can…

Sometimes the lesson you need to learn is to move on. Sometimes the lesson you need to learn is not to allow them to keep doing the things that they do.

Exactly.

Dick, how do people keep on being individual souls in the context of a relationship?

I think that it's a challenge.   I try to write about that in the book I wrote on couples. It's challenging because we all create these exiles inside of us. Parts get hurt and they become inconvenient, so we lock them up, and those parts are desperate to be cared for. They don't think we're going to.

We're also bombarded with these messages that there is somebody out there who will make us feel a lot better. They all start to focus on this redeeming person, which I think also has parallels to Christianity and Christians who come looking for redemption from Jesus. It's really these exiles who are desperate and don't think they can get much from us and think it has to be some supreme being that redeems them. We're looking for that, to find somebody that fits the profile of the redeemer. Our exiles glom onto that person and, because these parts are still not unburdened, they are still extremely needy. They either will smother our partner, or try to control our partner, or as our partner hurts them or gets close enough to hurt them, other protective parts will distance from that person and cut them off.

So the only solution I've found to that is to help people become what I call the primary caretaker of their own exiles, which frees up their partner to be the secondary caretaker. And that fosters what I call "courageous love," where you have the courage to love somebody without condition, without controlling, without having to smother them, because you know no matter what happens with them you're going to be okay, because you've got yourself and whatever connection you have with Self.

It seems like that would fit with what we sometimes say in the church, that we look for things in our human relationships that aren't humanly possible. We go into relationships with our burdens and unhealed parts but those needs can really get met only through a relationship with Self, or as we would say, with Holy Spirit. We take ourselves into places where we can't get what we need, it's not possible, and then that causes a lot of pain. And also we try to help couples who come with that kind of pain understand that it's not necessarily a bad thing. That marriage or relationship issue gives them a chance to turn

back toward a relationship with Spirit or to God for the
healing that can take place there.

But, aren't we supposed to marry the other person in order to
become complete?

No, we're not.

Aren't they supposed to take care of us, Dick?

They're supposed to torment us.

It's safe to say they do that.

As I mentioned earlier, Martin Buber talks about the ultimate
in human connection, and it takes place at a spiritual level.
The problem is that we treat people as "It," as "Other." The
best relationships are the connections that we make Spirit to
Spirit, or as I and Thou. That seemed to me to correspond
pretty closely to Self to Self connection.

Yeah, that would be a translation for that, sure.

Obviously people don't have to be religious or spiritual in
order to benefit from the model?

Right, yeah.

Do you notice any difference in the work when people do
come with a spiritual orientation of one kind or another?

Actually, not so much.

IFS attracts people from many different religions and

followers of lots of different paths. How do you explain the broad appeal to such a diverse group of spiritual seekers who might otherwise not be in the same room?

I think it's very simple, maybe elegantly simple, and not attached to any particular religion. Different believers will see the model and say, oh, this is really Buddhism, or this is really Hinduism, or this is really Christianity, or this is really Judaism. I have had very serious scholars from all of those different traditions come and say, you can't believe the parallels to what we believe.

I think partly because I'm not attached to any of those, it's also made people freer to take a look at them. It does seem to solve many of the conundrums that people get into with the certain limited ways that their religion is interpreted in the basic prophecies and teachings.

From what you can tell, does IFS fit more naturally with any particular religion or spiritual orientation?

Not actually. The ones I'm most familiar which would be, in order of familiarity, Buddhism, now Christianity, and Hinduism less and to a lesser degree Judaism, and particularly mystical Judaism and then very little. I'm not very familiar with Islam. But of the ones I'm familiar with, I would say not, so far.

You present yourself as not being particularly spiritual when you were younger, but you did have a picture of Jesus on your dorm wall when you were in college. What was that about?

I'd seen it in a magazine and I immediately felt drawn to it. It's actually on my mantle right now. It's a picture of him with a big grin laughing, like laughing at the world, I guess. It was such a contrast to the way Jesus is typically depicted as so pious and gentle. He's not only laughing but laughing in a kind of bravado almost. Some of the reason I picked it out was, I think, some of my rebellious part. And then books like Gary Wills later just confirmed my sense of Jesus as being much more radical and much more of a rebel than what I had been taught. I don't know other than that. I wasn't very religious at all.

At this point it might be safe to say that you've become a spiritual teacher in your own right.

An accidental tourist.

How's that for you? Rabbi Schwartz?

It's okay. Partly because I've become much clearer that I'm not this wise being who can convey this information. It's coming through me and I'm proud of the fact that I opened enough to let it come through me. But I don't have my ego tied up in it the way that you might think, in the way that some people in my position seem to be.

So it feels good. I mean, it would feel weird if I did ride some kind of roller coaster about how much people were believing me, or liked me, or thought I was god. But I don't honestly… I really… I think initially I started out on this path in part for the adoration of it. Another thing I feel proud of is that I don't really need that now. I worked on the parts that needed that enough that my motives are a lot purer.

Can you make any generalizations about the kind of Christians that are attracted to IFS?

Well, I would have said more liberal, less fundamentalist types but we did these two trainings in Mississippi and it was

304

mostly Evangelical Fundamentalists. While there were some very heated debates, they also seemed to embrace it. I don't know that they knew all my positions on things but they liked the model as it was presented to them.

I think the place where I get into it the most with Christians is this idea that Jesus is the only way, the only path, because as I said earlier, I feel like there are many different... I didn't say that earlier, but I do feel like there are many different paths. As I've gotten to know what Jesus actually said more, I think that Jesus can be a really good one, but isn't the only one. Most of the people who come to IFS and stay with it are not as attached to the idea that Jesus is the only savior as some people are.

It seems to me that people who do have that understanding of Jesus as the only way can still benefit from the model.

Yeah. I mean, clearly the people in Mississippi did, and many of them, as I understand it, still use it a lot.

They use the model with people who are not believers and find that those people have this thing I call Self, even though they haven't been saved. How do they reconcile that with the belief that people only get that after they have been saved?

They're using it even with those kinds of contradictions. The other contradiction which we worked out down there is this belief that people are basically full of sin and don't have any positive qualities until they are saved by Jesus. We had to go several rounds about that. People with that belief system initially have trouble buying this idea of Self.

That would be one of the belief differences that would make it hard to use the model at all.

305

Yeah, and this is where we could compromise down there. They could go with the idea that there is some kernel of goodness that maybe hasn't sprouted but is in people someplace.

For people who are not spiritual, can the model still work, and if so, how?

Yeah, it's the nice thing about it, it doesn't require any particular kind of belief other than that you have parts.

It's very empirical, and so if I'm working with somebody, they can be a total atheist, and they'd still be able to find different parts of them. Then as I get other parts to separate, they will spontaneously enter this state called Self, and I won't have to talk about it as a big spiritual deal; it's just okay. That's good that your Self is here... now what do you want to say to this part... how do you want to be with it? They'll know just what to do just like everybody else, and we don't have to ever mention spirituality or anything. They'll still be able to do a huge amount of healing.

I have a big value on not imposing anything on anybody with this stuff. While for me it's quite spiritual now, it wasn't for a long time and I wasn't. I have no judgment about people who don't believe in these things and no need for them to. And this may be different from other psycho-spiritual systems, or systems that maybe combine religion and psychology. There are many IFS therapists who don't share any of these beliefs and use it perfectly well, and are much more agnostic or atheist. When I teach this stuff, I teach it only to people who are interested. I teach it as: take it or leave it.

When you say "this stuff," you mean the spiritual pieces?

Spiritual pieces, yeah. And I don't expect anybody to share these beliefs. I'm just a reporter. I'm just relaying what I was taught.

How do you introduce the concept of Self to people who say they aren't spiritual?

Are you talking about therapists that I'm teaching, or are you talking about clients?

Clients.

I'll help them enter that state simply by getting parts to separate, but I don't teach much to clients about it. I just help them do it. I help them do it. If they get curious about it, I'll tell them what I think about it. A lot of clients like the intro book about it. There are many clients, if you asked about Self and spiritual Self or managers, exiles or firefighters, they wouldn't know what you are talking about.   I have a big value on people figuring out themselves. I'm a minimalist when it comes to imposing and it works just fine without believing all that.

Are there basic assumptions about IFS that people need to accept in order to benefit from the model?

That clients need to accept? Just that there are parts.

And even that isn't necessarily an intellectual thing, just part of the process.

Yeah, and they don't need to call them that, just that there are these sort of discrete little clumps in there that carry emotions and moods that they can work with. Aside from that, there's really not more that people have to swallow that's different from what they ordinarily would.

307

Why doesn't IFS work for everyone?

Because Self can still be easily constrained by certain parts and because people live in extreme environments that, no matter how hard you were to work to heal parts and to help Self leadership… there are elements of clients' environments that would never allow Self to emerge because parts would not think it was safe. If you get to a point where you can get some safety and access to Self, then most people do heal.

Clients that I haven't been able to help, I guess would fall into a couple of categories. One is people who clearly, when we got to their exiles, had secrets that other parts felt like they couldn't afford to reveal. We'd circle around and we'd look at glimpses, and then these backlash parts would come in and erase it, or say that it couldn't be possible.

It's been just a handful of clients in my career where we never really got there. We were never able to heal these exiles because it was just really clear, their protective parts weren't willing to go through the consequences, mainly in the external world, that would be the fallout of knowing these secrets. So that's one and I've had to learn to respect that.

It's not my call if people choose not to totally disrupt their lives. What I try to do is negotiate and make it clear that it doesn't have to lead to that; they don't have to confront anybody or tell anything about what they find outside the session. There are people who have parts that wouldn't sit still knowing, but without doing something about it, and that's their right, too. Anyway, I've just had to become more sanguine about this, or be much more okay with the choices the parts make. It's not my… they don't have to do it all in this lifetime, and so on. So that would be one class.

The other class, I think, is situations where the external environment is just too scary. The protectors don't feel like there is space enough to really separate it out, to get Self to come out. That's pretty rare because of the population I work with. It would be much more common if I worked a lot more with kids.

I was going to ask for an example, say, with kids.

When I did a lot more work with kids, and where we started all this was at the Institute for Juvenile Research, we worked a lot with street kids, gang kids, and some of them were actually interested in doing this but they just felt like they could never afford to be vulnerable anywhere, and there was some reality to that. While that was the case, it was tough to get inside, although there were some kids where we could negotiate a kind of volunteer fire department where, on the street, these firefighters would be up all the time, but in my office, or maybe sometimes at home, they could relax a little bit. And then those kids could do some really good work.

Given the notion that everyone has a Self and that the model is basically hopeful for everyone, how do you know when to walk away from a relationship, whether you're the therapist in a client relationship or in our personal lives? Because it seems like that kind of optimistic approach would kind of encourage one to just hang in there.

Yeah. It is a tough one for a lot of clients and I work with lots of couple situations where that's a chronic question. As I wrote in that couples book, I do believe that when you're with somebody it shouldn't all be smooth sailing, that they're there to help with your learning by tormenting you and by pulling up parts that you need to heal. And I also believe that at some point you matriculate. You get all the learning you can get from one particular person, especially as you heal the stuff they bring up, and then if they're continuing to be hurtful, then it's time to leave. Most people do at that point.

A lot of what happens is, as clients begin to take the phenomenon more seriously, to take seriously that these are real parts of them, real children inside them. I've said to a number of clients: if this was really your daughter would you constantly bring her to somebody who constantly beat her up? If you really thought that was a child of yours, are you willing to take these inner children as seriously as you might an external child in terms of being abused? And that really wakes people up sometimes.

As people get more Self led, they're more interested in connecting at that level with someone, with a partner. And the original parts contracts that got people into relationship, if one person is doing the work and the other is not, those become outmoded and unnecessary to the person doing the work. The person doing the work is looking for somebody else that they can access the Self with. That's the danger of doing this work with couples when they're not both doing it. It's not a danger in the sense that it's bad for the person doing the work, it's just not necessarily going to keep the marriage together. So I try to warn people if they come in and they want to do the work separate from their partner and their partner is not doing the work, it could be hazardous to their marriage.

As a therapist, when do you know that you shouldn't be working with a particular client, because we'd like to think that we have enough Self to work with anybody who walks in?

What I teach students is, that if therapy gets stuck, it's generally because of a part of you the therapist is triggered and

310

if you can't get it to not take over, you'll always be triggered at different points with certain clients in particular. But if you can't come back to Self and you can't make a good repair, and/or if you're not even aware that a part has taken over and has a protector, then it's really unhealthy for your client to invite you to go into these very vulnerable places.

So for me, the essence of supervision now is really helping therapists find the parts that are getting triggered and blocking. You get them to step back and get back to Self leadership with their clients. But where that's not possible, it's better to refer, because it's really harmful to your client. I had a couple clients where I clearly harmed them because I was triggered and I didn't do the work to get out of the part. I was so blended with the protector that I felt in the right about it, and it wasn't good for my client.

Knowing when to set limits, or end a relationship, is a difficult issue for spiritual communities and people who are trying to be faithful. We have the idea that we should welcome everyone, forgive everything and, as a result, we end up with bullies and predators among us -- real problems. And the same thing happens on an individual level where some very nice, good people end up in bad relationships or dangerous situations. How does that happen to people with such good spiritual intentions?

I think it's a misinterpretation of Jesus' message, if you're speaking about Christians. Buddhists have elements of that too. There are elements of that in a lot of traditions and there is this sense that -- who are we to judge, and turn the other cheek, and stuff like that -- that you should love everybody regardless of what they do to you.

I think it's a kind of misinterpretation of a fairly deep

311

teaching. In my point of view, if you're Self led, you can see behind the protectors of whoever it is that's hurting you. You can see the pain that drives them so you can have compassion for them, even maybe love for them, even while you're putting them in jail or you're doing whatever you need to do to stop them from hurting you.

So I talk about these 8 C's of Self leadership, and three of them involve Clarity, Confidence and Courage, all of which come into play in terms of acting to protect. As I said earlier, when you take seriously that these are almost literal children of yours, it is still your mandate, as Self, to protect those, and then you don't subject them to all kinds of abuse from people. Self doesn't do that. And I don't believe Jesus would do that.

So you're discerning. You have clarity. You can tell. You're not distorted and see everybody as dangerous. Or you're not distorted the other way, this over-trusting part that causes you to see everybody as a friend. You can see dangerous parts in people; you can see through that to the pain that drives them. If you can't reach that pain, you'll definitely protect your parts, your family's parts, your tribe's parts from those people.

I think where things got distorted was… it's two different levels. At this very high level, you can see all that. You have x-ray vision into peoples' systems and you can love them and have compassion for them. But at this other earthly level, you also need to protect, and you can be at both levels even while you are protecting. I think that some of the Samurai's, a lot of their teaching, was to… even while you have tremendous respect for your opponent, you still fight them.

People that do take on that over-loving position have certain parts that are sort of managerial but also some of these exiles that can be overly trusting.

What kinds of parts incline people to that over-loving position? The spiritualizing parts or the exiled parts?

There are parts, the "should" parts, that keep saying that you should be loving, you should forgive people, you should see beyond their sins, and so on. And they'll take passages from the Bible to support that. And then there are other parts that just are young and naïve and want to believe. They're sort of idealistic, and some of them have burdens, too. They are sort of desperate to be taken care of too, and so they sort of want to see everybody as good, or as a potential caretaker, or as a potential friend. They can blind you. They can distort your perceptions so you don't see obvious red flags.

To some people it's a combination of those. They're destructive because they constantly get people hurt, and then that means that they have to have, in reserve, all these angry parts who are locked up and will come out in manipulative ways, because they can't express their anger directly.

Seems like the challenging thing is that those parts can sound close enough to a spiritual message but not really be Self.

Right.

How can you tell the difference between a state of trance and the experience of Self? How do you differentiate between authentic mystical moments and parts that might numb you out in a way that mimic it?

Trance, I don't use that word, or hypnosis, because they conjure up such… they carry so many connotations in our culture.

313

So, for me, what's called trance is anytime people focus inside, they enter this other world. There is -- my point of view now -- there is a kind of other world inside of all of us that's, in a way, as real as the outside world. What I try to do is help clients simply focus in there and into that other world. And it seems like they're in a trance as it has been traditionally thought of, where you are somewhat oblivious to what's happening in the outside world, not totally by any means, but your focus is elsewhere. Your focus is in this other world. People are no less in a trance when they are in the outside world when they're totally ignoring the inside world.

It's like there are these two different worlds. Some people are totally stuck in one; others are totally stuck in the other. The goal is to be fluid, and to go back and forth. Because we've been so socialized to only be in the outside world, we call somebody who spends time in the inside world in a trance or hypnotized or meditating. They're doing this activity that's very esoteric when really there should be, in my mind, a balance between those two worlds.

I remember working with somebody once who got to this particular... what she described as an "oceanic state," and suddenly realized that this was a part, but for many years she had thought that it was a genuine spiritual state.

There's sort of these charlatan parts inside that can pretend to be spiritual. They do pretend. Yeah, there are parts that will try to do it for you, or give what they think is being strived for in terms of the spiritual experience to you and will try to keep you in that. I've worked with a lot of meditators from different kinds of traditions, and I'll run into those kinds of parts, and they're always shocked to find this was just a part.

How do you know it's a part? How do you get to that?

I'm trying to recall.

I think I just got suspicious because there were some telltale signs, like what they were experiencing in that state had an agenda to it. I can't remember exactly. Some of it is, it was still encouraging them to stay away from other parts, like the exiles.

It's about leaving.

It's about getting out.

There's an escape clause.

Exactly. It's kind of a fire-fighting escape quality which... When I started meditating, which was in '74, I was doing TM and that's what I was using it for – escape. It was totally about escape, and it worked well to get me into Self, and helped to get me above all my exiles, which were driving me crazy. It helped me a lot, but it didn't heal my exiles. It helped me become more Self led. Once I shifted out of meditation as a way of healing and toward IFS, I was able to go back to my exiles. I was probably better able to heal them because of the meditating.

I worked with other meditators where that state wasn't Self, really. It was kind of a pseudo Self-like state that was partly put on for that. It was usually all designed to get away from my exiles; it was just another kind of firefighter.

So some of it may have to do with intent?

With intent of the part, yeah, or of the state.

There's a difference between Self and Self leadership. There are spiritual aspects of helping people meditate or reach that transcendent sort of state of Self and then they kind of end there. To me, there's an important connection between Self and Self leadership.

Right. A lot of traditions use techniques to get you into that oceanic state that I just call Self but other traditions call higher self, or nirvana, or enlightenment, or whatever. I could do that ultimately with TM. I was in some really, seemingly probably really high states, and it was very, very pleasant. There were times where I could literally feel myself leaving my body and going to these places. I have nothing against that. In fact, I think once people get to a certain level, it can be a really wonderful journey.

It seems that my work is not so much exploring those higher realms while I'm in this incarnation, but it's helping bring some of that, more of that, here to this world for the purpose of healing this world. The danger with meditative traditions is that they've put their emphasis on exploring those upper worlds. There are parts that will become addicted to the practice as a way to get away from exiles, like any other kind of firefighter activity. So for me, that kind of practice is fine as an occasional "let's go get a break and go up here" and feel what really is possible up here and then bring that back, until you reach a certain level of healing, at which point it is just fine to just go and spend a lot of time up there.

The problem I see is that a lot of traditions will take people that aren't very healed and will encourage them to do that and maybe become addicted to it. They're walking around all the time above their parts and they're getting into trouble because their parts haven't been healed. They're confused because: I thought I was doing this practice that's only good and

316

here my parts are... here I'm doing these other behaviors that are really destructive.

I think that's the downfall of us gurus, and a lot of evangelical Christians, and so on, that they're trying to spend all their time in this holy state and they're not bringing it to heal, to heal their wounds.

The other kind of curious thing, I don't know if it's curious... I can't remember if I talked about this before, but for people who have suffered a lot of abuse, they're in this sort of quandary where they are more hooked up spiritually because their parts took off, left the body, went to these other realms, and they have access to other realms. A lot of them are still kind of up there and they haven't come back. So they get a lot of information, they can get a lot of intuitive information. A lot of psychics I think have that kind of background. In this world, that information is powerful and impressive; it impresses them, it impresses people who hear about it.

But they also, because of the abuse, carry huge burdens still, and the burdens can distort the information. I mean the information is often valid but then filtered through these parts and gets distorted, and they sometimes are elevated to positions that can cause a lot of damage too, because they haven't really healed.

There are a lot of other survivors that I treat who are very plugged in spiritually that way but they haven't exploited it, they haven't been using it. It's just that they're plugged in because they left, and that we can actually use their connections for their healing.

But the people who don't realize how hurt they are, they are the ones who are dangerous.

They may have some very valid legitimate spiritual experiences, teachings, but they're not connected or their parts aren't healed, so ...

Parts aren't healed so it gets distorted. They'll use the power of their teachings to exploit people.

The parts will?

The parts will. I also have to say to my credit, I sense that, because I think that, at some point, I realized that what I was teaching was powerful and could be exploited. I really needed to work on the deep parts that might be tempted to do that.

Your own parts?

My own parts. Which is an ongoing process; it's still a work in progress.

As practitioners of the model, how do we honor our own belief systems and yet remain open to whatever might show up in a session, even if it's contrary to what we believe?

You mean spiritual belief systems, religious beliefs?

It's an issue with political or social convictions as well, but, yeah, the spiritual. Although really it does go across the board, right? I mean, it's a challenge for us anytime we have clients who show up with stuff that's really contrary to what we believe -- about prejudice, for example, or anything else.

One of the nice things about the model is that you don't have to... like someone comes in with a belief that's totally antithetical to your own… you don't have to convince them of the wrongness of their belief. You can simply have them focus on the part that carries the belief and ask questions of it about where it got it. They do their own sort of deconstructing of extreme beliefs a lot of the time just through the act of focusing on the part, asking where it's stuck in the past, seeing where the belief came in, seeing where it does protect, and then unburdening it.

I can totally stay out of all that with my belief system, other than asking them to focus on the part, which much of the time they're curious about anyway. And the model is a kind of a Rorschach for different religions so when Hindus hear about it, they say: oh, this is a Hindu model. When Buddhists hear about it: this is applied Buddhism. When Christians hear about it: this is really Christ inside. So, it seems to not threaten. The basic tenets of it don't seem to threaten any particular religion and most religions can identify with it in some way.

I don't put it forth as packaged, as some particular religious approach. I have had some reluctance in writing this book because I don't want the model to become too closely associated with Christianity, for example. At some point I hope to write a book on Buddhism, and maybe other religions, so IFS is presented as the framework that has spiritual components to it, but it's not associated with any particular teaching, any particular school.

People can go wherever they want to with it. I'm fine with that. We worked with these evangelical Christians and fundamentalist people in Mississippi and ultimately we all kind of came around about a lot of this stuff, even though we started out with huge gaps in our belief systems.

The model has a lot of good systemic approaches that focus on

319

the process and lets clients deal with their own content. If we find ourselves getting activated by any of the content, then that's our parts, and then we have to work with our own parts around whatever it is.

Yeah, and, generally, if you're really present with clients and they have hurtful belief systems, those will shake out as they start to do the work. Not start to, but often, down the road at some point, they'll start to shift a whole lot on their own as Self becomes more a presence in there. I don't have to do any of the re-educating or any of that.

I have a particular personality that I've come to think of as myself, that I'm rather fond of, or at least, I seem to be pretty attached to it. In the IFS model, does that personality derive solely from my constellation of parts or is Self involved as well?

No, Self is involved. Your Self is in there but it's blended with a lot of different parts, which, if they're unburdened and collaborating, just make for the spice of your life, your personality.

But if we're all in Self, won't we all be alike?

When we're in pure Self, we are pretty much alike. But the goal of this work is not to be there all the time at all. That's the misconception a lot of people have. Your parts are great when they're not getting you in trouble, when your burdens aren't driving you. It's great to have them blend with you and be with you and live your life, as long as they trust your leadership and they step back if you ask them to. There are certain parts that are really good at certain things and it's great that they all take the lead at different times.

320

In both my practice of Christianity and IFS, it's easy for me to get the idea that, as I go along, it's going to get easier.

At some point it will get easier, but it often gets a lot harder before it gets easier.

I think the mistake that many religions, I would say, most religions have made, is to hold up a prophet as a role model or a state of being as a goal and say that this is what you should be like. And tell people the way to get there is to pray or to control your behavior, your impulses, and just be like that. Of course, that means they have to exile many, many parts of them to try to achieve that.

We know that exiling parts means a couple things. One is that they'll try to throw a coup at different points and pull you down, or the firefighters that react to the exile will. And that you're not a complete person, because you've locked up so much of your richness that way. So that's another big thing that I've been trying to counter, to say, yeah, it would be great if you could be that way, but you can't be like that until you've healed all this stuff. That's your lesson plan.

And actually, once you get there, you'll be much wiser for having done the journey and the healing. What I've tried to provide is a very concrete way that people can attain some of that but to not have to push away all the parts that don't seem Christ-like or Buddha-like or what have you, along the journey.

The goal is in some ways the same, the end point, but the method is different. In some ways it is counter-intuitive and counter to what a lot of religious paths have taught. Maybe not just religious paths because there's psychotherapeutic paths and cultural paths that teach the same thing.

Exactly. There are some spiritual and some psychotherapeutic and some cultural paths that are in harmony with IFS, but it's a small minority, so I would agree with that.

It's counterintuitive - it's natural to go away from the pain. In many of the clients that I see who are willing to do the work, they are only willing because they tried all those other ways and they didn't work.

It's natural to go away from pain. It's natural to fight destructive impulses. So it's all natural and commonsensical. Unfortunately, both those things don't work, they don't get you there.

What do you understand about your personal journey?

I do think that a lot of my lesson plan has been around learning to trust, and it's been a hard one. It's still not totally there. I think that a lot of people who have rejected religion had similar concerns that I did, which is looking around the world and seeing all the damage that's done by religion. Trying to sort out what in spirituality is of value and what have been distortions that create the damage has been my lesson plan -- in coming to trust what I've discovered and working with parts that still have huge doubts, and sifting through the dogma, and not throwing the baby out with the bathwater … all of that.

To me that sounds like a great journey.

It's been a remarkable one. It's instilled in me a lot of confidence. It's helped me with my own parts, my insecure parts a lot.

For me that kind of trust has really changed always, whether

322

it's pastoral care or therapy, the context of the work -- being able to trust that it's not all up to me and what I can do. There's that sense of being an instrument or being a vehicle for something larger. Is that part of your experience as well?

Yeah, definitely.

It's also, I think, consistent with a lot of what is in the scriptures. If you look in the Old Testament and New, it's really encouraging to know that the Divine can work through anybody, no matter how much of a schmuck you may be, or how much you've messed up your own life -- that's not ultimately what matters. There is the potential for anyone to open to that Spirit working through them. It's very hopeful for a lot of people.

Yeah, that's true. That's true for IFS too. Everybody's got the Self, and no matter how much harm you've done to people in your life, it's still there and untarnished and it can still help you learn what you need to learn.

And you can still be a positive force in the world despite what you've done.

Right.

From your perspective, how does spirituality come to play in the relationship between therapist and client?

I think there are many therapies where the healing comes from the connection, and they're not overtly spiritual. For me, healing happens when Self is present. Self energy is a healing energy so any approach that fosters that will be spiritual even if it doesn't consider itself that.

323

For me, it is the ability of the therapist to be in Self, and that serves just like a tuning fork for the client's Self. As the client's Self awakens and separates and is more accessible, then there's a connection between the client's Self and the Self of the parts. All these kind of connecting-the-dots relationships are spiritual for me, because what I'm calling Self easily translates to "God in us," or God in our parts. So that's one level of answer.

And then, the unburdening, the release of burdens -- originally I thought that was the goal. But it's clear to me now that that is in the service of allowing more embodying of Self, and that does transform parts in and of itself: but for me, the more spiritual goal is clearing out space in people's bodies so Self can have more access to the client through embodiment.

There are many therapies that might facilitate that kind of release or access to Self but not consider themselves explicitly spiritual, might not name it as such, but it's inherent in what they do.

Yeah, because they don't think about what I'm calling Self per se. They don't have a concept for that really, most of them.

It might be more of an intuitive embodiment of Self.

Yeah, they'll talk about the qualities of the therapist that they strive to hold. A lot of times, but not always, these are Self qualities. But they don't necessarily see it as anything spiritual. It's just good therapy. But for me it's all become much more overtly spiritual.

Self can be present in the therapist and in the client, in the room, whether it's acknowledged or not.

And where healing occurs, that's my take on what's happening.

Because of the spiritual presence?

Yeah.

To the extent that we embody that kind of spiritual presence in any relationship, whether it's formally between a therapist and client, or not -- that's what makes it healing.

And for me that increasingly becomes the goal: it's to have those kinds of Self to Self relationships inside and outside, which doesn't mean there are never parts that come up, but they come up by choice, not automatically, and they'll step back when you ask them to. And if they come up automatically, out of some burden, then both parties notice it and work on it. When that's the case then relationships become the crucible, become this place where lots of healing happens, because key parts are accessed and honored and allowed to change.

Is that some of why we would consider IFS more than just a model of therapy, what makes it more in keeping with a spiritual practice or spiritual approach?

I guess so, because it is a kind of map for living your life both internally and externally versus just a psychotherapeutic approach. I think that's true. It seems to me that's what spiritual approaches are. And this allows people to actually embody what the prophets of these traditions advocate. To my mind, too, many religions have the sense of this role-model prophet who we should all be like, but no real tools to get there. So people walk around feeling guilty because they are not that person. They're given some tools, like prayer, and in different traditions, meditation, but those aren't necessarily unburdening practices. Basically, all the prophets are telling us to be in Self, to be Self-led, and as you unburden, you are automatically that way. You don't have to push or force or fight with yourself to make it happen or feel bad when it doesn't. You're very patient with yourself. The times when you're not that way, you say, OK, there's work I have to do.

What's next for you?   What's next for the model?

I'm not really clear what's next. I've had the impulse to bring it to larger systems, and I've started to do that in a couple different contexts. There are connections with people who are immersed in spiritual things who, I think, would like to take it further into those realms... like you. So it could become more of a spiritual practice in addition to therapy, which I think would be good. That's kind of a question. Should it be an adjunct to currently existing spiritual practices or become something of its own? I don't really have the answer to that.

This whole journey I've rarely been able to see much beyond headlights and just kind of follow whatever guidance is coming. It's the easy sense that life is going in that direction and you just go that way.

Acknowledgements

I would like to acknowledge everyone that I've ever met. I am grateful for the company, for all the love and learning along life's way. I would like to thank my friends in the Presbyterian Church, USA, and so many in the IFS community who not only bore compassionate witness to my personal work, but also suffered through early drafts of this work. Melanie Hammond Clark has lovingly supported me on this path, even though it led me away from the most amazing collegial relationship ever. I am grateful for Marcia Barthelow who makes me laugh and brings me back to Self. Jon Rubenstein is like a brother to me; he shares my passion for spirituality and was co-creator of the original Spirit-Led Life series at Covenant Presbyterian. Dorie Cameron, Melanie Hammond Clark, Susan McConnell, Victoria Millar, Kathy Miller and Carolyn Scherer have all been generous in their support and assistance. I am thankful for Mike Radke who pointed me to Dick's door. Dick Schwartz has been many things to me: mentor and tormentor, teacher and colleague, friend and guide: one of God's great gifts in my life. Thanks, Dick. I am frankly ecstatic about my children and my husband, David, oh, the places we've been! Thanks for being a constant companion, friend and lover, not to mention supportive presence and superb editor; I am deeply grateful for all your help and treasure your own commitment to a Spirit-led life.

Chapter Notes:

Chapter 2: Multiplicity And The War Within

Thich Nhat Hanh, *Peace is Every Step: the Path of Mindfulness in Everyday Life* (New York, Bantam Books, 1992) p. 53

Chapter 3: The Holy Canary

Richard C. Schwartz, *The Larger Self* (Psychotherapy Networker, May/June 2004)

Chapter 4: Treasure In Clay Jars; IFS And Incarnation

Richard C. Schwartz, "*Spirituality and Connectedness*" (unpublished)

Chapter 5: Living Waters, Source Of Self

Richard C. Schwartz, *Introduction to the Internal Family Systems Model* (Oak Park: Trailheads Publications) p. 36

Chapter 7: Trusting In Divine Transformation; No Bad Parts

Parker Palmer, *Let Your Life Speak* (San Francisco: Jossey-Bass, 2000) p. 68

Richard C. Schwartz, *Introduction to the Internal Family Systems Model* (Oak Park: Trailheads Publications) p. 97

Ann Lamott, "Loving Your President: Day 2," *Plan B: Further Thoughts on Faith* (New York, Berkley *Publishing*, Penguin Group, 2005) p 220

Chapter 8: Courageous Love, Life Lived In Relationship

Barbara Brown Taylor, *God in Pain* (Nashville, Abingdon Press, 1998) p. 20

Richard C. Schwartz, *You are the One You've Been Waiting For* (Oak Park, IL, Trailheads Publications, 2008) p. 7

Richard C. Schwartz, *You are the One You've Been Waiting For* (Oak Park, IL, Trailheads Publications, 2008) p. 121

Chapter 10: The Spirit-Led Life; The Priesthood Of All Believers

Augustine, De Quanat, Anim 13, 22
Augustine, De Mor. Eccles 1, 27, 52

Chapter 11: There Are Eight C's In Discernment

Sue Monk Kidd, *When the Heart Waits* (San Francisco, Harper & Row, 1990) p. 182

Calm

Richard C. Schwartz, *Introduction to the Internal Family Systems Model* (Oak Park: Trailheads Publications) p. 44

Clarity

Richard C. Schwartz, *Introduction to the Internal Family Systems Model* (Oak Park: Trailheads Publications) p. 45

Curiosity

Stuart Hample & Eric Marshall, *Children's Letters to God* (New York, Workman Publishing, 1991)

Alfred Einstein, *The Voice of Genius: Conversations with Nobel Scientists and Other Luminaries* (New York, Perseus Books Group) p. 405

Richard C. Schwartz, *Introduction to the Internal Family Systems Model* (Oak Park: Trailheads Publications) p. 47

Compassion

Oriah Mountain Dreamer, The *Invitation (*New York, Harper Collins, 1995)   p. 137

Richard C. Schwartz, *Introduction to the Internal Family Systems Model* (Oak Park: Trailheads Publications) p. 48

Confidence

Richard C. Schwartz, *Introduction to the Internal Family Systems Model* (Oak Park: Trailheads Publications) p. 50

Courage

Richard C. Schwartz, *Introduction to the Internal Family Systems Model* (Oak Park: Trailheads Publications) p. 52

Creativity

Alfred North Whitehead, *Dialogues of Alfred North Whitehead* (Jaffrey, New Hampshire, David R. Godine Publisher, 2001) p. 366

Richard C. Schwartz, *Introduction to the Internal Family Systems Model* (Oak Park: Trailheads Publications) p. 54

Chapter 12: The Meaning Of Life, Burdens As Lessons

Thomas Lynch, *The Under-taking: Life Studies from the Dismal Trade* (New York, W. W. Norton & Company, 1996) p. 20

Max Lucado, *Traveling Light: Releasing the Burdens You Were Never Intended to Bear* (Nashville: W Publishing, Division of Thomas Nelson, Inc.) p. 4

Permissions

I would like to acknowledge, with gratitude, the following authors and publishers for permission to quote from their works:

About the Authors

Mary Steege is a certified IFS therapist, a licensed marriage and family therapist, pastoral counselor, and pastor in the Presbyterian Church, U.S.A. She is a graduate of Pomona College, received a Master of Divinity from Duke Divinity School, and completed post-graduate training at the Family Therapy Training Institute. She has served as a church pastor, hospital and hospice chaplain. She maintains a practice in Racine, Wisconsin.

Richard C. Schwartz, PhD, LMFT, is a licensed marriage and family therapist, fellow of the American Association for Marriage and Family Therapy, and developer of the Internal Family Systems model. He was associated with the Institute for Juvenile Research at the University of Illinois at Chicago and more recently with The Family Institute at Northwestern University. He has published four books and over fifty articles about IFS. His books include *Internal Family Systems Therapy*, *Introduction to the Internal Family Systems Model*, and *The Mosaic Mind* (with Regina Goulding), as well as *Metaframeworks* (with Doug Breunlin and Betty Karrer). His most recent book, *You Are The One You've Been Waiting For*, addresses IFS and couple relationships.

In 2000, Dr. Schwartz established The Center for Self Leadership to support the development of the model and growth of the IFS community. He is a spiritual seeker known for his warmth, curiosity, and compassion.

About Internal Family Systems

Internal Family Systems^{SM} therapy is at the forefront of a movement in psychotherapy toward a more collaborative approach that relies on client's intuitive wisdom. As one of the fastest growing approaches in the field today, it has had a significant impact on the field of psychotherapy. Internal Family systems (IFS) offers a clear, non-pathologizing and empowering method of understanding human problems that has become widely embraced by the trauma community and by those interested in integrating spirituality with psychotherapy. It offers a philosophy of practice that allows both the therapist and client to enter a transformational relationship in which healing occurs. IFS is also expanding internationally into larger systems and human communities. It is being used to promote peace in areas of world conflict and is being developed as an important adjunct for healing within the medical community.

The Center for Self Leadership is dedicated to the healing transformation of lives and cultures through educating therapists, health care professionals and the public in the IFS psychotherapeutic model. The organization maintains the integrity of the IFS Model by supporting the development and growth of practitioners so that they, in turn, can provide the maximum healing benefits for individuals, families, and entire communities.

The Center for Self Leadership supports professional development and also provides resources for clients and the general public. For information and resources such as training programs, lists of IFS therapists, retreats, and conferences, publications, DVDs, and other materials, please visit www.selfleadership.org.

Made in the USA
Middletown, DE
16 August 2017